PENGUIN BUSINESS

FROM LEHMAN TO DEMONETIZATION

Tamal Bandyopadhyay, consulting editor at *Business Standard* and senior adviser at Jana Small Finance Bank, is an award-winning journalist and author. One of the most respected business journalists in India, he has kept a close watch on the financial sector for two and a half decades and has had a ringside view of the enormous changes in the Indian finance and banking sectors. His other books—*A Bank for the Buck*, *Sahara: The Untold Story*, *Bandhan: The Making of a Bank*, *HDFC 2.0: From Dawn to Digital* and *Pandemonium: The Great Indian Banking Tragedy*—have all been non-fiction bestsellers.

PRAISE FOR THE BOOK

'Tamal Bandyopadhyay is one of the foremost thoughtful journalists writing on Indian finance today. He has the knack of going beyond the obvious and asking the right questions. In this collection of articles and essays, Tamal takes the reader through a tumultuous decade, offering a ringside view of major developments in Indian banking and insights into the thinking of the major protagonists. It will be of value for anyone interested in India's financial development' —Raghuram Rajan, professor of finance, University of Chicago, and former governor, RBI

'Many of us are aware of financial developments, but to understand why they happen and what the implications are, one must read Tamal's columns. He brings in a rare insight into every policy development and explains things in a very lucid way, backed by sufficient data. Most importantly, he does not take any position, but leaves it to his readers to conclude whether it is good, bad or ugly. A rare quality for a columnist'—Deepak Parekh, chairman, HDFC Ltd

'An outstanding compilation of essays on contemporary issues in money and finance in India, reflecting Tamal's amazing grasp of the interplay of issues, ideologies, individuals and institutions—indeed, a collector's item'—Y.V. Reddy, former governor, RBI, and chairman of the fourteenth finance commission

'Authoritative and lucid, Tamal's columns have made him one of the most trusted and influential financial journalists of the country. Even the very discerning turn to his writings for guidance'—D. Subbarao, former governor, RBI

'An exceptional book on the events that unfolded in the last decade in Indian finance by one of its keenest observers. Macro in its ambition and yet adequately micro in its detailing, a must-read for every student, practitioner and policymaker in, or interested in, India'—Viral Acharya, deputy governor, RBI

'The book touches upon events right from the global financial crisis to the latest efforts of financial inclusion and demonetization in India'—Arundhati Bhattacharya, former chairman, SBI

PRAISE FOR *BANDHAN: THE MAKING OF A BANK*

'Tamal Bandyopadhyay is a gifted storyteller who combines the sharp vision of a finance expert with a journalist's skill for observation and narration'—Kaushik Basu, former senior vice president, World Bank

'The transformation of Bandhan, a microfinance company, into a universal bank is as unique as the transition of Tamal from a business journalist to an author. As governor of the Reserve Bank, I had grown to respect Tamal for his passion for financial journalism, his enormous talent and endearing professional integrity. He combines all those attributes to tell the remarkable behind-the-scenes story of what it takes to overcome the challenges of last-mile connectivity in Indian finance'—D. Subbarao, former governor, RBI

'As an acclaimed journalist with decades of experience in financial markets, Tamal brings an intensity along with sincerity and integrity to his writing. In this book, he has woven a colourful canvas which draws the attention of the reader and makes him read, think and deliberate'— U.K. Sinha, former chairman, SEBI

'This is a fascinating story, deserving to be chronicled. And who better to do so than Tamal. It is a very revealing study—a must-read for those even remotely interested in this sector. The story is narrated by a person as well informed as a hands-on banker and has all the attendant nuances'—Vinod Rai, former comptroller and auditor general of India

'Bandhan, India's youngest bank, has a deep and long history behind it. A first of its kind, the book takes the reader through India's journey towards financial inclusion. Tamal brilliantly captures a story of hope and what it takes to lift millions of Indians out of poverty'—Deepak Parekh, chairman, HDFC Ltd

'Replete with fascinating anecdotes and containing perceptive pen portraits of some of the pioneers in the industry, the book makes for compulsive reading for all those who want insights into the growth of microfinance in India'—Y.H. Malegam, chairman of the RBI subcommittee set up to study MFI concerns

'Tamal Bandyopadhyay brings alive one of the finest stories of Indian entrepreneurship'—V. Vaidyanathan, *Business Today*

'Arguably the best banking journalist in India, Tamal spent most of his journalistic career covering banking and finance at several newspapers . . . Tamal brings both a storyteller's gift and an expert's knowledge to bear on his subjects'—R. Jagannathan, *Swarajya*

'The name Tamal Bandyopadhyay is synonymous with banking, and his views on any aspect of the subject are compelling . . . He is able to keep the reader glued'—Madan Sabnavis, *Financial Express*

'An outstanding book that gave me tremendous insights into the world of finance in India. A must-read'—Suhel Seth

'Recommended reading for those looking for inspiration'—Ashok Chawla, former chairperson, Competition Commission of India

PRAISE FOR THE AUTHOR

'In a period of great financial illiteracy, it's refreshing to have a book written by somebody very literate about matters relating to finance'—P. Chidambaram, former finance minister

'Tamal has set a new trend in the dissemination of knowledge' —Y.V. Reddy, former governor, RBI

'Tamal is able to bring two sets of skills to bear on his writing. He obviously has deep domain knowledge . . . He also follows a critical journalistic principle, which is to never assume that you know everything about the subject you are writing on'—Subir Gokarn, former deputy governor, RBI

'Tamal's sharp reporting instincts as well as eye for detail help him paint a profile that accurately reflects the original'—T.N. Ninan, chairman and editorial director, *Business Standard*

'India's most-respected and well-sourced banking and financial journalist'—Raju Narisetti, senior vice president, strategy, News Corporation

'Bandyopadhyay does not pass judgements but lays open the issues and arguments of both sides. This balancing act is quite remarkable' —*Business World*

FROM LEHMAN TO DEMONETIZATION

A Decade of Disruptions, Reforms and Misadventures

TAMAL BANDYOPADHYAY

Foreword by K.V. Kamath

PENGUIN
BUSINESS

An imprint of Penguin Random House

PENGUIN BUSINESS

USA | Canada | UK | Ireland | Australia
New Zealand | India | South Africa | China | Singapore

Penguin Business is part of the Penguin Random House group of companies whose addresses can be found at global.penguinrandomhouse.com

Published by Penguin Random House India Pvt. Ltd
4th Floor, Capital Tower 1, MG Road,
Gurugram 122 002, Haryana, India

First published in Portfolio by Penguin Random House India 2017
Published in Penguin Business 2021

10 9 8 7 6 5 4 3 2

ISBN 9780143456391

Typeset in Adobe Garamond Pro by Manipal Digital Systems, Manipal
Printed at Manipal Technologies Limited, India

www.penguin.co.in

To my elder brother, Tapas, who fought cancer with courage and grace.
I never knew we were so close to each other.

Contents

Acknowledgements

At the outset, let me admit that I am not a student of finance. Being a student of English literature, I would never have been able to understand the complexities of the world of banking and finance and appreciate the nuances hadn't many bankers, bond and foreign exchange dealers, economists, analysts and central bankers taught me continuously. They handheld me through the tricky terrain, and answered my naive questions with enormous patience and indulgence.

They do this even now as I am a slow learner. No word can express my gratitude to them. I am refraining from mentioning their names as the catalogue would run a few pages.

A special thanks to K.V. Kamath, president of New Development Bank of BRICS countries, for writing the Foreword. The first time I met him was the day he took over as CEO of the erstwhile development finance institution ICICI Ltd in the mid-1990s; I had then just about started my career as a banking reporter. When I approached him for the Foreword, he agreed—without even looking at the manuscript—with the selfsame warmth that he had always shown me. Needless to say, he features prominently in the list of my teachers that I mentioned in the beginning.

Barring two, all columns and interviews in this book appeared in *Mint* where I am now a consulting editor. R. Sukumar, editor of *Mint*, was kind and gracious enough to allow me to use these without any precondition. Thank you, Sukumar.

My thanks also to *Mint*'s Jayachandran Nanu for the lovely illustrations done at a very short notice.

Two of my colleagues in *Mint*'s research department, Ashwin Ramarathinam and Ravindra Sonavane, have crunched data for many of my columns. But for their assistance, I could not have written some of the pieces. Also, thanks to three other colleagues in *Mint*—Ramesh Pathania, Pradeep Gaur and Abhijit Bhatlekar—for the photographs of the governors and finance ministers, which we used on the cover. And to Abel Robinson, the national creative director of *Mint*.

I have also used two interviews from my previous paper *Business Standard*. Thank you, *BS*.

A special thanks to Penguin's commissioning editor Lohit Jagwani for his endless excitement over this project and for putting me under relentless pressure to meet the deadline! Also, my copy editor, Shanuj V.C., for his meticulous care and a hawk-eye for details.

Finally, I owe a big thanks to my wife and son, the self-proclaimed severest critic of my writings, for tolerating all my idiosyncrasies—often disappearing for days together for so-called research or selfishly spending days and nights in the confinement of my study without exchanging even bare pleasantries with them.

I will donate a part of the royalty earned for this book to Bal Asha Trust, a childcare institution providing quality care to destitute children in Mumbai.

Foreword

Tamal is a prolific writer and writes well. He has a unique ability to be witty, pithy, sharp and tongue-in-cheek—all at the same time. Because of this, for a long time he has kept his readers hooked. He is a mythical bowler who can bowl left-handed, right-handed, fast, leg spin, off spin, googly, and every variation in between. His ability to dig for facts while leveraging his deep pool of contacts amongst business, government and regulators gives him a unique credibility.

This book covers a range of topics that spans what can be termed as the modern-day history of the Indian financial services industry. To see how far we have come, you need to only read Part I of the book, which gives a reference point starting fifteen years back. While reading the book for this Foreword, I felt as if I was on a voyage in time. It was almost as if the author took me back into time and then forward again.

The Lehman days were indeed frightful in the Indian context. It was not because we did something wrong, but because the market would hold us accountable and responsible for someone else's sins. The judgement was not just limited to the market! To make our case to all stakeholders and at the same time to hold on to our ratings, required vast pools of energy and self-belief. It was a belief that we had not done anything wrong. In all this turbulence, the government and the regulator took steps, to help, facilitate and handhold, Indian business and banks.

Financial inclusion was a subject which I felt very strongly about very early in my career. It was a horizon for growth. The intersection of demand and technology appeared to make the task not so difficult. Unfortunately, the technology available then was not adequate. There were other challenges too that the industry was facing, all of which have been brought out very well by Tamal.

Why this industry will thrive has also been argued well. Measures like Jan-Dhan, Aadhaar and the criss-crossing of even more advanced technologies, reach, cost of transaction, data analytics, artificial intelligence, and the continuing demand for credit have opened up a new chapter in this business.

Tamal has covered public-sector institutions in detail. They have done the common man a lot of service under challenging conditions. These institutions face difficult times for a variety of reasons. How they and the majority shareholder navigate through these times will be the subject of yet another book on the fast-moving Indian financial sector. At this juncture in India's economic development, these institutions are critically important and hence it is imperative that they remain strong and healthy.

A large number of Tamal's essays cover the issue of bad loans. This is an extremely vast and complex subject. Loans go bad for a variety of reasons. Remember the 'stranded assets' that were talked of a few years back; or the microfinance crises; or the retail lending issues, about ten years back. If loans go bad, the challenge is to have resolution mechanisms in place.

While a series of steps have been taken in the last few months, what is needed is quick resolution. Non-performing assets (NPAs) sitting in the books and no growth in fresh lending is a lethal combination for banks. It is especially troubling if in such cases, lending rates are in the teens. It will take only six years for the principal amount of NPA to double at 12 per cent interest rate.

Tamal writes about the relationship between the policymakers in government and the regulatory set-up. Indeed, there is a need for harmony to ensure that the opportunities at hand are seized and India grows at its full potential.

Demonetization, I believe, is the single biggest, boldest and broad-reaching step taken by any government in India. The courage to take this step and to drive it is beyond imagination. The speed, agility and precision with which this was driven point to the fact that if we, as a nation, set our mind to a task, we can deliver. The fruits of demonetization will be harvested, that is for sure. And the harvest will be rich.

As one reads through history, and indeed to me this book is history, untainted and as it happened, one cannot but ponder what next. That there will be change is certain. This change will be breathtaking, as technology challenges all the paradigms that we have known so far. This technology will drive us to a new tomorrow. And Tamal, I am sure, will chronicle it.

K.V. Kamath

Shanghai
September 2017

Introduction

On 15 September 2008, Lehman Brothers Holdings Inc. filed for bankruptcy. The collapse of the iconic US investment bank, with $639 billion in assets and almost an equal quantum of debt and 25,000 employees worldwide, led to the global financial crisis and recession in many parts of the world. But India was largely unaffected. Its banking system was ring-fenced by its conservative, risk-averse Reserve Bank of India (RBI) Governor Y.V. Reddy. He had laid down office just ten days before the Lehman collapse but made sure that the banks in India remained unaffected by the crisis that swept through the global financial markets.

The Indian economy too was resilient; the growth dropped below 5 per cent for only one quarter—March 2009—and bounced back fast. After three successive years of over 9 per cent growth, India's economic growth sagged but to a relatively healthy 6.72 per cent in 2009 even as the rest of the world struggled with recession. For the next two years, the growth rose further—8.59 and 8.91 per cent, respectively.

Parachuted from the finance ministry, Reddy's successor, D. Subbarao, responded to the global crisis by flooding the financial system with money and bringing down the policy rate to its historic low. Indian banks were also allowed to restructure those loans that had gone bad. It helped borrowers—affected by demand recession globally and the collapse of the exports markets—who were not in a position to pay back to the banks. India could stage a sharp, V-shaped recovery but the ultra-loose monetary policy and loan restructuring had sown the seeds of inflation and piles of bad assets. The inflation genie was bottled only after Subbarao's successor, Raghuram Rajan, launched a war against it but the bad-assets pile has still been growing, leading to banks' reluctance to lend.

This book is a humble attempt to chronicle a tumultuous decade—from the collapse of Lehman Brothers to Demonetization—for Indian banking and finance. Demonetization was an exercise that squeezed out 86 per cent of the currency in circulation in India in November–December 2016.

What a decade it has been! Reddy could save the banking system from the impact of Lehman collapse but India's microfinance industry—which had been growing at a breakneck speed—got almost wiped out. The event came to pass when the promulgation of a state law in Andhra Pradesh, the hotbed of microfinance, put severe restrictions on its activities. In 2010, SKS Microfinance Ltd got itself listed on the bourses, the second microfinance entity globally to do so after Banco Compartamos in Mexico in 2007, but months after that the Andhra Pradesh law nearly killed SKS and many others.

The state followed that path as it felt that the microfinance companies were too aggressive in their lending activities and held them responsible for many farmer suicides. Indeed, many MFIs (microfinance institutions) were too aggressive as they had an eye on private equity investors; they were eager to drum up their valuation by building larger loan books. However, with remarkable restraint and maturity, the industry came back from the verge of collapse in a few years. So much so that by 2016, eight of them got the RBI's nod to became small-finance banks. It has been a fascinating tale of death and resurrection.

This book has chronicled that and more. Some public-sector banks have been driving down the slow lane to death, loaded with bad assets. Many of the loans that had been restructured following the Lehman collapse continued to haunt them but they were in a denial mode till Rajan drove the first-of-its-kind asset quality review (AQR) for these banks. When it came to exposing their bad loans, they had been doing a belly dance but the AQR forced them to do a striptease. Some of the essays in the book have traced the rise in the bad debts of Indian banks and tried to go to the roots—

as to why assets go bad. Is it the inefficiency of the management? Is it the interference of the government? Rogue corporations? Or, is it about business cycles going bust?

Then there are other issues that dominated the decade, many of which signified banking reforms. For instance, in 2011, the Reserve Bank freed savings rates, the last bastion of mandated interest rate in Indian banking. For better monetary transmission, the central bank has also been continuously evolving the benchmark loan rates of banks—from prime lending rate to (PLR) base rate to MCLR, or marginal cost of funds-based lending rate. Currently, it is in search of yet another new benchmark to replace MCLR for greater transparency and transmission.

Then, there are other critical issues such as corruption in banking; political interference in the shape of frequent loan waivers for farmers; lack of reforms in critical areas or selling old wine in a new bottle in the name of reforms.

Most importantly, the decade has also seen the opening up of the sector known for repression; the resurgence of non-banking finance companies (NBFCs) and the RBI accepting the ritual of flexible inflation targeting. Indeed, the Indian central bank has changed. The monetary policy is no longer the governor's policy; it is now decided by a six-member monetary policy committee and the governor just has a casting vote in case there is a tie in the decision-making.

The central bank has also become more adventurous. Since bank nationalization in 1969, India got its first set of ten private banks in 1993 but not all of them survived. We had to wait for a decade to get another two banks. And then, suddenly we got approval for twenty-three banks in two years since August 2015—two universal banks, ten small banks and eleven payments banks. The RBI is now ready to offer bank licences on tap and experiment with different types of banks such as wholesale banks and depository ones.

There has been a radical shift in the regulator's approach to bank licences. Earlier, it was waiting for the public-sector banks to gain strength and be able to withstand competition before opening up the sector. But now, it is clearly telling the public-sector banks to fend for themselves while new banks are ushered in. It has also overcome the fear of failure. Even if some of the small banks and payments banks fail (some of the payments banks, in fact, have withdrawn from the fray and a few more may walk out), they will not shake the system.

Meanwhile, public-sector banks are steadily losing their market share. And finally, even though India believes in a bank-led financial system, the past few years have seen the emergence of NBFCs, both in terms of asset creation and return to the investors. A normally conservative central bank is also allowing commercial banks to embrace technology in a big way. Some of them are moving on this lane very aggressively and a few years down the line, they plan to transform themselves into technology companies and say, 'We also do banking!'

And, of course, there is a section on demonetization, the most controversial economic decision in independent India since 1978 when a similar exercise was carried out even as there is no sign of the debate on its short-term pains versus long-term gains dying down.

The essays in this book have tried to capture the most defining decade of Indian banking and look at what the future holds.

The second part of the book deals with fifteen personalities who have played a seminal role in shaping the decade. They are regulators, professionals and professionals-turned-entrepreneurs. Not all of them are hugely successful but they are there because either they made policies or influenced policymaking that shaped the decades or as pioneers in their fields or as professionals with a mission but unable to fulfil it because of external circumstances.

There are some repetitions when it comes to data or technical terms used in the book. They have been left there intentionally at the insistence of the editor. Some of these terms are explained more than once to reinforce them in the narrative and support the arguments. This gives the readers the freedom to read sections or columns selectively if any of them does not want to read the whole book. Similarly, some data are being repeated in different context to support the arguments.

Barring two, all the essays and profiles/interviews in this book have appeared in *Mint*, India's second-largest-read business daily where I write a weekly column Banker's Trust, every Monday. I have hand-picked these columns from a total of 600 that appeared in the last decade. They have discussed, dissected and analysed issues that transcend date and time.

The idea of bringing them between two covers is to tell this gripping story of Indian banking in the most happening decade, globally. This story also offers clues to the future of the Indian industry which many believe is the most exciting place to be in among all the emerging markets.

PART I
A Turbulent Decade

1

The Lehman Collapse Days

On the day US investment bank Lehman Brothers Holdings Inc. filed for bankruptcy, the chief executive officers of six large commercial banks assembled at a south Mumbai hotel to debate a topic close to every foreign banker's heart: 'Should India open up the financial sector?' Y.V. Reddy, former RBI governor, widely known for his views against the opening up of the sector, had retired just ten days before the collapse.

His successor, D. Subbarao, former finance secretary, was to be the chief guest at the conference but he excused himself because he could not have expressed his views on the subject in his new role as RBI governor. Owing to the newsflash that morning, the mood at the conference was sombre and even the traditionally aggressive foreign bankers, who always blame the Indian banking regulator for keeping the doors closed, were restrained in their arguments. The beer tasted flat that evening, the food stale, and a few panellists, including ICICI Bank Ltd's then managing director and CEO, K.V. Kamath, did not wait for the dinner and left immediately after the discussion was over.

The exposure of ICICI Bank, India's largest private-sector lender, to Lehman Brothers was $83 million, less than 0.1 per cent of its consolidated balance sheet, but investors rushed to sell the bank's stock and pulled it down by 15 per cent in the next few days as panic gripped the market. A few other banks, including State Bank of India (SBI) and Punjab National Bank, two large public-sector banks, had a small exposure to Lehman Brothers in various forms.

At a meeting with the executives of Lehman Brothers' Indian arm and local banks, V. Leeladhar, then deputy governor of RBI, told the US investment bank to close all transactions with Indian banks within twenty-four hours. Lehman Brothers did so in forty-eight hours. It was running a non-banking financial company in India, but its entire capital was invested in government bonds and bank deposits; so the money was safe. Its broking arm, Lehman Brothers Securities Pvt. Ltd, housed in Ceejay House—hemmed in between the Arabian Sea and the glass-walled Atria shopping mall on Annie Besant Road in midtown Mumbai, the most expensive office space in the city—was taken over by Japan's Nomura Holdings Inc. In October, Nomura also took over Lehman Brothers' back office operations, which employed 2200 people, in Powai, a western suburb of Mumbai.

The panic did not last long. The global financial system had plunged into an unprecedented liquidity crunch after the Lehman collapse but India shrugged it off relatively easily. The GDP growth dropped to 3.5 per cent in the March 2009 quarter, but in the very next quarter, it rose to 5.9 per cent and by the September 2009 quarter, it bounced back to 9.3 per cent.

We all celebrated how resilient the Indian banking system was. A cautious and conservative regulator ring-fenced the Indian banks by not allowing them to take excessive risk.

However, we celebrated too early. The monetary policy and fiscal stimulus that followed after the collapse to ward off its impact led to a V-shaped recovery at that point, but it didn't last long; seeds were sown for high inflation and bad assets. It took years to bottle the inflation genie but we are far from sorting out the problem of bad assets.

The first rate cut was announced on 20 October 2008, more than a month after the Lehman collapse and in the next six months, the policy rate was brought down from 9 per cent to 3.25 per cent (lower than the savings bank rate which was an administered rate then); the cash reserve ratio or the portion of deposits that banks keep with the RBI from 9 per cent to 5 per cent; and the floor for banks' government bond holding from 25 to 24 per cent. Collectively, the cut in the reserve requirement and the opening of new refinance windows pumped Rs 5.6 trillion into the Indian financial system.

As the growth picked up, RBI had to tighten the policy, but the process was slow. For fear of hurting growth, RBI Governor D. Subbarao took 'baby steps' in raising the policy rates. As a result of this, the year-on-year growth of inflation which already crossed double digits by October 2008 remained there for the most part of 2009 and 2010. By 2011, it cooled down, but only a tad, and rose again to double digits in 2013. It was contained much later after Governor Raghuram Rajan, who succeeded Subbarao in September 2013, launched a decisive war against inflation to rein in the erosion in the value of money.

While inflation has been contained, there is no relief for the banks from piling bad assets. By flooding the system with liquidity and bringing down the policy rate to a record low, RBI encouraged banks to give cheap credit. The regulator also allowed them to restructure those loans which the borrowers found difficult to service, as many markets collapsed and the world was in the grip of recession. The boom was short-lived, but the bust lasted far too long. The gross non-performing assets of the banking system which were 2.3 per cent of their loans in 2008 have progressively risen to 9.6 per cent in 2017. If we take into account those loans that have been restructured, then the stress for the banking system is much higher. For fear of accumulating more bad loans, banks are reluctant to give credit even as over-leveraged corporations are under pressure to pay back.

The following pieces in this chapter relive those days of turmoil and trauma and the role of the banking regulator in protecting the Indian financial system. The first one describes graphically how a young finance professional's world collapsed in India and the rest dissect the Lehman phenomenon in India and its legacy. Together, they represent a slice of history of Indian banking that even today feels the tremors of that crash.

HOW A YOUNG FINANCE PROFESSIONAL'S WORLD COLLAPSED

December 2008

This is a story of a young financial-sector professional who rode on the economic boom of the past few years, but lost his job when the wave of the global credit crunch hit India after the collapse of the Wall Street investment bank Lehman Brothers.

His story is very surreal. The young MBA changed three jobs in the past four years and his annual salary rose from Rs 60,000 to Rs 550,000 by hawking loans to small and medium entrepreneurs and mortgages. After he joined a large NBFC with footprints across India, he got a hefty bonus for the year ending March 2008. But the good time did not last long. The cracks started showing from January itself, with borrowers diverting money into the stock market and instances of rising defaults. The NBFC, with its headquarters in Mumbai, chose to look the other way till the liquidity crunch hit it hard. By end-September, the company started asking people to resign. He was the last person of his thirty-member team to be asked to go.

Here's a first-person account of how a buzzing office turned into a cemetery and the computer terminals became tombstones.

June 2007

I was on my way to office. XX, my former colleague and now with a big NBFC, called me. They were looking for a sales manager to handle their SME (small and medium enterprise) loan portfolio. I knew if I could make it, I would be on a fast track as the company is very aggressive. I was in my casual Saturday clothes but my former colleague insisted that I drop in at his office. It was a small office with DSAs (direct sales agents) swarming all around. There was no place to sit. Somehow he managed to find a sofa in one corner of the reception and my first interview was over in ten minutes. I was not even carrying my CV!

My key area of responsibility would be appointing DSAs, training them and generating business. We also discussed other key issues such as IRR (internal rate of return), fee income and cost of acquisition.

A day later, I got a call from the SME business head and it's another ten-minute interview on the phone. I could feel his aggression while talking on the phone. He agreed to all my terms and offered me the job, provided I join in a week. I got a 35 per cent raise in salary, but including other benefits, the hike was close to 60 per cent. Not bad, I thought.

First Day in Office

Got a warm welcome from all. From day one, expectations from me were very high. My target for July, August and September was decided on the spot. It was a very aggressive target.

July–September 2007

It was like a dream. Every month we exceeded our target by more than 30 per cent. We were working till midnight every day and it was great fun. Particularly, the construction equipment and commercial vehicle finance division was doing extremely well. They were far ahead of us. The personal loan division was also giving us a good contest. The mortgage (home loan and loan against property) and auto loan divisions were not doing that well compared to others.

October 2007

There was no semi-annual appraisal for me as I had not been there from the beginning of the year. But those who had been around then got a good hike. I was told that if I do well, I will get a bonus. The terms on which the appraisal was done were business volume, returns, defaults, etc. (October, November and December—we were going a bit slow. But it was a happy time for me as I became a father. I will have to be more responsible now.)

January 2008

We moved to a new office. It was a huge 25,000 sq. ft office and I got my little corner, an independent workstation. There were some 400 workstations and a large meeting room with all modern facilities, as well as a training room. We also got a huge cafeteria.

I started working harder as I wanted to get a good bonus. I could not afford to lose out on an excellent rating. Money motivates.

But then, instances of cheque bouncing started. The collection department had to work now. They have had a cushy time so far. Strangely, big-value loans started defaulting. One such loan involved a big confectionery firm in east India.

The collection managers looking after personal and auto loans were also under pressure.

But all efforts went in vain. Only a few made payments while the rest told us they could not pay as their business was not in good shape.

February 2008

The situation became worse. We were really scared.

We didn't have any mechanism to track the end use of funds. Part of our loans started flowing into the stock market. With the Sensex rising to its lifetime high, people became greedy. We got to know that the customers delinquent in our books were also defaulting with other private financiers. It was shocking. All customers turning delinquent had taken loan from multiple financiers, and the loans were not backed by any security.

My boss told me that I would not need to bother about delinquency as that's not my area. The credit appraisal process was more or less templated although we had to invite the customers personally for a formal business discussion.

April 2008

Time for reward, time for party.

Our new deputy CEO visited all metros to celebrate our achievement. We achieved Rs 70 billion worth of business in less than a year!

I got a good bonus and felt very happy.

The next year's budget was Rs 100-billion business for all products—mortgage, auto, personal loan, loans for construction equipment, commercial vehicle and SME. And the focus was on secured funding.

April–June 2008

Time of slow growth—the business volume was coming down. What contributed to this was also the rise in the policy rate of the Reserve Bank of India. It did so to fight rising inflation. We cut the DSA payout and the cost of acquisition was reduced to 1 per cent.

I could sense that difficult time was ahead. Only the customers desperate for funds would come to us. With the cut in the DSA payout, we also became the least preferred financier for the DSAs. By the time the loan proposal came to us, the customer was already overleveraged. So, the growth in loan approval started coming down.

And the delinquency rate was shooting up sharply to 8–9 per cent.

July–September 2008

No improvement in the volume of business or delinquency. The half-year business growth was bad.

I was scared. The cost of living was increasing every day. The inflation rate was close to 13 per cent.

4 October 2008

We stopped loan disbursements completely. The message from the top management was that it was only a short-term blip and we would start soon. The cost of fund was extremely high at that point of time.

All other financial institutions also either entirely stopped, or were doing very little business.

Every day I was going to office but there was no work. In the past six months, we had been going slow and not achieving the target, but at least there was work.

Every day we were hearing a new rumour, like the company might reduce the budget and there could be retrenchment.

October 8

The entire DSA team—some 200 people—was asked to go.

That was a clear signal. I started looking for jobs. I uploaded my CV on all the major job portals, but there was no response.

The tension was mounting. All my friends were suggesting, 'Don't move to a new place. Just hold on to your ground.'

My friends working with other NBFCs started losing jobs and a few of them managed some placements after taking huge pay cuts. I can't afford that. I have a baby at home and my wife is not working now. I have fixed liabilities for my car and house rent.

November

The ugliest month in my life. Some of my colleagues were asked to move to the collection department.

Initially, some of them resisted, but there was no choice. The message from the HR was firm: either go to collection or move out. From sales managers, overnight they became collection managers.

Someone told me that those transferred to the collection division were safe till March. I realized that later.

In the second week, many more were asked to resign. They were offered three months' salary. Now I found the chair next to me was empty. The poor guy had been transferred to the loan against property division.

We had a small party a few days back to celebrate his joining.

I escaped this time, but how long?

I could not sleep at night. For no reason, I was shouting at my wife. I was sweating and getting irritated frequently. I had to consult a doctor and was prescribed tranquilizers at bedtime for a month.

In the third week, another fifty guys were asked to leave.

One of my colleagues who had taken a transfer to western India hardly three months ago was given two options: resign immediately and take three months' salary or remain on the payroll till you get another job, but not more than three months.

The credit manager faced the same fate.

That left only me in my department. When will it come? The office became quiet. It was like a dead body in the ICU with all its support system gradually being taken away one after another. I started finding it difficult to breathe.

I started spending long hours on the Net looking for a job. I was sending my CV everywhere, but did not get a single call.

December

Got my first call from a brokerage. It was my worst performance in an interview in my life. I was down. My self-confidence had been shattered.

In my empty office, I started having hallucinations as rumours abounded of many of our offices closing down.

Then there was a ray of hope as I heard the company would start operations selectively. The focus would be on the quality of business and not its volume. I was the only person there in SME at the sales manager level. Will they consider me?

I started interacting with the DSAs. Who knows, I might need them.

One day, in the first week of December when I came back to the office after visiting some DSAs to discuss the new model of business that I plan to do when we restart our operations, I saw our HR manager sitting next to my workstation. We had tea and then he put his arm around me to say the two words which I had all along been fearing to hear: 'Please resign.'

HOW THE RBI FENCED INDIAN BANKS FROM THE TURMOIL

5 October 2008

Within hours after Lehman Brothers Holdings Inc. filed for Chapter 11 bankruptcy protection in September 2008, the Reserve Bank of India asked its Indian arm to close all transactions with Indian banks immediately. The central bank followed this up by asking the Indian banks to furnish data on their exposure to other troubled financial entities, including Wachovia Corp, Fortis NV, American International Group Inc. (AIG) and Washington Mutual Inc. India's largest private-sector lender ICICI Bank Ltd's exposure to Lehman Brothers was $83 million, less than 0.1 per cent of its consolidated balance sheet. State Bank of India, Bank of India, Bank of Baroda, Punjab National Bank, Axis Bank Ltd and a few other Indian banks had a small exposure to the Wall Street bank in various forms, and part of this had already been closed.

Lehman Brothers ran an NBFC in India but its entire capital, some Rs 8 billion, was invested in government securities and bank deposits, and hence there was no cause for alarm. Similarly, there is no immediate problem for the local insurance ventures that have Fortis and AIG as partners. In future, Fortis and AIG may not be able to bring in fresh capital, but their stakes can always be sold to others. Finally, Wachovia holds a banking licence in India, but that will be cancelled as such licences are non-transferable. Overall, there is very little impact of the battered and bruised global investment banks and mortgage firms on the Indian financial system. The local banks are healthy, with adequate capital and very little net non-performing loans. So, how did RBI ring-fence the Indian banks from the turmoil?

Before answering this question, let's first look at the root of the global problem. It started with the US housing market, where a lot of imprudent loans were given to sub-prime borrowers who couldn't afford to repay them. These faulty loans were sliced, mixed with good loans and sold to other banks across the globe. This is loosely called securitization. Banks, insurance firms, pension funds, and even state governments bought those rated assets without batting an eyelid, as there was plenty of liquidity and interest rates were low.

The bubble burst when interest rates started climbing and house prices started falling. The problem was magnified with the proliferation of derivatives on these loans which were affected by the meltdown in the values of the underlying assets. How did India escape this? A cautious and conservative RBI has not allowed banks to take excessive risk. The work started in 2000 when the RBI first conducted a stress test of the banks' investment portfolios in a scenario of increasing interest rate.

This was done to strengthen the banks' ability to absorb the shock when interest rates rise. In a low-interest regime, banks make tonnes of money trading bonds, but when the interest rates rise, they are hit as they need to 'mark to market'(MTM) their bond portfolio. 'Mark to market' is the accounting system which calls for valuing bonds at their prevailing market price and not at the historical price of acquisition. The price of bonds and their yield move in opposite directions.

The yield on the benchmark ten-year bond dropped to its historic low of 4.97 per cent in October 2003, but well before that, in January 2002, the RBI advised banks to meet the adverse impact of interest-rate risk by building up an investment fluctuation reserve, or IFR. When a reversal of rate movement started in late 2004, this helped banks absorb the impact of rising interest rates and MTM losses.

Similarly, the RBI sensed the real estate bubble ahead of other regulators, and in June 2005, it directed banks to have a board-mandated policy in respect of their real estate exposure limits, collaterals and margins. It also increased the risk weight on banks' exposure to commercial real estate from 100 per cent to 125 per cent in July 2005, and 150 per cent in April 2006. A higher risk weight means banks need more capital to give loans and hence their cost of money goes up. The idea was to discourage them from aggressively disbursing real estate loans.

The risk weight on housing loans to individuals against the mortgage of properties was also increased from 50 per cent to 75 per cent in December 2004 (this was subsequently reduced for housing loans up to Rs 300,000). The RBI also increased the risk weight for consumer credit and capital market exposures from 100 per cent to 125 per cent. Unable to rein in the scorching loan growth in the real estate sector, personal loans, credit card receivables, and loans against shares, and apprehending a higher default rate in such loans, the RBI progressively raised the provisions for standard assets in November 2005, May 2006 and January 2007.

Till that time, a bank needed to set aside money or provide for only when a loan turned bad. The RBI asked them to set aside money even when a loan has not turned bad or is a standard asset. This is a preemptive action. These loans now attract 2 per cent provisions for standard assets, while loans to agriculture and small and medium enterprises continue to attract 0.25 per cent provisions, and all other loans 0.40 per cent. The RBI has also clamped down on interbank liabilities and banks are not allowed to borrow more than 200 per cent of their net worth or capital and reserves from other banks.

Banks typically borrow from other banks in the interbank market to meet their short-term requirements; they do not give loans by borrowing from this overnight market. The limit for such exposure for exceptionally well-capitalized banks is 300 per cent of their net worth. At the same time, NBFCs as well as banks and financial institutions are not encouraged to securitize their exposure and create more liquidity. A February 2006 RBI norm on securitization, in fact, virtually killed the market as securitization does not bring down capital requirement any more.

Finally, the RBI has also resorted to strong 'moral suasion' to dampen banks' appetite for risk. A 'moral suasion' is a persuasion tactic used by an authority to influence and pressure, but not force, banks into adhering to policy. They now closely monitor unhedged foreign currency exposures of their corporate clients and do not dare to venture into selling complex derivatives in order to help firms tide over currency fluctuations. As a result of all these, sophisticated credit derivatives market and financial innovation in India are still at an embryonic stage, but very few are complaining as it seems better to feel safe than sorry.

LIQUIDITY CRISIS: WHERE HAS ALL THE MONEY GONE?

13 October 2008

A one and a half percentage points cut in banks' cash reserve ratio (CRR), which defines the amount of cash that commercial banks need to keep with the RBI, has infused Rs 600 billion into the liquidity-starved Indian financial system on Saturday. CRR is held in cash and cash equivalents parked with the central bank to ensure that banks do not run out of cash to meet the payment demands of their depositors. It is a monetary policy tool used for controlling money supply in an economy.

There have been occasions in the past when CRR was cut by more than one and a half percentage points. For instance, in November 2001, it was cut by one and a three-quarter percentage points to 5.75 per cent, and in July 1974, the cut was even sharper—by two percentage points, to 5 per cent of the deposits. But in its seventy-three-year history, the RBI has never announced a second round of CRR cut even before the first cut takes effect—something it did last week.

This shows the seriousness with which the Indian central bank is viewing the liquidity crisis. Till recently, the system had plenty of money. In fact, the RBI had to raise CRR by one and a half percentage points in stages since April to drain the excess money that was stoking inflation. Where has all the money gone? What is the root of the sudden liquidity crunch?

The main source of money in the system in the past two years has been the RBI's dollar buying. The seemingly unending dollar flow pushed the level of the local currency to 39.20 a dollar early this year. An appreciating rupee hurts the competitiveness of exporters as their real income in local currency goes down. So, the RBI was buying dollars from the market to stem the rise of the rupee and, for every dollar it bought, an equivalent amount in rupees was injected into the system. As a result of this, India's foreign exchange reserve rose to a record $316 billion in May. At the same time, the rupee liquidity in the system increased phenomenally.

The excess liquidity was mopped up by the banking regulator through a series of hikes in CRR and the flotation of special bonds under the monetary stabilization scheme, or MSS. Under this scheme, the RBI floated dated securities as well as short-term treasury bills to soak up excess liquidity. They were not part of the government's annual borrowing programme to raise money to bridge the fiscal deficit. The RBI is not buying dollars any more as the supply has dried up. It is, in fact, selling dollars to protect the sharp erosion in the value of the local currency as a weak rupee increases the cost of import and adds to the inflation.

The rupee has lost some 18 per cent since January and at Friday's lowest level (49.30 to a dollar), the deprecation was more than 20 per cent. While the RBI's dollar buying added to the rupee liquidity in the financial system, for every dollar it sells now, an equivalent amount in rupees is sucked out of the system.

In October alone, the market estimates that the central bank has sold at least $5 billion. The latest data show that for the week that ended on 3 October, India's foreign exchange reserve declined by $7.8 billion—the highest in a week in the past two years—to $283.9 billion. Both dollar sale and revaluation of global currencies contributed to the fall in reserves. Overall, India's foreign exchange reserve has gone down by more than 10 per cent, or $32 billion, since May, signalling the RBI's presence in the currency market as a seller.

The RBI needs to supply dollar in the market as other sources are fast drying up. Foreign institutional investors, or FIIs, the main drivers of Indian equity markets, have sold Indian stocks worth $10.18 billion net this year after pumping in $17.36 billion in 2007. The volume of Indian firms' overseas borrowing is also coming down sharply as money is becoming more expensive overseas following the global credit crisis.

Finally, exporters, who earn dollars and sell them in the local market, too do not have too much of greenback in their kitty as most of them sold their dollar receivables in the forward market, apprehending further appreciation of the rupee. The trend has reversed and they have been caught off guard. The only source of dollar at this point is foreign direct investment (FDI), but that can take care of only a very small part of the demand. On the other hand, importers are buying dollar aggressively as they fear the rupee can depreciate further.

In the first five months of the current fiscal year, between April and August 2008, the trade deficit, or the gap between the cost that India incurred for importing goods, including oil, and its earnings on exports, is close to $51 billion and it has been rising every month. For instance, in July, the trade deficit was $10.79 billion and it rose to $13.94 billion in August. Even if the trade deficit remains at the August level, the RBI needs to sell about $690 million daily in the foreign exchange market in the absence of any other supplier. The RBI's dollar sale is just one of the causes of the liquidity crunch. Oil and fertilizer firms seem to be the biggest guzzler of bank credit, which has risen by 24.8 per cent year-on-year till 10 October.

Oil marketing firms need money to bridge the gap between the cost of importing oil and the price at which the product is sold in the domestic market. The government is supposed to take care of the deficit by issuing oil bonds to these firms. The deficit for the past year was some Rs 140 billion and despite the 50 per cent fall in international crude prices from its peak, this year's deficit could be around Rs 250 billion. Since the government has not issued oil bonds yet, the banking system is bearing the burden. Similarly, banks have also been lending big money to fertilizer firms since government subsidy has not yet been released. This amount could be as much as Rs 300 billion. The banking system has not yet been reimbursed by the government for the Rs 664.77-billion farm loan waiver and debt relief that was completed in June.

The pressure on the banking system has been further aggravated by the problems faced by a section of the Indian mutual fund industry—the so-called liquid funds which invest in money market instruments.

Some of these funds have invested in short-term commercial papers (CPs) and certificate of deposits (CDs) issued by NBFCs, and in real estate companies to earn high returns. Commercial paper is an unsecured short-term loan, usually issued at a discount, and CDs are like bank deposits with a fixed interest rate and fixed maturity period.

They have also invested in asset-backed securities and bought pools of retail loans in the form of truck finance, car loans, etc. These securities, known as 'pass through certificates', or PTCs, offer higher interest, but are illiquid and there are risks of default. Banks were parking their excess money in these funds but now, facing a liquidity crunch, they are withdrawing money from such funds. This is shrinking the size of the funds and, at the same time, drying up resources for firms that were raising money through CPs and CDs. They are now turning to banks for funds, adding to the liquidity pressure. In August, liquid funds were managing assets worth Rs 890 billion, about 18 per cent of the total assets under the management of the Indian mutual fund industry. According to industry estimates, in the past one week, Rs 300 billion has been withdrawn from liquid and other debt funds, and in the past three months, the withdrawal could be as much as Rs 1 trillion.

Finally, the growing mistrust among global banks and their refusal to lend to each other is also affecting domestic liquidity. Most large Indian banks, both state-run as well as private ones, have an overseas presence. The aggressive ones have been building assets overseas by rolling over their liabilities, raised from the interbank market. But these money lines are now fast drying up and it is difficult to replenish them as overseas banks are not rolling over credit any more even though the London interbank offered rate (LIBOR), an international benchmark for interest rate, is soaring.

So, if an Indian bank faces a liquidity crunch abroad, it is now being forced to borrow from India, convert the money into foreign currency, and then quickly export the funds to support the bank's overseas operations. Last Friday, the government cancelled auctions of two bonds slated to raise Rs 100 billion, but sooner or later, it has to enter the market as part of its borrowing programme (around Rs 390 billion) is yet to be completed this fiscal year. So, the pressure on liquidity can only rise.

How does the RBI tackle the crisis? Apart from cutting CRR, it has been infusing money through its repurchase, or repo window, every day. Under this arrangement, banks borrow from the RBI at 9 per cent, offering government bonds as collaterals. In October, on average, the RBI has been infusing about Rs 750 billion daily into the system. Theoretically, the RBI can cut CRR to zero in stages and the seven and a half percentage point cut—the current level of CRR—can infuse Rs 3 trillion into the system. This allows the RBI to sell about $60 billion in the foreign exchange market, at the current rupee–dollar exchange rate, to support the local currency. This is a little more than 20 per cent of the country's foreign exchange reserves and double that of what the RBI has sold since May.

MSS bonds can also be unwound to create liquidity. The outstanding MSS bonds are worth Rs 1.73 trillion. Unwinding these bonds will release liquidity not into the entire system but into those banks that had bought the MSS bonds.

However, the RBI cannot do this because Indian banks are required to invest certain portion of their deposits in government bonds known as SLR (statutory liquidity ratio—or the ratio of their funds that banks are required to maintain in liquid instruments) securities. Under the law, 25 per cent of bank deposits must be invested in SLR bonds. The RBI has recently brought down the level to 24 per cent, thereby offering a temporary relief to banks. If the RBI wants to buy back MSS bonds from the banks, their SLR level will go down below 24 per cent. So, along with the CRR cut, the RBI also needs to bring down the SLR requirement to free up money.

The RBI can also open a special repo window for mutual funds, large NBFCs and housing finance firms, and money can be offered in exchange of AAA-rated (AAA is the best rating) securities as collaterals. This will not only ease the pressure on the banking system, but also avert the impending collapse of some of the funds and NBFCs.

Unlike banks, mutual funds have very small capital and some of the liquid funds may see their entire capital being wiped out by losses. Once the government gets Parliament's nod for oil bonds and subsidy for fertilizer firms, and reimburses banks for the farm loan waiver package, money will flow into the system. Besides, this will enable the oil-marketing firms to buy dollars directly from the RBI, pledging the oil bonds, and this will ease the pressure on the foreign exchange market.

In a late-night statement on Friday, RBI governor D. Subbarao said the central bank 'has taken action to inject liquidity into the system as warranted by the situation' and it is 'ready to take appropriate, effective and swift action'. The challenge before RBI now, apart from injecting liquidity, is to break the expectation of a daily depreciating rupee. It has been selling dollars every day in the past few weeks and the pattern of its intervention is predictable, allowing the foreign exchange market to form a view on the currency.

This needs to be broken fast. With $284 billion in its kitty, the fourth-largest foreign currency chest outside the eurozone, after Japan, China and Russia, it can afford to be bold in its currency-management strategy which is now inseparable from liquidity management.

A DESPERATE RBI NEEDS TO BE CREATIVE IN CRISIS MANAGEMENT

24 October 2008

Over the last fortnight, the Indian central bank has cut its policy rate by 100 basis points and banks' cash reserve ratio with the RBI by 250 basis points, thereby releasing Rs 1 trillion into the cash-starved Indian financial system. One basis point is one-hundredth of a percentage point.

Besides, interest rates on non-resident Indian, or NRI, deposits have been raised; norms on raising external commercial borrowings relaxed; and a special Rs 200-billion liquidity window has been opened to help mutual funds facing redemption pressure.

Clearly, the objective is to bring down interest rates, create adequate liquidity in the system and keep the rupee–dollar exchange rate at a reasonable level.

With global commodity prices declining sharply, the fear of rising inflation is disappearing fast and growth is back on the Reserve Bank of India's agenda. And, along with growth, it wants to maintain financial stability at *any* cost.

In a sense, liquidity, interest rates and exchange rate are interlinked. The RBI has cut its policy rate to improve sentiment, but that has weakened the rupee further, pushing it down to a lifetime low, as the attraction for rupee assets for overseas investors has waned with the interest rate differential between India and the US shrinking.

Similarly, the RBI's dollar sales in the foreign exchange market are affecting rupee liquidity, as for every dollar it sells, an equivalent amount in rupee is drained from the system. So, if the RBI continues to sell dollars to stem the fall of the local currency, it will need to cut CRR again and again to infuse liquidity into the financial system. The RBI needs to be proactive to address the unprecedented liquidity crunch and the banks' extreme risk aversion for lending, but overall, the central bank's measures smack of adhocracy, nervousness and desperation. It seems to be trying to do too many things and expecting results overnight.

With the general elections round the corner, the government has no time to wait for what in economics is called the 'lead-lag' effect, but the central bank possibly needs to show more patience. Also, it needs to be more creative in its crisis-management strategy.

Let's take a closer look at what the markets expect the RBI to do on Friday:

Policy Rate Cut

Unlike the US Federal Reserve and most other central banks, the RBI has two policy rates—the repo rate, or the rate at which it injects liquidity into the system, and reverse repo rate, or the rate at which it sucks out liquidity.

In a liquidity-surplus situation, the effective policy rate is reverse repo rate, currently at 6 per cent. Similarly, in a liquidity-starved situation, 8 per cent is the policy rate.

The gap between the two rates forms a corridor within which the cost of overnight money should move. Those who are pitching for a rate cut argue that the repo rate should be brought down to 7.5 per cent, narrowing the corridor to 150 basis points. This will bring down the volatility in the overnight call money market.

This is a sensible thing to do but by bringing down the rate, the RBI will end up making the rupee more vulnerable. If it wants to send a strong signal to banks and make them cut their lending rates, it needs to make sure that there is ample liquidity in the system.

This will automatically make the reverse repo rate the effective policy rate. In other words, without announcing any rate cut, the RBI will bring down the policy rate by 200 basis points.

Another Cut in CRR

This is inevitable, even though it may not happen on Friday. In this week alone, the RBI might have spent at least $4 billion (Rs 199.2 billion) in the foreign exchange market to stem the fall of the rupee, which has already lost more than 20 per cent this year. A weaker rupee pushes up the cost of imports and negates the benefit of the falling prices of crude to the economy, among other things. To that extent, it adds to the inflationary pressures.

As long as the RBI sells dollars, it will have to continue to increase rupee liquidity in the system by cutting CRR. Every 100 basis points cut in CRR releases about Rs 400 billion. There is no floor for CRR under banking law, which means it can be brought down to zero, but if that is done the banking regulator will not be able to talk loudly on the safety of Indian banks.

The level of CRR is an indication of the banking system's safety, as, in case of a collapse, the money kept with the central bank acts as a sort of insurance for depositors.

Cut in SLR

Under the law, Indian banks are required to invest 25 per cent of their deposits in government bonds, known as SLR, and any excess bond holdings can be used to borrow from the RBI.

The SLR level has recently been brought to 23.5 per cent, as a temporary measure, to help the banks and the mutual funds that have been seeing huge redemptions to use the money borrowed from the RBI to lend.

An SLR cut will encourage banks to lend as they will have more money at their disposal. On the flip side, the government will find it difficult to sell its papers and raise money from the market when the SLR level goes down. Two government bond auctions worth Rs 100 billion each have been cancelled this month because of lack of liquidity in the system.

The government plans to borrow Rs 390 billion between now and March 2009, and Finance Minister P. Chidambaram has indicated that the borrowing programme will go up to bridge a higher fiscal deficit this year.

Clearly, a cut in SLR will inconvenience the government that is staring at a high fiscal deficit, but it will go a long way in goading banks to lend to companies and individuals.

What Else?

The RBI needs to show more creativity if it wants a faster solution to the problem. For instance, it can pay interest on the banks' CRR balance. Till last year, it was paying interest on CRR, but discontinued it after the amendment of an Act which allows the central bank to bring down CRR to zero (against a 3 per cent floor kept earlier). Interest needs to be paid not to protect banks' profitability, but to enable them to lend at lower rates.

Similarly, the RBI can bring down the risk weights for certain segments such as home loans. The regulator had earlier raised the risk weights for some sectors, including real estate and personal loans, to discourage banks from aggressive lending.

Lower risk weight will bring down the cost of capital for banks.

Finally, the RBI must find ways for the most productive use of its $274-billion foreign exchange reserves. It has already spent about $40 billion to defend the currency without any success. If it uses an equivalent amount to offer support to Indian banks and corporations, overnight the sentiment will change dramatically. It needs to convince Indian companies and the banking system that there won't be any liquidity problem tomorrow. A dollar line from the RBI will also take the pressure off the currency.

What's the point in piling up such a huge foreign exchange reserve unless the central bank uses it when it's needed the most?

IS THE CENTRAL BANK AT RISK OF LOSING ITS CLOTHES?

3 November 2008

The Reserve Bank of India seems to have started throwing the kitchen sink at the liquidity problem that has been plaguing the financial system since Wall Street icon Lehman Brothers filed for bankruptcy in mid-September, plunging global credit markets into a deep crisis.

One week after unveiling a measureless monetary policy review, the Indian central bank on Saturday cut its policy rate, CRR, or the portion of deposits that commercial banks are required to keep with it, and SLR, or the portion banks need to invest in government bonds. The steps are meant to increase banks' resources and ease constraints on credit.

Apart from these, the RBI has announced many more measures, including a Rs 400-billion three-month refinance facility for banks and a buy-back of government bonds offered under MSS. These bonds are not part of the government's annual borrowing programme under which the Indian government raises money from the market every year to be bridge its fiscal deficit. They were floated by the RBI in the past few years to soak up excess liquidity generated by its dollar buying to stem the rise of the local currency. For every dollar it had bought, an equivalent amount in rupee flowed into the system. Now, the situation has reversed and the RBI has been continuously selling dollars, sucking out rupee liquidity.

The buy-back of the MSS bonds will release liquidity. Along with the SLR cut, the central bank has also allowed banks to borrow up to 1.5 per cent of their SLR holdings—Rs 600 billion—temporarily to meet the cash requirements of mutual funds and NBFCs. What has changed between 24 October, when RBI announced its mid-year review of monetary policy, and now?

The overnight call money rate that dropped to about 6.5 per cent, following a cut in CRR and policy rate in the third week of October, crossed 20 per cent last Friday as liquidity tightened again, worsening the growth prospects for the economy, while the wholesale price-based inflation dropped below 11 per cent for the first time since May. Then there was a report by the industry chamber Assocham that forecast a 25–30 per cent loss in jobs in certain sectors after Diwali (it was subsequently withdrawn).

Globally, there has been a series of rate cuts by central banks. The US Federal Reserve took the lead; it was followed by five Asian central banks—in China, Hong Kong, South Korea, Taiwan and Japan. The Bank of England and the European Central Bank too are expected to cut their policy rates sooner than later. This explains the RBI decision to cut its policy rate, but what's the rationale behind the cut in CRR and SLR? Why didn't the central bank pare the level of CRR and SLR on 24 October when it reviewed its monetary policy?

The sudden rise in the overnight call money rate and the tightness in liquidity should not come as a surprise to the RBI. Traditionally, the Indian financial system witnesses this during Diwali as consumers withdraw money from banks and keep the cash with them for festival shopping. The amount of 'money in circulation', as this is called in finance parlance, during the festive time varies between Rs 150 billion and Rs 200 billion.

Another contributing factor to the tightness is a string of bank holidays during the time. As these holidays are not uniform across India, banks tend to keep more cash with them to meet consumer demand.

Finally, the RBI's massive dollar sales are drying up rupee liquidity. In fact, in seven days between 17 October and 24 October, India's foreign exchange reserves dipped by a record $15.4 billion. This means that at the current exchange rate, the RBI had drained close to Rs 770 billion from the system by selling dollars. So, a CRR cut was inevitable, but why did the RBI refrain from doing this in its October policy announcement? The cut in SLR too has not surprised the market, but the timing of the reduction strikes a discordant note. A week ago, the RBI had left it unchanged and defended the action, saying a higher

SLR is symbolic of the safety of the Indian banking system as a bank's investment in government bonds can be liquidated at a short notice and generate cash to meet the depositors' demand. Along with a high capital adequacy ratio, reserve requirements such as CRR and SLR lend strength to the Indian banking system.

Then, why the sudden change in approach? The RBI governor, D. Subbarao, had last week said he could not let his guard slip on inflation, but now it's clear that concerns over inflation have been thrown out of the window, and growth and financial stability are higher on the central bank's priority list. With global commodity prices declining and oil prices going down steadily, India's inflation will fall rapidly in the next few weeks and there will probably be one more round of rate cut this month as the government is expected to cut the administered prices of petrol and diesel before the state elections start in November.

There is nothing wrong in the RBI's focus on growth and financial stability that prompted the aggressive cuts in the policy rate and reserve requirements. In fact, they are in sync with Subbarao's commitment to respond swiftly in an evolving situation. But was there enough provocation for such measures over a weekend? Did the growth prospects dramatically deteriorate in the past week? Was the financial stability massively threatened in the last few days?

It's difficult to justify the RBI's inaction on 24 October and the series of measures a week later. One hopes that the Prime Minister's Office and the finance ministry aren't calling all the shots. In abnormal times, coordination between the central bank and the government is fine, but if the trend continues, the RBI risks losing its clothes.

WE SHOULD SEND FLOWERS TO INDIAN BANKERS

31 May 2009

Last week, Moody's Investors Service threatened to downgrade thirteen Indian banks. The ratings agency is reviewing India's ability to provide support to its banking system. The combined fiscal deficit of the Centre and the state governments, including oil and fertilizer subsidies, is around 11 per cent of India's gross domestic product(GDP), and such a high deficit curbs the government's ability to support the banking system through a capital infusion, if needed.

In its assessment of systemic support, Moody's will consider the size of the banking system in relation to government resources, the level of stress in the banking system and its foreign currency obligations relative to the government's own foreign exchange resources, among other things.

Early in May, US President Barack Obama's administration conducted stress tests of the US banking system and there was no surprise in the result: ten of the largest nineteen US banks need $65 billion (around Rs 3.07 trillion) in funds to boost their capital. US Treasury Secretary Timothy Geithner is 'reasonably' confident that the banks could raise the capital on their own, but the government will not shy away from providing capital, if necessary. The nineteen banks, tested by 150 examiners of the US treasury and the Federal Reserve, account for two-thirds of the total assets of the US banking system, and at least 50 per cent of the total credit in the US economy.

I am not qualified to conduct stress tests of Indian banks. But it may not be a bad idea to take a close look at some of their critical financial parameters and the impact of the global credit crunch on their balance sheets. Except for a few banks such as Jammu and Kashmir Bank Ltd, Development Credit Bank Ltd, City Union Bank Ltd and Lakshmi Vilas Bank Ltd in the private sector and United Bank of India and Punjab and Sind Bank in the public sector, all Indian banks have announced their earnings for fiscal 2009. Since foreign banks operating in India account for just about 8 per cent of banking assets, the performance of state-run and private banks provides a fair idea of the health of the national banking system. The findings are quite revealing.

Going by the published data, , only two banks had less than 11per cent capital adequacy ratio (CAR) in March 2009. They are Dena Bank (10.73 per cent) and State Bank of Hyderabad (10.58 per cent). Under the current norms, banks in India are required to maintain 9 per cent CAR, expressed as a ratio of capital to risk-weighted assets. In other words, for every Rs 100 worth of assets, a bank needs Rs 9 of capital. This is a very critical indicator of a bank's health.

Twenty-eight of the thirty-five banks that have announced their 2009 earnings so far have at least 12 per cent CAR or more, and some of them have even a far higher capital cushion. For instance, Federal Bank Ltd has 20 per cent CAR; Yes Bank Ltd 17 per cent CAR; and ICICI Bank Ltd, India's largest private-sector lender, 15.53 per cent CAR.

Another key parameter to judge the banking system's health is the level of its stressed assets. With corporate earnings shrinking and many individuals losing jobs in a slowing economy, it is only natural that banks' NPAs will grow. A rise in NPAs affect banks' health as they do not earn anything on such assets, and on top of that, banks need to set aside a portion of their income to provide for stressed assets. Even in the worst year for the financial sector in independent India, local banks have not seen any dramatic increase in their NPAs.

In fact, twenty-five out of thirty-five banks that have announced their earnings so far have less than 1 per cent of their advances categorized as net NPAs, and ten of them have even less than fifty basis points net NPAs. After money is set aside to cover gross NPAs, net NPAs are arrived at. Only two banks have at least 2 per cent net NPAs. They are Kotak Mahindra Bank Ltd, 2.39 per cent, and ICICI Bank, 2.09 per cent. State Bank of India, the country's largest lender, has 1.76 per cent net NPAs. Punjab National Bank's net NPAs are seventeen basis points and that of Andhra Bank, eighteen basis points.

Indeed, the RBI's insistence on restructuring those loans where borrowers are not in a position to pay on time has helped banks to arrest the rise of stressed assets, but with fledgling signs of recovery in sight in various pockets of the economy, most of these loans are unlikely to add to the banks' bad assets. The gross NPA level is relatively higher at two banks, ICICI Bank and Kotak Mahindra Bank—holding around 4.3 per cent gross NPAs each—and Federal Bank, carrying 5.57 per cent gross NPAs. However, the overall industry does not project an alarming picture.

Higher provisions have brought down the level of net NPAs and banks have been able to make such provisions because they recorded hefty profits. Net profits of thirty-five banks rose by 27.20 per cent in fiscal 2009 to Rs 415.4554 billion. Public-sector banks, as a group, performed better than their counterparts in the private sector, collectively posting close to a 31 per cent increase in their net profits while private banks' profits on an average have gone up by 16.75 per cent.

At least nine banks' net profits have gone up by 50 per cent or more in 2009 and only four in the pack of thirty-five banks that have so far announced their earnings have shown a drop in their net profits. They are ICICI Bank and Kotak Mahindra Bank in the private sector, and Allahabad Bank and Vijaya Bank in the public sector.

Indian banks remain healthy and profitable even in the worst of times. Shouldn't we send flowers to our bankers to say thanks?

Postscript

In retrospect, the last bit reads like a joke. Now I feel it was too early to congratulate them.

2

Microfinance: To Hell and Back

Eight out of ten small-finance banks in India have migrated from the business of microfinance to banking. Ahead of them, another microfinance entity became a universal bank. This sums up the two-decade journey of this set of financial intermediaries.

The columns in this chapter focus on the evolution of financial inclusion in India and the aggressive expansion of the microfinance industry. The microfinance institutions (MFIs), by and large, have been driven by a desire to fill the gap in the Indian financial system where high-street banks typically don't reach out to the credit-starved poor people. However, for a few of them, the guiding principle was the greed to make money by attracting investors. This greed saw the enactment of a law in the southern state of Andhra Pradesh in October 2010 which almost killed the industry.

In the five years between 2005 and 2010, the Indian microfinance sector emerged as one of the largest in the world, but the autumn of 2010 changed the face of the industry. About Rs 9.5 million loans by an estimated 6.5 million borrowers in the southern state turned defaulters—the largest number of defaulters in any single location in the world.

Since then, the storyline has changed. The Reserve Bank of India stepped in with regulations capping the interest rate, quantum of loans and the number of borrowers a microfinance company can entertain; credit bureaus have been formed; and the two industry bodies—Sa-Dhan and Microfinance Institutions Network (MFIN)— have transformed themselves into self-regulatory organizations. Breaking away from the concentration in Andhra Pradesh, the industry has also expanded to different geographies. And, finally, eight of them have become banks. The story of Indian microfinance industry is a story of resurrection.

The columns in this chapter dissect the crisis triggered by the Andhra Pradesh law, the industry's journey through hell and back, and its display of maturity and resilience. The underlying theme through all the columns remains financial inclusion. Unfortunately, not everyone has learnt lessons from the Andhra crisis and hence we see new hotspots. Demonetization and frequent farm loan waivers have also impacted their health. The pieces in this chapter catch all these and offer pointers to the future.

FINANCIAL INCLUSION AND MY DRIVER, RAJU

10 August 2009

In April, India had around 403 million mobile users. About 46 per cent of them, or 187 million, did not have bank accounts. My colleague Ravi doesn't find this surprising. 'People can do without bank accounts but not mobile phones. My mom and aunt don't have bank accounts, but they use mobile phones to stay connected with others,' Ravi says. My driver, Raju too doesn't have a bank account, but he carries a cell phone. He has not been able to get an account as he doesn't have a proof of address and can't fulfil the KYC (know your customer) norms, essential for opening a bank account.

A bank account is not all about financial inclusion, but it is still an important indicator. How many Indians have bank accounts? Anil Ambani, the billionaire chairman of Reliance–Anil Dhirubhai Ambani Group, said in a recent annual general meeting of one of his group firms that nearly 400 million Indians have bank accounts. That's less than 40 per cent of the country's population.

The Reserve Bank of India's deputy governor, K.C. Chakrabarty, in a recent presentation in Mumbai on financial inclusion, said about 40 per cent Indians have check-in accounts. Going by his presentation, fifty-one out of every 100 Indians had bank accounts in 1993. This marginally went up to fifty-four in 2007.

Yet another presentation by another central banker, a few years back, had said that 59 per cent of the adult population in India had bank accounts and that there was a large gap between the coverage of banking services in urban and rural pockets. In rural India, the coverage among the adult population is 39 per cent as against 60 per cent in urban India.

This, of course, doesn't necessarily mean that sixty out of every 100 Indian adults in cities have bank accounts, as many people operate multiple accounts. The sources of these information are different and I cannot vouch for their accuracy, but the fact remains that the coverage of banking services in the world's second-fastest-growing major economy is very low, compared to a developed country.

A British Bankers' Association survey says that 92–94 per cent of the population in the UK has either current or savings accounts. The low coverage is true of other financial services as well. Ambani's presentation says that barely forty-five million Indians invest in mutual funds. This is about 4 per cent of India's population. The comparable figure for the US is 31 per cent.

When it comes to direct investment in equities, the number drops drastically and only fifteen million Indians hold Demat (electronic share) accounts that one needs to buy stocks.

Nearly 80 per cent of the Indian population is without life, health and non-life insurance coverage. While life insurance penetration is 4 per cent, the non-life cover is even lower at 0.6 per cent. The per capita spend on life and non-life insurance is just about Rs 2000 and Rs 300 respectively, compared to a global average of at least Rs 18,000 and Rs 13,000.

Some other relevant data will help us understand the criticality of the issue. Only 5.2 per cent of India's 650,000 villages have bank branches even though 39.7 per cent of the overall branch network of banks, or 31,727, are in rural India. Overall, the population covered by each branch came down from 63,000 in 1969 to 16,000 in 2007, and the total number of check-in accounts held at commercial banks, regional rural banks, primary agricultural credit societies, urban cooperative banks and post offices during this period rose from 454.6 million to 610.3 million. Still, very few people in the low-income bracket have access to formal banking channels. Only 34 per cent of people with annual earnings less than Rs 50,000 in urban India had a bank account in 2007. The comparative figure in rural India was even lower at 26.8 per cent.

The situation has definitely changed for the better, with banks aggressively opening 'no-frill accounts', which require very low or zero minimum balance; but a recent study by Skoch Development Foundation, a strategy and management consultancy based in New Delhi, says only 11 per cent of 25.1 million such basic banking accounts—opened between April 2007 and May 2009—are operational. This means the banking correspondent (BC) model that the Indian central bank is using to spread banking services across the country has failed. This model allows non-governmental organizations, self-help groups, microfinance organizations, farmers' clubs, post offices, cooperatives, panchayats and many others, including IT-enabled rural outlets of corporate entities and insurance agents, to act as intermediaries on commission.

The Skoch study, based on twenty-eight financial inclusion projects and a large banking correspondent scheme in Andhra Pradesh, finds that the BC model is not commercially viable. The gap between what the banks are paying the BCs or vendors and what actually such entities spend in two years works out to be Rs 26.25 per account. The regulator and the banks need to address this immediately. Mere opening of accounts and branch expansion will not solve the problem.

The biggest challenge before Indian banks is lowering the transaction costs for small loans and deposits, using technology. For instance, South Africa has a large rural population with no access to the traditional banking channel, but high mobile penetration. Its banks have developed many innovative products, using mobile telephony and the postal network, to spread financial inclusion.

There are many regulatory issues that need to be addressed in the Indian context, but for the time being, commercial banks and mobile service providers seem to be busy using each other's database to sell products and not spread banking. My driver, Raju, is often penalized by the traffic police for using his cell phone while driving. He can't resist taking calls from the 'ladies' who call him 'sir' and offer him credit cards and consumer loans. But that's a different story of inclusion.

MFIS NEED TO ALTER BUSINESS MODEL

21 November 2010

India's finance minister Pranab Mukherjee says the government doesn't want to 'strangulate' the microfinance industry that is in the business of giving tiny loans to poor people. At the same time, he asserts that the industry should bring down interest rates to a 'reasonable' level and stop using 'coercive methods' to recover loans. Mukherjee is also in no hurry to act. He wants to wait until a panel, appointed by the Reserve Bank of India, prepares its report on the state of affairs in the sector by December-end even as many feel that the Rs 330-billion industry, involving thirty million consumers, is facing a grave crisis that is intensifying every day.

Shares of the country's largest and only listed microfinance firm, SKS Microfinance Ltd, last Thursday lost nearly 20 per cent to close at Rs 641, far less than half the stock's lifetime high of Rs 1491 recorded in September. In August, it had raised money from the public at Rs 985 per share. The stock fell after the company sent a note to the stock exchanges, saying there could be a 'material impact' on its earnings and asset quality because collections have fallen sharply over the last one month due to the changes in rules for microfinance companies in Andhra Pradesh.

An ordinance in the southern state, which is yet to become a law, seeks to check alleged coercive methods used by the MFIs, and prohibit them from taking their business to doorsteps, giving multiple loans to borrowers and collecting weekly repayments. The day after the free fall, SKS issued another statement, saying it is confident that the regulation will actually strengthen the industry and benefit well-funded ethical lenders like SKS. Its chairman, Vikram Akula, said the company had dropped the interest rate to 24.5 per cent from 26.7 per cent as it has benefited from economies of scale. The 2.2 percentage point difference was for insurance cover for which the borrower was earlier paying, and the company will now absorb the cost.

Following the promulgation of the ordinance, the MFIs are able to collect repayment for only 70 per cent of their loans in Andhra

Pradesh. SKS is not too worried about this because the state accounts for only a little over one-fourth of its loan assets and the company operates in eighteen other states where its collection record is 99 per cent. But there is no guarantee that the Andhra Pradesh experience will not spill over to a few other states. The Indian government's Rs 700-billion farm loan waiver in fiscal 2008–09 encouraged many small and marginal farmers not to repay bank loans. Those who track the microfinance industry closely say the Andhra Pradesh ordinance will push up the default rate in other states as well, sooner than later, as borrowers of tiny loans will not be in a hurry to pay up.

The ordinance and the finance ministry note that has advised banks not to give loans to microfinance units unless they bring down their loan rates to a reasonable 22–24 per cent band will change the face of the industry. Public-sector banks that roughly account for about 70 per cent of the Indian banking industry have been giving tiny loans through the self-help groups, or SHGs. The SHG–bank linkage programme started in 1992 owing to advocacy by some of the NGOs, and the RBI approving a pilot project to link 3000 SHGs with bank branches all over the country in three years. At the moment, there are about five million such groups and seventy million consumers across India. In Andhra Pradesh, loans given by banks to the SHGs were worth around Rs 780 billion.

While the SHG–bank linkage programme was emerging as a tool to take care of the financial needs of the poor, another stream started feeling the pulse of the people—the MFIs. The first MFI in India was set up in 1996. Most of the MFIs follow the joint liability group, or JLG model. Here, loans are given to individual households, but the liability is collective when it comes to repayment.

The MFIs borrow money from public-sector, foreign and private banks, and lend it to JLGs, keeping a margin. Typically, five women form a JLG, and six to eight JLGs form a centre. Such centres meet every week at the same time and place—generally at the courtyard of one of the borrowers—and loan repayment instalments are collected. The MFIs have about seven million customers in Andhra Pradesh and their exposure per customer is between Rs 12,000 and Rs 14,000. Now, every three out of ten such customers are not paying back. Worried banks are going slow in giving money to MFIs. The equity flow to the sector will also dry up as there aren't too many investors who are willing to take political risk.

There are about forty for-profit MFIs that are all non-banking finance companies. The big ones are SKS, Share Microfin Ltd, Spandana Sphoorty Financial Ltd, Bandhan Financial Services Pvt. Ltd and Bhartiya Samruddhi Finance Ltd. The big MFIs' consumer base varies between 1.8 million and 7.4 million each. The rest of them are small (an NBFC needs only Rs 20 million of capital), but they have been dreaming of making it big. Now, they will be left with no choice but to merge with the relatively stronger NBFCs as it will not be easy to get fresh equity, 90 per cent of which come from foreign funds. They will also need to change their business model.

Most MFIs have been giving money to landless and marginal farmers and women labourers, who are at the bottom of the pyramid, and the repayment cycle is daily or weekly, in sync with their cash flow. Now they will have to reach out to the petty traders and non-farmer entrepreneurs and contract farmers whose cash-flow cycle is longer, and hence it will be easy to shift to the monthly repayment schedule. This will bring down the transaction cost and help MFIs pare their interest rates.

Finally, they will also need to focus on fee income by selling microinsurance, mutual funds and other financial products, along with giving loans. For survival, the industry needs to consolidate and curb its obsession with growth. As one microfinance expert puts it: it needs to figure out which way to grow—as a eucalyptus tree or a teak tree? The eucalyptus grows faster, but teak wood lasts longer.

HOW CAN WE SAVE INDIA'S MICROFINANCE INDUSTRY

1 August 2011

A decade and a half ago, the state-run Indian Bank came very close to a collapse when its accumulated losses wiped out its equity and reserves. The Chennai-based lender had made huge losses as it had to set aside money to provide for its bad assets. Now, the Vijay Mahajan–promoted Bhartiya Samruddhi Finance Ltd (BSFL), India's oldest MFI is also collapsing under the burden of bad loans. However, the similarity between the two ends here.

Indian Bank's bad assets swelled because of indiscriminate lending by its management and the lack of monitoring of bad loans. In the case of BSFL, popularly known as Basix, borrowers in Andhra Pradesh are refusing to pay, encouraged by a state law. Some of Indian Bank's peers in the mid-1990s celebrated its impending demise and put up billboards in Chennai, asking depositors of Indian Bank to migrate to them, but Basix's ill health has spread a pall of gloom across the Rs 200-billion microfinance industry as other MFIs with big exposure to Andhra Pradesh may face the same fate. Out of fourteen million small borrowers in India's fifth-largest state, 9.2 million have turned defaulters.

Under banking law, once a borrower is not able to repay for a quarter, or ninety days, the loan turns bad and banks have to provide for it. For profit-making microlenders, categorized as NBFCs, a loan turns bad when a borrower does not pay for 180 days. Initially, an MFI needs to set aside 10 per cent, but if the loan is not serviced for two years, the entire exposure needs to be provided for. As of 30 June, BSFL's net worth was Rs 1.28 billion, down from Rs 2.3 billion in September 2010, and this will be completely eroded in the next eighteen months because of accumulated bad loans of Rs 4.5 billion.

BSFL's loan book has shrunk from Rs 18 billion to Rs 10 billion, and Andhra Pradesh accounts for around Rs 4.5 billion of this. Since repayment in the southern state has dropped to 10 per cent, the only way to increase income would be to aggressively lend in other states where repayments are assured. But BSFL cannot do so as banks are not giving it fresh money. MFIs borrow from banks and lend to the poor, keeping aside a margin. Mahajan has been looking for a Rs 4.42-billion equity infusion and a Rs 10-billion bank loan for survival.

Andhra Pradesh passed a law in October to control moneylending, after a spate of reported suicides following alleged coercive recovery practices adopted by some of the microlenders. Among other things, the law restricts MFIs from collecting weekly repayments and makes government approval mandatory if a borrower takes more than one loan. Early July, the Union government released the draft of a proposed legislation to govern MFIs that seeks to take them outside the purview of state law and to give more powers to the RBI to regulate MFIs.

However, the battle over regulating MFIs is far from over, with Andhra Pradesh remaining firm on retaining its own law. The state finds the SHG model more cost-effective for poor borrowers than the MFI model. There are about a million SHGs in the state with twelve million members. The state has spent $600 million in World Bank money to develop SHGs. The Centre also plans to develop SHGs across India under its National Rural Livelihood Mission for which the World Bank recently offered a $1-billion long-term soft loan.

Typically, SHGs get bank loans at a concessional rate of 8–9 per cent, but the actual cost for the borrowers is much less as the state government offers a huge subsidy. Andhra Pradesh has spent around Rs 40 billion so far to subsidize such loans. The MFI model, where a microlender borrows money from banks at 12–13 per cent and offers small loans to poor borrowers at 24–26 per cent, is based on recovery of cost in contrast to the highly subsidized SHG model. However, the actual cost for both is almost the same. Andhra Pradesh accounts for at least one quarter of the microfinance industry, and if borrowers do not repay, it will deal a blow to the industry. Even the SHG channel is disturbed now, with the recovery rate dropping to 40 per cent. There are reasons behind the MFI concentration in the southern state.

The profile of rural economy in Andhra Pradesh is different from other Indian states as farmers here shifted from subsistence farming to commercial crops ahead of others—groundnut in southern Andhra (Rayalaseema) and cotton in the northern part (Telangana), even as the eastern part, or coastal Andhra, continues to produce paddy. Besides, after they won the anti-arrack (country liquor) movement and forced the then state chief minister N.T. Rama Rao to announce prohibition in the state, agitating women in the southern state were looking for a different cause to channel their energy and organizational skill, and *podupulakshmi* (savings and credit) offered that platform.

When N. Chandrababu Naidu replaced Rama Rao as chief minister, he nurtured the movement to reap political mileage. Now, there are around two million borrowers from MFIs, many of whom are members of SHGs too.

Allowing multiple channels to work and compete with each other is the best solution to the MFI problem. Besides, the RBI can force them to reveal their cost of funds and justify the loan rates, cap investors' stakes in MFIs at 5 per cent, and make its approval mandatory for the emolument of the top brass—norms that banks follow. Both the Centre and the state also need to look for a political solution to the Andhra impasse before it's too late. Let us also remember that half of India's population still does not have access to banking services.

WE NEED MFIS TILL BANKS GET READY TO SERVE THE POOR

15 January 2012

The government and the Reserve Bank of India must draw an MFI survival strategy before it's too late. We need them at least till such time the banks are ready to reach out to the masses. Andhra Pradesh, India's fourth-largest state by area and fifth largest by population, has set a world record. About 9.2 million borrowers in the southern state have defaulted in repaying money borrowed from MFIs—the largest number of defaulters in any location in the world. As Andhra Pradesh has a population of 84.6 million (2011 census provisional figure), theoretically one in every eleven Andhraites is a defaulter.

This, however, is not the actual case as most such borrowers have more than one account. By industry estimates, around four million people of the state—almost all women—have turned defaulters. As the female population in Andhra Pradesh is 42.1 million, one in every ten women in this state has borrowed from MFIs but not repaid.

To put the Andhra phenomenon in perspective, in 2008, when the Indian government announced a Rs 600-billion debt-waiver scheme for farmers across the nation, some forty million farmers didn't repay debt. Indeed, the money involved in Andhra Pradesh is minuscule compared to the national debt-waiver scheme, but the point to note is that in this case, the debt has not been waived even though a section of the local politicians has created that impression and encouraged borrowers not to pay back.

The microfinance industry's total exposure to Andhra Pradesh was around Rs 72 billion in 2010 and they have been able to collect from the borrowers only 10 per cent of this money. They are carrying in their books Rs 65 billion worth of bad assets, and when they write off this amount in March, at the end of the current fiscal, many of India's big MFIs' net worth will turn negative. Unless the RBI relaxes the prudential norms that stipulate a 15 per cent capital adequacy ratio (Rs 15 as capital for every Rs 100 worth of loans) for this set of financial intermediaries, many will have to shut shop. The MFIs that will bear the brunt will include the country's lone listed microlender SKS Microfinance Ltd, Spandana Sphoorty Financial Ltd, Share Microfin Ltd, Asmitha Microfin Ltd and the Vijay Mahajan–promoted Bhartiya Samruddhi Finance Ltd—India's oldest MFI.

In this pack, SKS Microfinance will be the least affected as it had raised money from the public through its capital float in August 2010; the others are in a bad shape. Some are restructuring the debt taken from banks. But even then, keeping themselves afloat is not an easy task as commercial banks, which provide 90 per cent of resources that MFIs need for business, are not forthcoming in giving money for fear of piling up bad assets. Interestingly, even MFIs which do not have any direct exposure to Andhra Pradesh are being shunned by the banks.

For instance, Arohan Financial Services Ltd, an MFI in West Bengal, hasn't got any money from banks ever since the Andhra crisis broke out, even though it doesn't have a single borrower in the southern state. For lack of resources, it is shrinking its assets and closing down offices. Utkarsh Micro Finance Pvt. Ltd of Varanasi is another instance. It lends to poor people in eastern Uttar Pradesh and Bihar. In 2010 and early 2011, banks withdrew all lines of credit. Subsequently, a few banks have started sanctioning loans but they are not releasing money.

With no fresh money in the kitty and Andhra Pradesh borrowers not repaying loans, MFIs are forced to shrink loan books, close down offices and retrench employees. The outstanding loan book of the industry, which was Rs 300 billion in October 2010, has shrunk to Rs 150 billion in January, and at least 30 per cent of 150,00,00 employees have been shown the doors.

The origin of the crisis was in October 2010 when Andhra Pradesh, which accounted for at least a quarter of the microlending industry, promulgated a law to control microlenders after a spate of reported suicides following alleged coercive recovery practices adopted by some. The law, which restricted MFIs from collecting money from borrowers on a weekly basis, made government approval mandatory for borrowers taking more than one loan. Subsequently, an RBI panel, headed by noted chartered accountant Y.H. Malegam, capped the loan rate by MFIs at 26 per cent and the margin at 12 per cent.

These norms were fine when banks were giving money to MFIs at 11 per cent. With the increase in interest rates, banks are now charging more; and if we add to that the processing fee and the cash margin that MFIs need to keep with the banks, the effective cost of money is at least 17 per cent. No wonder then that most MFIs are making losses.

There are a few exceptions though. Janalakshmi Financial Services Ltd, which takes care of the tiny loan needs of the urban poor, is one of them. The Bengaluru-based firm has grown its assets from Rs 800 million in March 2010 to Rs 2.6 billion now. Apart from giving tiny loans, Janalakshmi distributes financial products such as pension and insurance, and sells mortgages and enterprise loans through sixty-six branches across forty-one cities in eleven states. The Kolkata-based Bandhan Financial Services Pvt. Ltd is another MFI. It has recently overtaken SKS in terms of the loan book size. In January itself, it achieved the year-end target and may end the fiscal with a loan book of Rs 35 billion. Its bad assets have grown but are still way below 1 per cent of the total assets, and it is making profits.

The death of the microfinance industry will push the poor into the grip of moneylenders and deal a blow to the government's financial inclusion drive. The government and the RBI must draw an MFI survival strategy before it's too late. We need them at least till such time the banks are ready to reach out to the masses. At the same time, the industry needs to get rid of its obsession with growth and learn from the Bandhan and Janalakshmi experiments to reorient its business models.

MICROFINANCE: TO HELL AND BACK

19 October 2014

Alok Prasad, chief executive officer of MFIN, a lobby group for the Indian microfinance industry that recently got the status of a self-regulatory organization from the banking regulator, says 'we did not waste a good crisis', on the fourth anniversary of the microfinance crisis that originated in Andhra Pradesh.

This statement is generally attributed to Rahm Emanuel, a former White House chief of staff, in response to the Wall Street meltdown, but actually comes from a comment made by Niccolò Machiavelli, a well-known Italian political thinker of the fifteenth century, who wrote, 'Never waste the opportunity offered by a good crisis.'

'That's exactly what the microfinance industry has done. It took a hard look at itself; it reformed and moved on, doing what it knows best—providing microloans to low-income households,' Prasad told me, sitting at his Gurgaon office. In a nation of 1.2 billion people, half of whom are not served by the formal banking system, the microfinance industry acquired a halo in the early part of the last decade. A highly successful listing of SKS Microfinance Ltd in July 2010, and strong all-round growth of loan assets, created a situation when new funding was on demand in an industry that was then lightly regulated by the RBI.

Then in October 2010, the cookie crumbled, with the Andhra Pradesh government promulgating an ordinance to curb the activities of microfinance companies. The provocation was allegedly the coercive collection policy of the MFIs that drove many borrowers to commit suicide. It mandated MFIs to specify their area of operation, rate of interest and recovery practices. It also became mandatory for MFIs to seek the state government's approval before issuing any fresh loans.

Following the liberalization of India's economy in 1991, the private sector increasingly started extending credit to fill the gaps created by the banks' reluctance to step in. In the five years between 2005 and 2010, the Indian microfinance sector emerged as one of the largest in the world, with Andhra Pradesh—dubbed by *The Economist* as 'the state that would reform India'—as its hub. However, the autumn of 2010 changed the face of the industry; the Andhra Pradesh ordinance was a death warrant and the operations of all MFIs in the state came to a grinding halt. The ripples created by the crisis were felt in almost every state, with bad loans piling up, as borrowers refused to pay back and banks declined to give loans to MFIs.

The crisis triggered a strong response from the RBI. Based on the recommendation of a high-powered committee, headed by Y.H. Malegam, a member of the central bank's board, the RBI put in place regulations for the industry in December 2011. The margin between the cost of borrowing and the price at which loans were given was capped, interest rates were regulated and loan norms were defined. The central government too chipped in by introducing a Bill in Parliament to provide a statutory framework for regulating and developing the microfinance industry.

Over the past four years, the industry has seen more changes, including the creation of two credit bureaus—Equifax Credit Information Services Pvt. Ltd and CRIF High Mark Credit Information Services Pvt. Ltd—to help it take appropriate credit decisions and arrest multiple lending; the introduction of a code of conduct; diversification of the product basket; and adoption of new practices to focus on customers' needs. The code of conduct ensures governance and client protection, and creates an ethos for responsible lending, something many MFIs did not do till the crisis broke out. The credit bureaus are now a repository of at least 100 million loan records.

The inevitable fallout of the Andhra Pradesh crisis was that the industry spread out to other geographies. The latest regional exposure data are indicative of the spread, with the west and the east accounting for 23 per cent and 28 per cent respectively, of the gross loan portfolio of MFIs in 2013–14. Loan disbursements are evenly spread out in Maharashtra, West Bengal and Tamil Nadu. I will not be surprised if some of the entities plan to morph into small banks, the draft licensing norms for which have already been circulated by the RBI.

That said, it is absolutely critical for microfinance firms, particularly those MFIs that operate as NBFCs, to be continuously on guard and not succumb to the greed of expanding business at any cost—something they did to keep their private equity investors happy before the Andhra Pradesh crisis broke out. There are around fifty such companies, less than one-fourth of the MFIs that exist in India, but they account for at least 90 per cent of the business. Rapid growth always carries high risks and the industry will not be able to live through another crisis if that happens. Responsible lending has to be the mantra, now and always.

As of 30 June 2014, NBFC–MFIs had a client base of at least twenty-eight million, with the base growing 23 per cent in the first quarter of the current fiscal year from a year earlier. The aggregate gross loan portfolio in June stood at Rs 270 billion, a growth of 44 per cent over the first quarter of 2013–14. Disbursements of loans in the first quarter of the current fiscal year increased by 48 per cent and the number of loan accounts grew by 34 per cent.

The good news for the industry is that the political risks seem to be diminishing, with states, including Assam and Kerala, accepting the RBI as the sole regulator for the industry. Unlike in 2010, microfinance today is a highly regulated industry, with the segment of clients, size of loans, purpose and even price being regulated. Microfinanciers are in dialogue with the RBI for relaxation of the tight framework of rules and regulations, but it should take a while as the central bank needs to be convinced about the maturity that the industry claims to have attained.

THE LIFE, DEATH AND RESURRECTION OF INDIAN MICROFINANCE

18 September 2015

After giving licences to eleven payments banks in August, the central bank on Wednesday announced a fresh set of ten licences—this time for small-finance banks. Eight of them are from the microfinance industry, which was on the verge of collapse just five years back.

Some seventeen MFIs applied for licences and nearly 50 per cent of them succeeded in convincing the Reserve Bank of India about their ability to offer banking services to the masses in Asia's third-largest economy. It's an economy where, according to a 2012 working paper by the World Bank, half of the adult population does not have access to formal banking services.

Indeed, the RBI has been liberal in opening up the sector. One new universal bank launched in August and another will see the light of day next month. Yet, twenty-one more banks with a special focus on certain segments of business will open shop over the next year and a half. Seen against the backdrop of thirteen banks opening in the past two decades—quite a few of them do not exist today—this is a banking revolution.

Equally importantly, it is the resurrection of the microfinance industry, nearly buried in scandal in 2010, when the Andhra Pradesh government promulgated an ordinance to curb its activities.

In the preceding five years, between 2005 and 2010, the Indian microfinance sector had become one of the largest in the world. After the Andhra Pradesh ordinance, the operations of all MFIs in the southern state came to a grinding halt. The impact of the crisis was felt in almost every state. Bad loans piled up as borrowers refused to service their debts and banks stopped lending to MFIs.

Since then, the RBI has stepped in, putting in place regulations for the industry, capping the margin between the cost of borrowing and the price at which loans are given, and defining loan norms.

The formation of credit bureaus, the introduction of a code of conduct, diversification of the product basket and adoption of new practices to focus on customers' needs have combined to ensure governance and client protection, and created an ecosystem for responsible lending.

The industry has now expanded to other geographies, paring the concentration risk.

The granting of eight licences to MFIs for small-finance banks signals that all is well now with the industry. Indeed, MFIs play a critical role in countries such as Bangladesh, Pakistan, Indonesia and the Philippines—and some of them become banks.

Nowhere in the world has the industry seen such a dramatic turnaround.

Of the eight MFIs that have been given licences, two each are in Chennai and Bengaluru, and the remaining four are headquartered in Guwahati, Navi Mumbai, Ahmedabad and Varanasi—well spread out across India. All eight have over 99 per cent standard assets. The founders of at least four of them are former bankers: Ramesh Ramanathan of Janalakshmi Financial Services Pvt. Ltd (Citibank), Samit Ghosh of Ujjivan Financial Services Pvt. Ltd (Citibank and HDFC Bank Ltd), P.N. Vasudevan of Equitas Holdings Ltd (DCB Bank Ltd) and Govind Singh of Utkarsh Micro Finance Pvt. Ltd (ICICI Bank Ltd).

Once these eight MFIs become banks, the for-profit microfinance industry will shrink by around 40 per cent. After the erstwhile Bandhan Financial Services Pvt. Ltd became a bank with around Rs 105-billion loan assets, the industry shrank to Rs 320 billion. These eight MFIs collectively have a loan book of close to Rs 135 billion. This means that once again, the industry size will shrink to around Rs 185 billion.

But nobody will complain.

There will be around forty-five for-profit MFIs after these eight become banks. Around 200 not-for-profit MFIs have a collective loan book of close to Rs 50 billion. Shri Kshetra Dharmasthala Rural Development Project (Karnataka) and Cashpor Micro

Credit (Uttar Pradesh) constitute 90 per cent of the loan book of these MFIs.

Among the relatively large for-profit MFIs that have not got an RBI nod for becoming small banks are SKS Microfinance Ltd and Satin Creditcare Network Ltd. Another name is Arohan Financial Services Pvt. Ltd, even though it does not have a large loan book. Of course, there are others who fell by the wayside, bearing the brunt of the Andhra crisis: Spandana Sphoorty Financial Ltd, Share Microfin Ltd, Asmitha Microfin Ltd and the Vijay Mahajan–promoted Bhartiya Samruddhi Finance Ltd—India's oldest MFI.

Small-finance banks can function almost like any other commercial bank, but on a smaller scale. They will be in the mass market and 75 per cent of the loans given by these banks should qualify for the so-called priority-sector loans.

The maximum loan exposure to a single or group company is capped at 10 per cent and 15 per cent of their capital respectively, and small loans of up to Rs 25,00,000 should constitute at least 50 per cent of the loan portfolio.

There are challenges ahead. The successful candidates will need to meet all the conditions of the regulator to get the final nod in the next eighteen months. It will not be easy to scale up, acquire market relevance and become commercially successful, but the industry should savour this moment and celebrate.

In due course, the successful small banks can graduate to universal banks. In the meantime, MFIs who have failed to make it this time should not lose heart. If those who have got the licence can demonstrate success, others will join the league when the RBI puts banking licences on the tap.

That day's not far away.

INDIAN MICROFINANCE INSTITUTIONS HAVE JUST BUSTED A MYTH

19 October 2015

By definition, microfinance is the business of giving tiny loans to people who do not have access to formal banking services. The Investopedia website defines microfinance as a type of banking service that is provided to unemployed or low-income individuals or groups who would otherwise have no other means of gaining financial services. 'The goal of microfinance is to give low income people an opportunity to become self-sufficient by providing a means of saving money, borrowing money and insurance,' it says. In India, MFIs cannot collect deposits, but sell insurance products, besides offering small loans that are typically paid back in weekly or monthly instalments.

Such institutions operate in the hinterland where traditional banks baulk at serving. Or so we believed. The scene has changed. MFIs have shifted their focus from rural pockets to urban India. For the first time in its twenty-five-year history, Indian MFIs have more urban clients than rural ones. The latest data, compiled by the industry self-regulatory organization Sa-Dhan show that 67 per cent of the thirty-seven million MFI customers live in urban India.

The share of rural customers was 69 per cent in the fiscal year 2012. That dropped marginally to 67 per cent in 2013. In the following two years, the share of rural customers has declined drastically. In 2014, rural customers constituted 56 per cent of the total. It dropped further to 33 per cent in the following year. This busts the myth that Indian microfinance is predominantly a rural phenomenon, very different from what we see in Latin America and large parts of Africa and Asia.

The industry's outreach to urban clients was increasing every year and it has now outstripped that of rural customers. Why has this happened? Before we look for an answer, let's look at the broader picture. The industry had a customer base of 37.1 million in March 2015, up from thirty-three million a year ago. It included 6.5 million customers of Bandhan Financial Services Ltd, the largest MFI that turned into a bank in August. The proportion of women customers remained unchanged at 97 per cent, while the share of Scheduled Caste and Scheduled Tribe customers rose from 19 per cent to 28 per cent. The loan portfolio was close to Rs 400 billion and 80 per cent of it was for income-generating activities. The average loan per borrower in the year end of 31 March rose to Rs 13,162 from Rs 10,079 at the end of the previous fiscal.

The quality of assets has improved. If we leave aside a few MFIs that had been affected by the crisis that gripped the industry following the Andhra Pradesh state law five years ago, the industry's non-performing assets were to the tune of thirteen basis points as of 31 March. (One basis point is one-hundredth of a percentage point.)

Such MFIs were referred to the corporate debt restructuring cell as their equity and reserves were eroded by accumulated bad loans. About 80 per cent of 250-odd MFIs have less than 1 per cent of their loan portfolios at risk. About 12 per cent of MFIs have 1–3 per cent of their loan portfolio at risk, and 8 per cent of MFIs have more than 5 per cent of their loan portfolio in the risk category. The loans at risk are those that have not been serviced for thirty days.

In contrast, the quality of small loans distributed through the so-called self-help group (SHG) model is inferior. The number of SHGs shrank to 7.71 million in 2015 from 7.43 million in the previous year even though the number of families involved in SHGs increased from ninety-seven million to 101 million. SHGs' total savings stood at Rs 113.07 billion in 2015 and the loan portfolio was Rs 517.27 billion. The average loan outstanding per SHG was Rs 115,000 and NPAs were 7.4 per cent, up from 6.8 per cent in the previous year.

One reason behind the rise in urban customers is the phenomenal growth of a few urban-focused MFIs such as Janalakshmi Financial Services Pvt. Ltd, Ujjivan Financial Services Pvt. Ltd and Satin Credit Card Network Ltd. These three collectively had around 5.7 million customers in March. Their growth last year had been higher than the average industry growth and most of their customers live in urban India. Till it became a bank, Bandhan had an 18 per cent market share of customers, followed by SKS Microfinance Ltd and

Shri Kshethra Dharmasthala Rural Development Project. Others among the top ten are Janalakshmi, Equitus Microfinance Pvt. Ltd, Spandana Spoorty Financial Ltd, Share Microfin Ltd, Satin and Grameen Koota Financial Services Pvt. Ltd.

Janalakshmi, Ujjivan and Equitus have received in-principle approval from the RBI to become small-finance banks.

Another reason behind the growth in urban customers is the shift in the business models of many MFIs. They are becoming increasingly urban-centric to cut down operational expenses and maximize operational efficiency. Under the priority-sector lending norms, banks in India are required to give 40 per cent of their loans to small borrowers. As they do not have the reach, they give money to the MFIs to on-lend to such borrowers. While fixing the loan price for small borrowers, the MFIs cannot charge more than 10 per cent over the cost of loans taken from banks. This means their profitability solely depends on operational efficiency as the cost of raising resources is almost the same for all MFIs.

The rise in urban clients of MFIs also tells us that banks in India have a cultural problem—they don't like small borrowers, be they in rural or urban India. The official reason for not reaching out to small borrowers are many—ranging from higher transaction costs and lack of reach to the absence of a competent rural cadre. These probably explain the banks' absence in remote villages. What about urban India? Our drivers and housemaids, vegetable vendors and fishermen in Mumbai and Delhi are being serviced by MFIs as the banks refuse to see business there.

THE NEW HOTSPOTS OF INDIAN MICROFINANCE

28 November 2016

P. Satish, executive director of Sa-Dhan, the oldest industry body for Indian microfinance, and Ratna Vishwanathan, chief executive of Microfinance Institutions Network, a relatively younger body which has all large, for-profit microfinance institutions as its members, aren't very happy these days. Yes, the historic decision to ban Rs 1000 and Rs 500 notes has contributed to their unhappiness, as this has affected the entire industry—particularly those entities which operate in rural India. However, this could be a temporary phenomenon. The reason behind their grumpiness is something that the industry has been grappling with for quite some time now. An October newspaper report spoke about this—loan defaults in ten villages of Wardha district in Maharashtra.

A very high level of indebtedness and tough recovery techniques adopted by MFIs have led to many villagers seeking government intervention, the Marathi daily *Loksatta* reported. Quoting the report, a flash note by Religare Institutional Research in the last week of October (written by Parag Jariwala and Vikesh Mehta) said the Wardha phenomenon 'epitomises a widespread problem for the MFIs, placing the sector on the brink of a sharp correction that will ratchet up NPAs and credit costs'.

Vishwanathan organized a meeting of the for-profit MFIs, small-finance banks, banking correspondents and the banks—all lenders to low-income clients—in Mumbai in the first week of November to frame a common set of principles or compliance framework, even as Satish sent a Sa-Dhan inspection team to Tamil Nadu, Madhya Pradesh and West Bengal, where certain districts were being overheated by aggressive lending. This was the third such on-field inspection being undertaken by Sa-Dhan.

As self-regulatory organizations (SROs), both Sa-Dhan and MFIN have tough tasks ahead as the Rs 640-billion Indian microfinance industry has started seeing defaults, pipelining (a group of borrowers being used as a proxy for one person who is taking the money) and overlending in some pockets.

What was complicating the situation further was that many moneylenders were masquerading as MFIs. During the field visits, the Sa-Dhan team identified at least twenty such entities operating in Mysuru. Sri Chamundeshwari Finance, Sri Siddarameshwara Finance, Sowbhagya Laxmi, Srirama Finance, Kaveri Sphoorthi Finance, Mahalaxmi Finance and many others, posing as MFIs, were charging more than 40 per cent interest and also collecting a security deposit of 7 per cent on loan amount and a service charge of 3.5 per cent.

Under the RBI guidelines, an MFI cannot charge more than 26 per cent interest rate; for relatively large MFIs, the spread between the cost of money taken from banks and the interest rate charged on the borrowers is capped at 10 per cent. Besides, they are also not allowed to ask for security deposits. Almost 70 per cent of large MFIs currently charge an interest rate of 24 per cent or less.

Armed with political links, these unregulated entities are creating huge reputation risks for the responsible MFIs. The existence of similar outfits has been reported from Uttar Pradesh (UP) and West Bengal also. One such entity is 'Turanta' in Mirzapur in eastern UP. The lending and recovery by this entity are both *turant* (fast)and implemented with strong-arm tactics.

While this is a law and order issue and the SROs can do very little except for seeking help from the local administration, another area of concern is the high growth of some of the MFIs. At least, fourteen MFIs have grown by no less than 100 per cent and up to 421 per cent in fiscal 2016, even as the industry grew by 31 per cent, with the share of the for-profit MFIs at least 88 per cent. The top ten MFIs account for 69 per cent, or Rs 438.87, of the loan portfolio. The total number of clients served by the industry rose to 39.9 million last year and a majority of these clients are being served by large for-profit MFIs. In fact, large MFIs with at least Rs 5 billion loan portfolios are responsible for reaching out to a little more than 85 per cent of the clients.

The list of MFIs that had been growing very aggressively till the recent turmoil includes Hindusthan Microfinance Pvt. Ltd (421 per cent), Janalakshmi Financial Services Ltd (191 per cent), Sarala Development and Microfinance Pvt. Ltd (175 per cent), SV Creditline Pvt. Ltd (142 per cent), Annapurna Microfinance Pvt. Ltd (132 per cent), Samasta Microfinance Ltd (128 per cent), Village Financial Services Pvt. Ltd and ASA International India Microfinance Pvt. Ltd (both 126 per cent). These figures pertain to the fiscal year 2016, ending in March.

While Janalakshmi will become a small-finance bank, another small-finance bank licence holder, RGVN (North-east) Microfinance Ltd too has reported more than 100 per cent loan growth (113 per cent, to be exact).

Based on data from credit information bureaus in terms of the number of MFIs present in a district, growth in loan portfolios, active clients and disbursements, Sa-Dhan had identified ten districts as overheated. They were North 24 Parganas and South 24 Parganas (West Bengal); Kanchipuram, Cuddalore and Coimbatore (Tamil Nadu); Mysuru and Hassan (Karnataka); Indore (Madhya Pradesh); Pune (Maharashtra); and Thrissur (Kerala). Statewise, Himachal Pradesh recorded the maximum loan growth last year (1075 per cent), albeit on a minuscule base, followed by Haryana (129 per cent), Punjab (120 per cent), Puducherry (115 per cent) and Kerala (105 per cent).

Two disturbing trends were being noticed. One, some of the large MFIs had started playing the role of predators. They were swooping on the customers brought to the credit fold who had been nurtured by relatively smaller not-for-profit MFIs. And two, the growth in the loan portfolio of some of the large MFIs was not in sync with the growth in their customer base.

Last year, the RBI had raised the maximum loan limit for a single borrower from Rs 50,000 to Rs 100,000. That encouraged many large MFIs to push more money down the throats of borrowers, leading to over-indebtedness, even though some of them have voluntarily capped the exposure to individual borrowers at Rs 60,000, following the code of conduct devised by the SROs.

In fact, more than 80 per cent of the MFIs have bad loans, or the so-called portfolio at risk (when a loan instalment is not paid for more than thirty days) of less than 1 per cent, and only 6 per cent of MFIs have such loans exceeding 5 per cent of their loan books, but the emerging trends can play spoilsport.

The RBI's silence on a critical issue is also adding to the complications. Currently, a borrower cannot take money from more than two MFIs, but once eight large MFIs become small-finance banks, can a customer continue with her loan exposure to such entities and raise fresh loans from other MFIs? Technically, she can, as small-finance banks and MFIs are different entities. If the RBI allows this, we may find many small borrowers being overleveraged and not in a position to pay back. Not a happy omen for an industry that came back from the brink of collapse just five years ago.

Of course, both Satish and Vishwanathan have a bigger task in hand. They need to find ways to tide over the latest crisis, however temporary it is, arising out of the demonetization move. The RBI too has stepped in, relaxing the income recognition norms. For all you know, this could be a blessing in disguise for the industry—the over-aggressiveness of some of the MFIs will abate and hotspots will get cooler after this.

3

Public-sector Banks: Fall from Grace

The government-owned banks' market share has been shrinking and some of them are fast losing their relevance. There have been talks on consolidation as we do not need a bunch of stressed public-sector banks who continue to collect deposits with the backing of the government, but are reluctant to give loans for fear of piling up more bad assets.

Written over a period of time, the columns in this chapter focus on the importance of reforms in the PSU (Public Sector Undertaking) banks, the key to which is acceptance of the fact that regulations should be ownership-neutral. There have been certain steps taken by the government, the majority owner of these banks, such as splitting the top post in a public-sector bank (between a non-executive chairman and a CEO and managing director) and changing the selection process of the chiefs, but these changes seem cosmetic. Many PSU banks lack efficiency, expertise and the right governance structure to keep pace with their fast-moving private peers; their existence is becoming anachronistic.

They have many handicaps too. For instance, unlike private players, PSU banks are subject to investigation by the Central Bureau of Investigation (CBI) and the Central Vigilance Commission (CVC). They are also under the lens of India's chief auditor—the Comptroller and Auditor General of India (CAG). Besides, they are covered by the Right to Information Act. All these inhibit the decision-making process.

(The CVC can also now probe allegations of corruption in private-sector banks and against their employees after the Supreme Court ruled in 2016 that the chairman, the managing director and other officers of a private bank could be seen as public servants under the Prevention of Corruption [PC Act], 1988.)

Reforms in public-sector banks at every level—from the constitution of the board to the tenure of the CEO—are imperative. The biggest beneficiary of such reforms will be the government as the banks will become competitive; with the rise in efficiency, their market value will rise and free the government from the burden of pumping in capital into these banks.

The pieces in this chapter raise questions, offer suggestions, report the changes or lack of them, and witness the fall from grace of many PSU banks for multiple reasons.

THE SAAS–BAHU SYNDROME IN INDIAN BANKING

8 November 2009

Despite a slowdown in loan growth, the quarter ending September has been quite interesting for the Indian banking industry. The banks are not aggressive in pushing home, automobile and consumer loans, but approvals for infrastructure loan proposals are rising and when such loans are disbursed, banks' loan book will grow. The net interest margin, or the difference between the cost of funds and the income on loans, a key indicator of bank profitability, has also increased at most banks as they have redeemed high-cost bulk deposits and cut the rates on fresh deposits.

One area of concern is the quality of assets, but there are no visible signs of deterioration as yet, as the regulator has allowed banks to restructure loans that borrowers were not in a position to repay when the economic growth had slowed.

A nasty surprise among public-sector banks, which make up roughly three-fourth of the industry's assets, has been Bank of India. Its net profit has fallen from Rs 7.6286 billion in September 2008 to Rs 3.2334 in September 2009. The main reason behind the decline has been higher provisions for bad loans—Rs 6.0213 billion against Rs 2.8675 billion. It had to set aside more money to take care of rising bad loans. Overall, its gross bad assets have risen from Rs 19.78 billion a year ago to Rs 39.2 billion in September, and net bad loans, or the bad assets net of provisions, have risen from Rs 6.08 billion to Rs 16.05 billion. The bank's gross bad loans, as a percentage of its total loans, is now 2.61 per cent (up from 1.53 per cent a year ago) and net bad loans 1.08 per cent (up from 0.48 per cent a year ago).

Bank of India would have been able to absorb the shock of higher provisions for bad assets had its overall performance been good. But that has not been the case. There has hardly been any growth in its interest income as well as fee income; as a result, its operating profit, which is calculated before provisions are made and is a key parameter for judging a bank's efficiency, has fallen from Rs 12.15 billion to Rs 12.06 billion.

Why has this happened? Had the reason been the economic slowdown, all other banks would have been equally affected. So, one should not blame the economy for this bank's bad performance.

One reason could be the change of guards at the bank. Its former chairman, T.S. Narayanasami, retired on 31 May. Alok Misra, who was till recently heading the Delhi-based Oriental Bank of Commerce, now heads Bank of India. An analysis done by a banking consultant shows there is a correlation between a public-sector bank's performance and the retirement of its chairman. This consultancy firm, which does not want to be named as it advises many banks on their business strategy, has reviewed the quarterly performance of public- sector banks in the past eight years and the results are quite startling. In six out of ten cases, there was a sharp drop in a bank's net profit and rise in its bad assets after a change in leadership.

Interestingly, this trend is evident in those cases where the chairman retires, but when the leader leaves one bank for another bank—normally the chairman of a relatively smaller bank gets promoted to head a relatively bigger bank after a few years—the balance sheet does not show any strain.

There are two reasons behind this trend. One, there is a tendency by the outgoing CEO to inflate profits as the leader always wants to leave the organization on a happy note. It's like a cricketer wanting to score a century in his last innings (in the case of a batsman) or take a handful of wickets (in the case of a bowler). Two, the new CEO normally wants to begin with a clean slate.

The quality of assets is seldom the headache of an outgoing chairman. His focus is on balance sheet expansion (higher loan growth earns higher interest income) and profits, and in the process the bank may end up piling bad assets that eats into its profits in the future. Similarly, the new chairman often wants to tell the world, 'I'm here holding a can of worms', and embarks on a clean-up drive immediately after taking up the assignment.

It is another matter that the incumbent retires one day and may repeat his predecessor's exercise. I call this the *saas–bahu* syndrome in

Indian banking. Many new brides feel unhappy about the way they are treated by their mothers-in-law, but they end up doing the same thing to their own daughters-in-law!

How can one stop this practice? Since the salary of the CEOs of public-sector banks is not linked to the performance of the banks, one should not presume that the focus on balance sheet and profit growth is linked to greed. Yes, they earn a performance-linked incentive, but that's too small an amount and is linked not to profit alone but various other parameters too. Bankers often do this to protect their reputation. If they sign off on a good note, they are assured of a post-retirement assignment at some other government-run organization.

One way of tackling this phenomenon could be not offering any post-retirement job to any retired banker till such time as the regulator is convinced that the bank's health had not been compromised for higher profit. The regulator also needs to be hawk-eyed on the auditors of those banks that show wild fluctuations in net profit.

GOVERNMENT, THE BIGGEST RISK FACTOR FOR PUBLIC-SECTOR BANKS

2 March 2008

In 2004, the finance ministry first told banks where to lend their money and how much. This was followed up by fixing the interest rates for such loans. Finally, the third act of this absurd drama was scripted in Budget 2008, with the largest-ever loan waiver. Agriculture credit doubled in the first two years of the United Progressive Alliance's (UPA) rule after Finance Minister P. Chidambaram directed banks to do so. In the current fiscal that ends this month, banks will disburse Rs 2.4 trillion of farm loans and the target for FY 09 is Rs 2.8 trillion. On government directive, banks extend such loans at 7 per cent interest. Despite this, the indebtedness of Indian farmers is rising. The government wants to address this through a Rs 600-billion loan waiver.

The scheme covers all loans disbursed by commercial banks, regional rural banks and cooperative credit institutions up to March 2007 and not paid till December. Small and marginal farmers won't have to pay anything and big farmers will get a 25 per cent discount on loan repayment. The scheme will be implemented in four months. There is no budgetary provision for the loan waiver, and Chidambaram, in his post-Budget interface with the media spoke about 'liquidity support to banks in the next three years'.

The banks are not aware of the nature of the liquidity support, but seem happy as this will help them clean their balance sheets and the government will bear the burden. The stock market too seems to have been convinced of this theory. Almost all bank stocks that were in the red when Chidambaram was reading out the Budget proposals in Parliament on Friday, bounced back before the market closed after bankers and analysts started explaining how the loan waiver will actually help the system by cleaning up bad credit. However, if the scheme is to be implemented by June, why would the banks need to wait for three years to get their dues? Will they get cash or bonds? Will they get money even for the loan write-offs done, or the provisions already created for stressed agriculture loans?

As yet, nobody knows the answers to these questions. But that's not surprising considering the fact that normally, public-sector banks do not question the wisdom of the government, which owns a majority stake in them. And many of the critical decisions taken by their CEOs are equally baffling. For instance, State Bank of India, India's largest lender, and Canara Bank cut their benchmark prime lending rates by fifty basis points in two stages last month. Other banks such as Bank of Baroda, Bank of India, Union Bank of India and Punjab National Bank have cut their rates by fifty basis points at one go, but after SBI and Canara Bank announced the rate cuts. What happened between 11 February and 20 February? During this time, market rates actually went up. For instance, the yield on the benchmark ten-year paper rose from 7.44 per cent to 7.62 per cent. And the yield on five-year government bonds rose from 6.68 per cent to 8.95 per cent. So, there was reason to raise rates and not pare them.

Still, why did they do this? The answer: pressure from the government. The finance ministry does not believe only in telling banks to cut rates; it also decides on the quantum of the rate cut. This makes government interference the biggest risk for the state-run banks, which account for about three-fourth of the Indian banking industry. No wonder the government features prominently among the risk factors cited by SBI in its offer document for a rights issue that is currently on.

Let me reproduce a few risk factors from the document verbatim:

> As the bank's majority shareholder, the government controls the bank and may cause the bank to take actions which are not in the interest of the bank or of the holders of the equity shares. . . . The government, after consultation with the RBI and the chairman of the bank, may issue directives on matters of policy involving public interest, which may affect the conduct of the business affairs of the bank.
>
> The legal requirement that the government (must) maintain a majority shareholding interest in the bank of at least 55%

> may limit the ability of the bank to raise appropriate levels of capital. . . . As the Indian economy grows, more businesses and individuals will require capital financing . . . the bank will need to accrete its capital base, whether through organic growth or . . . capital market financing schemes.
>
> Other risk factors cited in the document include SBI's inability to attract and retain talent as it cannot offer market related salary and its 'significant' exposure to the farm sector: The loan portfolio contains significant advances to the agriculture sector, amounting to Rs 38,140 crore, or 15.9% of net bank credit as of 30 September 2007. The government's proposed agriculture lending plans may contemplate state-owned banks . . . lending at below market rates in the agriculture sector . . .
>
> The market may perceive the exposure of [the] state-owned banks to the agriculture sector to involve higher risks, whether or not the government mandates lending. This may . . . affect the risk-adjusted returns or state-owned banks and . . . State Bank's business, future financial performance and the trading price of the equity shares.

It is obvious that the State Bank is talking on behalf of all government-owned banks.

ARE PSU BANK HEADS FEUDAL LORDS?

29 May 2011

What does the chairman of a public-sector bank do if he can't get into the car that is supposed to ferry him to the bank's guest house from an airport? He will catch a taxi, right? Well, partially. Indeed, he will catch a taxi, but he will also suspend the senior executive who is at the airport to receive him.

Believe me, I am not cooking up this story. It happened in Mumbai in the third week of May. On a Thursday evening, the chairman of a public-sector bank took a flight from a southern city to Mumbai. The liaison officer of the bank was at the airport to receive him, along with a general manager who heads the bank's Mumbai operations. The liaison officer went inside the airport to greet his chairman and the general manager preferred to wait outside while the air conditioner was on to keep the car cool on a hot and humid evening. While the chairman's suitcase was being loaded in the car's boot by the driver, the doors got locked, with the key in the ignition.

As it was not possible to get another office car at that time (it was well past 9.30 p.m.), the liaison officer first tried to arrange for a Cool Cab, but the queue at the airport counter was long. Finally, he hailed a Meru cab to take the chairman to the bank's guest house in Cuffe Parade in south Mumbai, but by that time, the chairman had lost precious forty-five minutes and his cool. The delivery of the suitcase at 1 a.m. to the guest house and the apology of the general manager next morning (he even touched the chairman's feet, I am told) cut no ice with the chairman, who suspended him on Friday. The suspension order was revoked after a national daily narrated the story graphically last week.

I am not naming the particular bank and its chairman as this incident is symbolic of the culture in public-sector banks that account for a little more than 70 per cent of the Indian banking industry. The chiefs here are always under a lot of stress—they are not only answerable to their board, but also to officials of the Ministry of Finance and even politicians, at times. Moreover, they are not paid well. But when it comes to managing the bank, at least some of them behave like feudal lords.

Using guest houses for personal purposes such as accommodating relatives when their children get married is not uncommon for the bosses. In the executive lunchroom of one public-sector bank, I have seen a particular table being reserved for the chairman where no one is allowed to sit. In yet another bank's lunchroom, I have seen the chairman eating green chillies till beads of sweat trickled down his bald head and somebody wipes it with a white towel before serving dessert.

The suspension of a senior executive for being stranded at an airport for about an hour may be a little too much, but a few years back another senior executive of another bank got transferred to the North-east—traditionally seen as a punishment posting for a banker—after a guest house elevator got stuck at midnight, with the chairman and his wife inside. To pacify his wife, who was very upset, the chairman had to leave the guest house immediately and at night shifted to the guest house of another organization that he had previously headed. The general manager was handed his transfer letter the next morning. Apparently, the general manager had told the chairman that the lift might get stuck if both got in and suggested that they should use it one at a time.

How do private-sector bankers deal with such situations? Differently. This is not because they get higher compensation packages and have more patience and less stress in work. Most private banks have facility management divisions that look after logistics and other related issues, and normally the senior managers do not get involved in arranging the chief executive's vehicle at the airport or food at the guest house. Only when it comes to fixing appointments in the finance ministry or the regulator in Mumbai do senior managers get involved.

They attend such meetings with the chief executives, take notes, and oversee the follow-up actions. However, greeting the boss at the airport, and arranging vehicles and flowers at the guest house are the responsibility of the facility management division.

I spoke to a Mumbai-based psychiatrist to understand why such things happen in the public-sector banking industry. Are the bosses a pampered lot? Is it outright feudalism? The psychiatrist—she doesn't want to be named—blames both the culture as well as individuals for such incidents.

According to her, one should not generalize such problems and instead focus on an individual's behaviour. After all, everybody does not suffer from road rage. She also wants to know why the general manager went to the airport to receive his chairman. I am told the rule book does not say that a senior executive needs to be present at the airport, but by tradition, most go. Of course, there are bosses who actively discourage this practice as it's sheer waste of time that can be better utilized for soliciting business or recovering a bad asset.

After discussing these episodes with the psychiatrist, I feel a bit relieved, as such incidents could be exceptions and not norms. Meanwhile, here is a piece of advice to the reinstated general manager. Next time he goes to receive the chairman at the airport, he can carry a tennis ball with a hole drilled in it. Apparently, if you place the tennis ball against the outside lock where you would normally insert your key, and push as hard as you can, the air pressure will pop the inside lock open. Needless to say, I found this on the Internet and have not tried it yet.

HOW THE GOVERNMENT CHOOSES PSU BANK CEOS

3 March 2013

How does the Government of India, majority owner of public-sector banks, a key growth driver in the world's tenth-largest economy, choose the chief executives of such banks? A peek into the boardroom at the RBI's regional office on Delhi's Parliament Street, on 11 February, would have given you an idea. On that day, a committee consisting of Rajiv Takru, secretary, department of financial services; Anand Sinha, deputy governor, RBI; Jagdish Capoor, former RBI deputy governor; and Debashis Chatterjee, director, Indian Institute of Management, Kozhikode, interviewed eighteen executive directors for nine posts of CEOs that will fall vacant between now and January 2014.

The original idea was to interview six EDs between 9 a.m. and 11 a.m., another six from 11 a.m. till lunch and the rest in the afternoon, post-lunch. But for some reason, the committee could not start interviewing the candidates before 10 a.m., and by lunchtime only seven of them had their turns. The post-lunch session started at around 3.30 p.m. and since eleven candidates were to be accommodated, the panel could hardly spend more than ten minutes with any one of them.

By the end of February, the list of successful candidates was ready and the office of the Central Vigilance Commission is now screening the names. Those who could not make it to the final list are upset and some of them allege that the eligibility criterion for the candidates appearing before the panel was tweaked to accommodate at least a couple of them. How has this been done? Typically, EDs of nationalized banks, deputy managing directors of IDBI Bank Ltd and the managing directors of associate banks of State Bank of India are called for such interviews, provided they have completed two years in the current position and have a residual service of two years as of 1 April of a financial year in which the vacancies arise.

The allegations are that quite a few of the candidates in the list of eighteen have not completed even one year of service as an ED and have less than two years' service left. The government relaxed the eligibility criterion to six months of completed service and twenty-one months of residual service, but it is entitled to such relaxations when it does not find enough candidates to compete for the vacancies. Under the norms, the number of candidates interviewed for such positions should be one and a half times the number of positions vacant. This means, for nine vacancies, at least fifteen candidates should be interviewed. The norms were relaxed as the banking system does not have fifteen executive directors with two years of completed service and with two years to retire. Three more candidates were added to the list who had appeared for the interview last year but could not make it.

While there is nothing illegal about calling relatively junior professionals for the interview and even selecting them, the question remains: how does one pick the right candidates to head a bank in ten minutes? The typical questions asked in such interviews are on financial inclusion, risk management, implementation of Basel III and international banking norms, which any smart business school student can answer without a blink.

Another critical factor to consider is that seventy out of 100 marks—the maximum which a candidate can score—comes from a professional's confidential reports of the past seven years, signed by the proximate boss. Since very few candidates have had a two-year tenure as ED, confidential reports of the past seven years mostly pertain to their career as general managers and deputy general managers. Even if one gets full marks in such reports—which most of them have got—how realistic is the idea of making this a key contributor to their promotion to a position that involves running a bank?

At those levels, a professional handles only a part of the banking business such as loan, treasury, resources or risk management, and excellence in any of these doesn't necessarily guarantee a broad vision, leadership and understanding of the macroeconomy required to run a bank.

The selection of the CEO is only the first stage of an imperfect system. At the second stage comes the selection of banks that such

CEOs will head. Should an ED first be made the chairman of a small bank and only after the government is convinced about his competence, should he be given the top job at a big bank? Or should one straightaway be made the head of a large bank? There is no rule for this.

It is high time the government puts in place a credible and transparent appointment policy for such banks. There are many ways to do it—expanding the talent pool by inviting applications from the market, giving weightage to seniority as well as professional brilliance and making all eligible candidates go through intensive grilling, including group discussions.

A wrong choice of CEO can kill a bank and yet the government is not willing to show professionalism in its approach when it comes to the appointment of CEOs of the institutions which it owns. For two years, the Unit Trust of India has been headless even as its business has been shrinking. Another glaring instance is the appointment of former chief of the Life Insurance Corporation of India (LIC), T.S. Vijayan, as the country's new insurance regulator. In 2011, he was demoted to the position of the managing director of LIC at the end of his five-year term as chairman since the government did not find him suitable to continue at the top. Both decisions—his demotion two years ago and being made the insurance regulator now—cannot be right. But it's too much to expect from the government to own up to its mistakes.

WHY WE NEED PSU BANK REFORMS

3 February 2014

Foreign investors gave a cold shoulder to State Bank of India's Rs 80-billion mega share sale last week. Had Life Insurance Corporation of India not come to its rescue by picking up more than one-third of the shares in the so-called qualified institutional placement, it would have been a huge embarrassment for India's largest lender, which, along with its associate banks, has about a 20 per cent share in India's banking assets. There is only one truth emerging from this episode: foreign investors are not enamoured of India's state-run banks, which are in dire need of reforms.

The RBI governor, Raghuram Rajan, has taken the first step by setting up a committee to review the governance of the boards of Indian banks. The eight-member committee, headed by P.J. Nayak, former chief of Axis Bank Ltd, is expected to submit its report within three months of holding its first meeting. The terms of reference of the committee include a review of the regulatory compliance requirements of the banks' boards; analysis of the representation on the banks' boards to see whether they have the right mix of capabilities and the necessary independence to govern the institutions; investigation of possible conflicts of interest in board representation, including among owner representatives and regulators; examination of whether adequate time is devoted to issues of strategy, growth, governance and risk management; and assessment and review of the so-called 'fit and proper' criterion for all categories of directors of banks, among other things.

The key reform in public-sector banks, which roughly account for 70 per cent of the Rs 82-trillion Indian banking industry, is acceptance of the fact that regulations should be ownership-neutral. This is not the case now. Private banks and public-sector banks are two different animals governed by different sets of regulations.

For instance, a public-sector bank is headed by a chairman and managing director, or CMD, while in a private bank, the top post is split between a chairman and a managing director. As a result of this, in a private bank, which is entirely board-driven, the chairman lends the vision, and the chief executive officer and managing director is in charge of execution of the strategy laid down by the board. In contrast, in a public-sector bank, the CMD is the last word on anything and everything. Indeed, there are executive directors (most public-sector banks have two executive directors), but their role is vague.

This is certainly not an ideal situation, particularly when the boards are weak and there aren't too many directors with expertise and strategic vision to guide the CMD. Splitting the top post in a public-sector bank is a critical component of reform, along with strengthening the board. The chairman should be in a non-executive role and the managing director should be a hands-on professional, supported by executive directors. This should be the administrative structure of State Bank of India as well as other state-run banks, although they are governed by separate acts of Parliament.

A relevant question in this context is: why should the Reserve Bank have its representative on a public-sector bank board, particularly when it does not have any director on a private-bank board? A representative of the regulator being present on the board of a regulated entity is a clear conflict of interest and it's high time the RBI withdrew all its directors from public-sector bank boards. If the idea behind keeping an RBI representative on a bank board is to ensure that the bank follows all regulations diligently, it doesn't always serve the purpose. A former RBI deputy governor who was on the board of State Bank of India could hardly play any role in its policy decisions, pushed by the bank's aggressive chairman.

Similarly, why should the regulator be involved in the process of appointment of the CMD in a public-sector bank while it stays away from private banks? An RBI representative is an integral part of the selection panel of public-sector banks where there is no set norm and the entire process is often marred by political interference. By being part of this process, the regulator loses its credibility. It should be entirely left to the owner of these banks—the government. It's another matter that the government needs to overhaul the entire selection process by being transparent and look for ideal candidates in the open market.

Finally, the concept of 'fit and proper' does not exist for public-sector bank boards. This criterion is not applicable to any director of the board, including the CMD and executive directors. Barring the representatives of shareholders and an RBI nominee, all directors on a public-sector bank board are nominees of the government. They represent different interest groups such as agriculture, small-scale industries and information technology, and most of them are political appointments. Nobody ever checks whether they are 'fit and proper' candidates to be on a bank's board.

As a result of this, there is very little contribution from such directors in terms of strategy and direction to a public-sector bank, where the CMD rules the roost.

It is clear that there is no level playing field for private and state-run banks, but it's not necessarily true that because of this, state-run banks always have had an advantage over their counterparts in the private sector. For instance, unlike private players, public-sector banks are subject to investigation by the Central Bureau of Investigation and the Central Vigilance Commission and audit by the Comptroller and Auditor General of India. They are also covered by the Right to Information Act.

All these inhibit the decision-making process in public-sector banks. They should be freed from these shackles to be able to take decisions without fear.

GOVERNMENT TO GAIN THE MOST FROM PSU BANK REFORMS

19 May 2014

Last week, a Reserve Bank of India panel set up to review the governance of bank boards suggested that the government—the majority owner of public-sector banks—should drastically change the governance structure at these banks. The objective is to make the banks competitive, push up their market value, and free the government from the burden of pumping in capital into these banks every year, despite a high fiscal deficit.

Put up on the RBI website for public comments, the 111-page report of the panel, constituted under the chairmanship of P.J. Nayak, former chairman of Axis Bank Ltd and erstwhile head of Morgan Stanley India Co. Pvt. Ltd, clinically dissected the reasons behind the inherent inefficiency of the public-sector banking industry that has been piling up bad assets.

Incidentally, weeks after the Nayak committee was constituted in January, the RBI wrote a long letter to the then financial services secretary Rajiv Takru on what ails the public-sector banks. Many of the issues that have been raised by the Nayak panel—ranging from tenure of the chairman to composition of a bank board and government ownership—were highlighted in the RBI letter. Takru got back to the RBI, defending the government's stance on almost each and every issue. He even took the blame for the rising non-performing assets of the public-sector banks as the government had pushed these banks to give many project loans in the wake of the North Atlantic financial crisis in 2008–09.

The central bank has subsequently written back to Takru's successor, G.S. Sandhu, refusing to accept the government's arguments and reiterating its stance on governance and other critical issues. Since this is a confidential communication between the RBI and the ministry, and I do not have a copy of the letters, I would not like to discuss their content, but most issues flagged by the RBI have been covered by the Nayak panel's report.

The timing of the release of the report and the exchange of letters between the RBI and the government is interesting. Clearly, the Indian central bank wants the new government to appreciate the problems that have been plaguing the sector and remedy them on a war footing before public-sector banks see more value erosion in the market. The industry's expectations from the Narendra Modi government are very high. Which is why the banking indices of both BSE Ltd and the National Stock Exchange in the past one month have risen the highest among all indices.

There is no surprise in most of the panel's recommendations. They are predictable and much discussed. For instance, it has suggested creation of a bank investment company to hold equity stakes in banks, currently held by the government. In the past, there had been discussions on creation of a holding company where the government can park its shares in the public-sector banks. This is to ensure greater freedom for banks. Besides, the government will also not need to pump in capital every year as the holding company can raise money from the market. Once the government interference in banks' operations comes down, their valuation will rise and the holding company will not face any difficulty in raising money from the market.

The panel has also suggested that the government consider reducing its holding in banks to less than 50 per cent to create a level playing field for public-sector banks vis-à-vis their peers in the private sector. Under the current norms, the government stake cannot come down below 51 per cent. Since the banks are majority-owned by the government, their executives are subjected to probe by the Central Bureau of Investigation as well as the Central Vigilance Commission, and often genuine commercial decisions that go wrong come under this scrutiny. Besides, the government ownership also restrains the bank management in giving market-related compensation to executives. The chief of State Bank of India is possibly earning one-fifth of the salary of the chief executive officer of a small private bank which is one-tenth of its size. This demoralizes public-sector bank executives.

The committee has also recommended a minimum tenure of five years for bank chairmen and a three-year tenure for executive directors—something which the RBI has been harping on for some time.

It has proposed that a category of authorized bank investors (ABIs) be created that would be able to own as much as 20 per cent in a private bank without regulatory approval. ABIs would include pension funds, long–short hedge funds (involving buying long equities that are expected to increase in value and selling short ones that are expected to decrease in value), exchange-traded funds and private equity funds. In distressed banks, private equity funds, including sovereign wealth funds, should be permitted to take a controlling stake of as much as 40 per cent. Under the current norms, a single investor is allowed to hold 5 per cent stake in a bank without regulatory approval.

The panel has also proposed that the ownership ceiling for a promoter in a private-sector bank be raised (from 10 per cent to 25 per cent) and the RBI should not force a new bank to list within a short time frame 'as premature listing could be injurious to minority shareholder interests'. I doubt how many takers will be there for ideas like a higher promoter's stake in private banks and longer time frame for a new bank's listing. HDFC Bank Ltd was listed even before it completed its first full year of operations and it is India's most valued bank. A few promoters, by exploiting regulatory loopholes, continue to hold stakes in banks higher than what is stipulated by the RBI.

However, reforms in public-sector banks at every level—from constitution of the board to tenure of the CEO—are imperative. The biggest beneficiary of such reforms will be the government itself as efficiency will raise their market value and, in turn, the value of the government's shareholding in these banks.

BANKING WITH A BROOM, PSU STYLE

13 October 2014

The chairman and managing director of Canara Bank, R.K. Dubey, and that of Oriental Bank of Commerce, S.L. Bansal, both retired on 30 September. Another large, listed state-run bank, Punjab National Bank, will see its boss R.J. Kamath's five-year term coming to an end on 30 October. Since Kamath is not sixty as yet, he may get another term, but four other listed public-sector banks haven't had CMDs for different reasons.

While Indian Overseas Bank's boss, M. Narendra, demitted office on 31 July, Archana Bhargava of United Bank of India had sought voluntary retirement in February, citing health reasons (her tenure would have ended in March 2015). Syndicate Bank chief S.K. Jain was suspended in the first week of August after he was arrested for accepting a bribe (the government sacked him on 22 September), and Bank of Baroda CMD, S.S. Mundra, was appointed as a deputy governor of the RBI on 31 July.

Why is it taking so long to fill the top posts? There are quite a few reasons. First, the Central Bureau of Investigation has found the appointment of Syndicate Bank's Jain not appropriate. The natural reaction from the government is to take a close look at all appointments and make sure that in future the investigative agency can't find fault with any appointment.

Typically, a short list of candidates is prepared well in advance—sometimes a year before a vacancy comes up. The process, of course, is not transparent; beyond competence and seniority, there are other reasons that influence such appointments.

Second, the government is also talking about consolidation in the public-sector banking industry. State Bank of India's merchant banking wing, SBI Capital Markets Ltd, is preparing a paper on it. If, indeed, the government decides to shrink the number of banks, there will be fewer CMD positions, and possibly the government wants to get a sense of the new scenario before filling in the vacancies.

Finally, a committee, headed by former Axis Bank Ltd chairman P.J. Nayak has suggested splitting the post of CMD into a chairman and a managing director, but no decision on this has been taken as yet. This too will have a bearing on the appointment of public-sector bank bosses.

Meanwhile, the RBI has raised the retirement age of private bank chiefs to seventy. This seems to be in sync with the provisions of the new Companies Act which stipulates that under Section 196(3), no company is allowed to employ any person as managing director and whole-time director who has attained the age of seventy years.

Earlier, no maximum age was specified for the CEOs of private banks and decisions were taken on a case-to-case basis. The Nayak committee, set up to look into corporate governance of banks, is in favour of bank chiefs retiring at sixty-five.

By allowing private banks to retain CEOs till they attain seventy years of age while chiefs of public-sector banks retire at sixty, the banking regulator has made it clear that there is no level playing field in the Indian banking sector. A longer tenure ensures continuity and stability which the public-sector banks lack as most CEOs remain at the helm for a couple of years. Contrast this with HDFC Bank Ltd, India's most valued bank: Aditya Puri, its managing director and CEO, has been heading the bank since its inception in 1994.

The tenure of the CEO is one of the many issues that have been plaguing the public-sector banks. The chiefs are not well looked after in terms of salary and they report to a board, often infested with incompetent directors. On top of all this, there is government interference. On 2 October, a public holiday, banks had to be kept open and bankers were seen sweeping the branch premises to show solidarity with Prime Minister Narendra Modi's Swachh Bharat Mission.

A bureaucrat from the finance ministry had written to the CMDs of all public-sector banks asking them to keep offices open on 2 October and the employees were directed to report at 9 a.m. 'A senior officer may be designated to administer (the) cleanliness pledge to all employees at 9.45 a.m. Thereafter, the officers will voluntarily carry out cleaning of their office premises from inside and outside . . . All the officers may also be motivated to contribute voluntarily towards cleaning of their residential premises, neighbourhood and social network premises so as to provide 100 hours of voluntary contribution during the year,' the letter said.

Predictably, there was a chain reaction, with the CMD's office forwarding the mail to the zonal offices, which in turn, alerted the branches. The objective of the bankers at the branch level was not necessarily to clean the premises, but somehow get photographed with a broom in hand. The photographs were promptly emailed to the zonal offices, which in turn, emailed them to the headquarters. I presume the CMDs of all public-sector banks have emailed such photographs to the finance ministry as proof of their participation in the cleanliness drive. I wonder whether they will clean up their balance sheets with equal aggression.

I have nothing against bankers coming to office on 2 October as they enjoy too many holidays, but the rush to be photographed with a broom lent a farcical element to the entire exercise, even though nobody can find fault with the objective of the mission. The much-touted Pradhan Mantri Jan-Dhan Yojana also runs the risks of turning into a farce with the bankers chasing the numbers and not real expansion of banking services. The joke doing the rounds is that nobody wants to walk on the pavement near a public-sector bank branch for fear of being dragged in to open an account.

4

Banking Reforms or Lack of It

This chapter is on reforms in Indian banking and the lack of it. After the economic liberalization in 1991, the Reserve Bank of India started freeing the loan rates as well as deposit rates in a phased manner. The RBI governor, C. Rangarjan (December 1992–November 1997), better known for abolishing ad hoc treasury bills, also pulled down the wall between the banks and the development financial institutions and started dismantling the administered rates, both for deposits as well as loans. From there to the deregulation of savings bank rate in 2011 has been a long road.

The columns in this chapter attempt to trace reforms in Indian banking and the regulator's relentless efforts to make monetary transmission seamless. There are also pieces which take a critical look at the functioning of the RBI as well as some of the institutions that the successive governments have built in this space—such as Bharatiya Mahila Bank (which got merged with State Bank of India in 2017), Mudra Bank (Micro Units Development Refinance Agency Bank) and the Banks Board Bureau—and question their efficacy. One piece also raises questions on the future of India Post Payments Bank.

Finally, there are pieces on the changes that the sector is witnessing—with the RBI willing to experiment with different kinds of banks, digitization on a fast lane, and intense competition among banks for customer acquisition and retention. One caveat though: the pieces need to be read in the context when they were written. For instance, Bharatiya Mahila Bank was a misadventure; Mudra Bank is merely creating a statistical illusion; and the Banks Board Bureau remains a toothless tiger while the Pradhan Mantri Jan-Dhan Yojana, despite many zero-balance or near-zero-balance accounts, remains a mission-mode project for achieving financial inclusion.

BANKS FOR BREAKFAST, LUNCH, DINNER

22 November 2009

Tourists at the Tadoba Andhari Tiger Reserve in Nagpur were recently treated to a rare sight. On an early morning in November, a healthy sambar was seen trying to dodge two tigers by entering the shallow waters of Telia Lake, only to be attacked by a pair of crocodiles. The sambar battled hard with the crocodiles for most part of the day before being mauled by the tigers in the evening when it came out of the lake trying to sneak into the forest. The tired crocodiles had given up, but the tigers were waiting for the kill.

For a moment, replace the sambar with some of the relatively smaller public-sector banks in India such as Dena Bank, Vijaya Bank, Andhra Bank and Corporation Bank. They are a bunch of efficient and not-so-efficient banks with assets ranging from Rs 400 billion to Rs 1 trillion. Then replace the tigers and crocodiles with the relatively bigger public-sector banks—Punjab National Bank, Bank of Baroda, Bank of India, Canara Bank, IDBI Bank Ltd and Union Bank of India, with assets between Rs 1.5 trillion–2.5 trillion. The Denas and Corporation Banks will be attacked by the Canaras and Bank of Indias the moment the government converts the Indian financial sector into a reserve forest of big banks.

A day after a few bureaucrats of the finance ministry held a meeting with the chief executive officers of five big banks on consolidation, Canara Bank Chairman A.C. Mahajan told reporters that he would look for acquisitions and an internal team would identify the potential targets. S.K. Goel, chief of the Kolkata-based UCO Bank, would draw up a blueprint to buy a smaller bank.

I am going by media reports and haven't spoken to Mahajan or Goel. I have, in fact, spoken to a few others who have not been quoted in the media, and most of them, given a choice, would love to have a small bank on their table for breakfast, lunch and dinner, much the same way the crocodiles wanted to kill the sambar, and the tigers devoured it.

I am not against consolidation. Neither am I against big bankers' appetite for a healthy meal. But there is something called dinner table etiquette in terms of dress code, use of napkins, knife and fork, and so on. Just because India's capital market regulator is not sensitive enough to the wishful market-moving statements, bank bosses should not compete with each other in fantasizing about who will take over whom.

After all, barring two, all such banks are listed, and investors rush to buy stocks when they hear the chiefs talking about identifying targets and setting up merger and acquisition teams for inorganic growth. The talk about consolidation of public-sector banks, which account for roughly three-fourth of the Indian banking industry, is at least five years old. In early 2004, the then banking secretary N.S. Sisodia had sought the views of large public-sector banks on consolidation at a meeting in Jaipur, kicking off the debate. At that meeting too, every banker wanted to be an acquirer.

To be sure, the Congress-led coalition government is in a better position to push for consolidation today than it was in 2004 as it does not depend now on the Left parties for its existence. The Left parties oppose bank mergers out of concern that such mergers will lead to large-scale job losses. Any merger between two public-sector banking entities takes place under an Act that stipulates that two banks can initiate merger talks, but the scheme of the merger must be finalized by the government in consultation with the central bank, and it must be placed in Parliament, which reserves the right to modify or reject the scheme. In case of a merger between a public-sector bank and a private bank too, parliamentary approval is a must.

This means that unless the government is in a position to push through any merger, consolidation in Indian banking cannot take place. Actually, a near-decimated Left gives the government a handle to ensure Parliament's approval for such mergers, but this alone cannot ensure consolidation.

From 1969, when Bank of Behar was merged with State Bank of India, till the union of Centurion Bank of Punjab Ltd with HDFC

Bank Ltd last year, most mergers have been an offshoot of the central bank's efforts to protect the financial system and depositors' money, and very few of them have been driven by the need for consolidation and growth. At this point, bankers are looking at different geographies to find their strategic fits. So, Canara Bank in the south is eyeing Dena Bank in the west; Bank of India in the west is looking at Oriental Bank of Commerce in the north; Union Bank in the west is wooing Corporation Bank in the south; and Bank of Baroda in the west seems comfortable with Vijaya Bank in the south. Geographical reach is one of the many critical issues that needs to be considered along with work culture, technology platform, business mix, and so on. Most importantly, who will head the merged entity?

The CEO of a small bank will never be excited about merger prospects as he runs the risk of losing his job. One way of tackling this could be initiating the process after the CEO of the bank to be acquired retires. Also, it's not acquisition, but amalgamation where the employees of small banks must be treated with the utmost respect.

Finally, the CEOs should not talk till they act. I love the way some of them run their banks, but I don't share their fantasy.

WHY THE RBI SHOULD KILL THE BANK RATE

14 February 2010

Can you ask Hindustan Unilever Ltd (HUL), India's largest packaged consumer goods maker, to give a break-up of the cost of vegetable oils, tallow, sodium hydroxide, pigments and fragrances that are used to make soap? And the cost of packaging, dealers' commission and the margin that it wants for every cake of soap sold? If you can't do that, why do you expect banks to be transparent and reveal their cost of funds, overheads and margins while pricing loans? A highly agitated senior banker told me this last week after the central bank issued a statement freeing all loan rates and replacing the benchmark prime lending rate (BPLR) with a new concept called 'base rate', below which no bank will be allowed to lend from the next fiscal, beginning 1 April.

The RBI wants banks to be transparent while fixing the rate. According to this banker, the RBI's move will deal a blow to the market economy. 'Let the borrowers reject the banks that are overcharging. Why does the RBI want to get into micromanagement?' he argued. Banking is not like selling soap, and money—the raw material that bankers use—is very different from what goes into making of Lifebuoy and Lux. Nirma Ltd could flood the rural market with its low-cost detergent and force HUL to rework its pricing strategy, but this kind of competition cannot take place in banking, a highly regulated business. This is why protection of consumers is the regulator's headache.

Banks are being asked to shift to the base rate because they were misusing BPLR by offering loans to many corporations below BPLR while overcharging others. Small and medium enterprises (SMEs) have been raising bank loans at 3–4 percentage points higher than BPLR in contrast to the top-rated corporations whose cost of loans is 3–4 percentage points lower than BPLR. In other words, SMEs were subsidizing the larger and stronger firms. The new base rate is nothing but MLR, or minimum lending rate, and many bankers are not comfortable with it for fear of losing the power of discretion in fixing loan rates.

Incidentally, the Telecom Regulatory Authority of India lays down the basic pricing norms for cellular phone firms. In the financial sector, the Securities and Exchange Board of India decides on how much commission a mutual fund can charge, and the Act that governs the insurance industry has fixed the ceiling for commission on the sale of insurance products.

Bankers will find it difficult to have one base rate for all loans. The cost of short-term money is less, and hence short-term loans will always be cheaper than long-term loans, they say. If that's really the case, why are they offering twenty-year mortgages at 8–8.5 per cent? There is something rotten in the current loan pricing system. If the long-term loans are floating-rate loans, where the price is adjusted periodically, then it's not very difficult to link all loans to the base rate, irrespective of their tenure. To be fair, bankers alone shouldn't be blamed for distortions in rates.

Unlike other developed markets, in India the policy rate does not have a direct bearing on banks' loan rates because the monetary transmission mechanism is very weak. Monetary transmission mechanism is the process by which asset prices and general economic conditions are affected as a result of monetary policy decisions. Such decisions are intended to influence the aggregate demand, interest rates and amounts of money and credit, in order to affect overall economic performance. This is why, despite a 5.75 percentage points drop in the policy rate since October 2008, in the wake of the collapse of Lehman Brothers, banks did not pare their BPLR by even half of it.

Also, there is no correlation between banks' loan rates and government bond yields. In the US, the prime rate, which is normally 3 percentage points higher that the Fed rate, is the benchmark rate for all consumer and retail loans while the London interbank offered rate, or LIBOR, is the reference point for all corporate loans. Similarly, in the UK, the Bank of England's base rate is the benchmark rate for consumer and retail loans while LIBOR influences commercial loans.

In India, neither repo (the rate at which the central bank infuses liquidity into the system) nor reverse repo (the rate at which the RBI sucks out liquidity from the system) has any bearing on the actual loan rate of banks. And the bank rate of the RBI, its medium-term signal rate, is defunct. It was last changed in April 2003.

LIBOR's Indian counterpart is MIBOR, or the Mumbai interbank offered rate—the rate at which banks can borrow funds from each other in the interbank market. Launched in June 1998, MIBOR is calculated daily by the National Stock Exchange as a weighted average of lending rates of a group of banks. The success of the overnight MIBOR encouraged the exchange to develop one-month and three-month MIBORs, but these term rates are not as effective as they should be. One of the key reasons why the term 'money market' virtually doesn't exist in India is an imperfect government bond market.

The government borrows from the market every year to bridge its fiscal deficit, and the RBI, the banking regulator, manages this programme. There is a clear clash of interest between the role of the RBI as a banking regulator and the government's debt manager, as it would always like to keep the yield on bonds at a low level to ensure smooth implementation of the borrowing programme at a low cost for the government.

Once the RBI steps out and an independent debt manager is appointed for managing the government's borrowing programme, it will help develop the term 'money market', as bond yields will be more realistic, but that may not happen until the fiscal deficit declines. We will wait for that, but meanwhile, the RBI should kill the bank rate. Nobody will miss it.

BANK BPLR: MAY IT REST IN PEACE

27 June 2010

If I were to write an epitaph on the tombstone of the benchmark prime lending rate, which will be buried on 31 June by the Indian banking industry, it will probably read: 'To be fair to small and medium borrowers, it had to die; a failure since birth, but can the bankers explain why?'

The top-rated Indian companies will shed tears on the grave because they will no longer be able to raise money at below BPLR. Since it was introduced in 2003 as a benchmark rate below which no bank should lend money, the bulk of bank loans have been disbursed at lower than BPLR. Why did bankers do that?

There is a structural problem here. Even though the industry is by and large deregulated, a few lending rates are still mandated and linked to banks' BPLR. For example, loans to exporters are given at 2.5 percentage points below BPLR. Similarly, all loans to small farmers are priced cheaper than BPLR. This has prevented banks from paring their BPLR as the moment this benchmark rate is cut, automatically the loan rate for exporters and small farmers declines. So, banks preferred to keep their BPLR at an artificially high level and charge most of their borrowers a rate much below the benchmark rate.

This is the only way they could prevent loan rates for exporters and small farmers from declining to a level that does not even cover their cost of funds. On 1 July, the base rate will replace BPLR and banks are banned from lending at below the base rate. Small farmers and exporters will, however, continue to get cheap loans even though the rate at which they will get money will not be linked to the base rate. The government gives a subsidy of two percentage points to banks on such loans.

Apart from small-ticket borrowers (loans of up to Rs 200,000) and exporters, two other categories of loans will not need to adhere to the base rate formula—loans to banks' own employees and loans against deposits. How will the banks calculate their base rate? They need to take into account their cost of funds, overheads such as the cost of running branches and employee wages.

Then there are other critical factors to be considered. For instance, banks do not earn any interest on the cash reserve ratio, or the portion of deposits they keep with the regulator. Currently, the CRR is pegged at 6 per cent. If it goes up, banks' earning will go down and that will have an impact on the calculation of the base rate. Similarly, the level of non-performing assets will also influence the base rate. Banks do not earn any interest on their NPAs, and hence, the higher such assets the lower their income.

The calculation for BPLR was no different. Despite that, most of the banks ended up having their BPLRs in the same range even though their cost of funds, overheads and level of non-performing assets were not alike.

Typically, State Bank of India takes the lead in setting the rate and others follow. There is no cap on the spread between the base rate and the actual rate that a bank can charge its customers. This means that a bank can keep its base rate at 8 per cent and still charge a customer 18 per cent. But to do this, it has to justify the spread of ten percentage points. The tenure of the loan, risk profile of the customer, the industry that the customer represents (real estate will carry higher risk than, say, a manufacturing unit) and even the geography (an individual borrower from the Dharavi slum in Mumbai will have a higher risk profile than one from upscale Bandra) will influence the spread.

The biggest difference between the BPLR regime and the base rate regime will be transparency, as the banks will be required to explain the rationale behind the actual loan rate—something they have not been doing. In a highly distorted financial world, efficient small and medium enterprises have been subsidizing top-rated companies; this may end now. But still there are ways how a bank can offer loans to top firms at below its base rate, indirectly though, and no regulator can stop the practice. It's fairly simple.

A bank can offer loan to a top-rated firm at its base rate and pay two percentage points higher than the market rate on the deposit that the firm keeps with the bank. To be sure, it's not easy to arrive at an ideal loan rate in India as the policy rate here, unlike in the developed markets, does not have a direct bearing on banks' loan rates. Also, there is no synergy between banks' loan rates and government bond yields.

As discussed earlier, in the US, the prime rate—normally three percentage points higher than the Federal Reserve rate—is the benchmark rate for all consumer and retail loans, and the London interbank offered rate is the reference point for all corporate loans. Similarly, in the UK, the Bank of England's base rate is the benchmark rate for consumer and retail loans, while LIBOR is the benchmark for commercial loans. LIBOR's Indian counterpart MIBOR is the rate at which banks can borrow funds from each other in the interbank market. However, this is an overnight rate and the efforts to develop one-month and three-month MIBORs have not yet met with success.

Two critical factors that can ensure a fair loan rate regime are a term money market and a vibrant bond market where the yields are not artificially suppressed to ensure that the government's huge annual borrowing programme goes through. We are nowhere close to either of them.

LIFE AFTER SAVINGS BANK DEREGULATION

30 October 2011

Hours after the Reserve Bank of India freed savings bank rate last week, Yes Bank Ltd raised the rate by two percentage points, and Kotak Mahindra Bank Ltd followed suit over the weekend. No other banks have responded yet to this move, but many fear there will be a rate war to woo savings bank depositors. If that happens, consumers will benefit and banks' cost of funds will rise. This will affect their net interest margin, or the difference between the cost of funds and earnings on the deployment of funds, the key to their profitability.

Since Yes Bank has only about Rs 7 billion worth of savings deposits, which is less than 2 per cent of its total deposits, a two percentage point hike in rate will raise its interest cost by Rs 0.14 billion a year. At this point, the Indian banking industry has a deposit base of Rs 56.25 trillion, and roughly 22 per cent of this, or Rs 12.38 trillion, is savings bank deposits. If all banks raise their savings bank deposit rate by an identical margin, the annual cost for the industry will be Rs 247.6 billion. Even if they decide to raise the rate by one percentage point, the interest cost will go up by Rs 123.8 billion, about 20 per cent of the industry's net profit in fiscal 2011. Will that happen?

A savings account is the most common operating account for individuals and others for non-commercial transactions—a hybrid of current account and term-deposit account, providing the convenience of easy withdrawals, writing of cheques and an avenue to park short-term funds that earn interest. Banks generally put a ceiling on the total number of withdrawals permitted and stipulate a certain minimum balance to be maintained in such accounts.

In the past decade, the composition of savings accounts has not changed and the household sector continues to have a share of about 85 per cent of such deposits despite a reduction in interest rates. This essentially means that even though the average inflation rate is higher and the real return from savings accounts is negative, Indian households continue to keep money in such accounts. This helps banks lower their average cost of money and this is why the focus of all banks has all along been to push up the proportion of current and savings accounts in their overall deposit portfolios. Banks do not pay any interest on current accounts. The savings account rate was last changed in April, after a gap of eight years, and raised from 3.5 per cent to 4 per cent. Until fiscal 2010, the average cost for banks for such accounts was even lower—at around 2.8 per cent—because they used to pay interest only on the minimum balance kept between the tenth and the end of a month. From April, they have been paying interest rate on a daily average basis.

Regulations of deposit rates came into being from September 1964 and before that, the rates were governed by voluntary agreements between large public-sector banks and foreign banks operating in India. The only exception was a short period of six months, between September 1960 and February 1961, when the RBI regulated the interest rates of deposits up to fourteen days. Eight years later, in September 1969, the RBI banned interest payment on current accounts and deposits of up to fourteen days. From 1979 onwards, almost all deposit rates were administered.

In April 1992, banks were given the freedom to fix interest rates on term deposits of forty-six days to three years and more within the ceiling prescribed by the RBI. The deposit rate structure was made more flexible in October 1995 by giving banks the freedom to fix rates on domestic term deposits over two years, and finally in October 1997, interest rates on term deposits were completely deregulated.

In April 1998, the minimum maturity of term deposits was reduced from thirty days to fifteen days and it dropped further to seven days in 2002, only for wholesale deposits of at least Rs 15,00,000. Now even retail customers can keep any amount for seven days.

Savings bank deposit was the last bastion of administered rates in Indian banking. Non-resident Indian deposits are the only other banking product that offers mandated rates, but they are related to the external sector and till India embraces capital account convertibility, they will probably continue to be regulated, as the RBI would need to have the lever to regulate the foreign money flow.

The RBI started seriously exploring the option of freeing the savings bank rate in 2006, but couldn't do that in the face of stiff resistance put up by the national bankers' lobby, the Indian Banks' Association. Will the Yes Bank move trigger a rate war and shake the system? I am not sure about that. When rates were freed for term deposits, which account for about 65 per cent of the overall deposits, there was no shake-out in the system.

One can argue that the competition was less intense at that time, but the counterargument is that the banking system is more mature now. Not too many banks are expected to match the Yes Bank offer as they are not as starved of savings bank deposits as Yes Bank is, but one thing for sure is that they will be forced to innovate. Consumers will gain a little extra interest income now when inflation is high, but at the cost of convenience, as banks will try to limit the number of transactions and other peripheral stuff such as accounts statements and cheque books for low-value customers in order to cut cost.

They will also discourage branch visits of customers as the cost per transaction in a bank branch is the highest. Alternative channels such as automated teller machines, Internet banking and phone banking will be encouraged to lower the cost of transactions.

Finally, the freeing up of savings bank accounts will encourage foreign and new private banks to enter rural India, the traditional stronghold of state-run banks, to raise relatively cheap money.

BHARATIYA MAHILA BANK: UPA'S RS 10-BILLION MISADVENTURE

24 November 2014

The 5000 sq. ft Bharatiya Mahila Bank Ltd branch at Nariman Point's landmark Air India building in Mumbai—the sole branch in Maharashtra till now—is managed by half a dozen employees. They outnumber customers most days of the week.

The scene is similar with many of the forty-odd branches of the one-year-old bank across Indian cities. Barring Jammu and Kashmir and some north-eastern states, the lender has opened branches in all states, but its business is yet to take off. There aren't too many people who know about this bank meant for women.

Bharatiya Mahila Bank is also finding it difficult to expand its branch network as landlords are not too excited about offering premises to it till they are told that it is wholly owned by the Government of India.

It is the only public-sector bank in the country entirely owned by the government, and is probably the last company to be incorporated under the old companies law of 1956. At its launch in Mumbai on 19 November last year—the ninety-sixth birth anniversary of former prime minister Indira Gandhi—the then finance minister P. Chidambaram had said the bank would break even in the next three to five years. Its total business—advances and deposits—would be Rs 600 billion by 2020 when it would have a 770-strong branch network and would be listed in the stock exchanges in due course. The then prime minister Manmohan Singh and the United Progressive Alliance chairperson Sonia Gandhi graced the occasion.

Chidambaram was guided by an Excel sheet prepared by SBI Capital Markets Ltd, the investment banking arm of State Bank of India, which drew the blueprint for this bank. A committee consisting of former Canara Bank chairman M.V.N. Rao, former Bank of Baroda chairman M.D. Mallya and SBI chairman Arundhati Bhattacharya, among others, gave its inputs for setting up the bank.

A year down the line, this bank has gone nowhere. It has a deposit base of around Rs 5.2 billion, advances of around Rs 2.75 billion and 75,000 customers, out of which 82 per cent are women. About 60 per cent of its 250 employees are women. In 2013–14, it had made a profit of close to Rs 130 million, primarily on treasury operations. Its Rs 10-billion capital is entirely invested in government securities. In the first half of the current financial year, its profit is around Rs 260 million, again based on treasury income.

With a minuscule branch network and no brand push (it does advertise on the baggage tag of Jet Airways), the challenge for the bank is business growth. While men also can keep money with it, when it comes to loans, it is exclusively focusing on women. Apart from women customers, any company headed by a woman chief executive officer can borrow from this bank.

Similarly, companies where 40 per cent of the board of directors are women or 50per cent of employees are women can be its customers. Moreover, a male entrepreneur running businesses for women such as a nursing college or an engineering college or producing hygiene products for women is also eligible to become a borrower.

The bank is also developing exclusive loan products for running crèches, kindergarten schools, home-catering services and beauty salons, which are typically run by women. Since in most states in India, barring Kerala and Meghalaya, women do not have the right to property and hence cannot offer collateral for a loan, Bharatiya Mahila Bank is ready to give them loans of up to Rs 10 million without security. Of course, the borrowers need to pay a little extra for the cover of the Credit Guarantee Trust for Micro and Small Enterprises. Despite this, business is not taking off simply because of a lack of awareness about this bank among women and its restricted reach.

In the beginning, its chairman wrote to 2000-odd Indian institutions—ranging from corporations to academic bodies—seeking business relationships, but there has been hardly any response. Since there are not too many takers for loans customized for women, it is giving money to intermediaries such as LIC Housing Finance

Ltd and GIC Housing Finance Ltd, Janalakshmi Financial Services Pvt. Ltd in Bengaluru and a microfinance outfit in Lucknow to buy cycle rickshaws and sewing machines, among others.

Desperate to expand, the bank is monitoring business daily. Unable to bear the pressure to perform, some employees have already gone back to the institutions from where they had come on deputation. This is an all-officer bank; there are no clerks on its payroll. Out of 250 executives, 100 have been on deputation from other banks. The incentive to join the bank was a one-grade promotion, but now frustrated employees are willing to go back, settling for a lower grade and salary.

The technology is in place and soon Internet banking will take off, but managing this small bank is not easy as employees have come from many banks, soaked in different cultures. For instance, its two general managers are from United Bank of India and Canara Bank, and six deputy general managers are from Punjab National Bank, Bank of Maharashtra, Vijaya Bank and an SBI associate bank.

If the early signs are any indication, Bharatiya Mahila Bank is set to become a political misadventure by the erstwhile UPA government. Nowhere in the world has a bank for women become successful. Pakistan was the first country to set up a women's bank—First Women Bank Ltd—in 1989. Founded by the late prime minister Benazir Bhutto to meet the needs of women entrepreneurs, it began business in December 1989, with five leading public-sector banks holding a 90 per cent stake and the government the rest. Subsequently, the government's stake has risen beyond 50 per cent.

First Women Bank gives loans to those companies where women have at least 50 per cent shareholding, or women employees constitute at least 40 per cent of the total number of employees, or those that have a woman CEO. For the year ending December 2013, it reported a loss of 222 million Pakistani rupees as it had to set aside 168 million Pakistani rupees for bad loans on an advance book of 8 billion Pakistani rupees.

Tanzania Women's Bank Ltd is another example. In 1999, a group of women entrepreneurs proposed the idea of the bank to the then president Benjamin William Mkapa. It was set up in 2007, with the government holding a 97 per cent equity stake and private entities the rest, but it started business only in July 2009. Based in Dar es Salaam, it focuses on low-income earners, small businesses and small and medium enterprises. Its name was changed to Tanzania Women's Bank Public Ltd Co. in 2012 when the lender planned to raise money from the public and list its shares.

If the UPA government was concerned about women not getting money from banks, the smartest way of sorting out this problem could have been to ask all Indian banks to dedicate 5 per cent of their branch network to cater to women customers. These branches could have been managed exclusively by women employees. At one stroke, we would have got 6000 branches across India to do the job.

Setting up this bank is a sheer waste of Rs 10 billion, particularly when the government is not in the pink of fiscal health.

DO WE NEED MUDRA BANK?

9 March 2015

For the quarter that ended on 31 December 2014, the aggregate loan portfolio of India's for-profit microfinance institutions registered with the Reserve Bank of India as non-banking financial companies were to the tune of Rs 314.50 billion, disbursed to 28.7 million borrowers. In the December quarter, loan disbursements in terms of amount rose by 46 per cent even as the number of loans grew by 33 per cent over the same period last year.

The coverage of such institutions is now geographically well disbursed, with southern and eastern India accounting for 29 per cent each of the market share, and the northern and western parts accounting for 21 per cent each. If we include the not-for-profit MFIs, the portfolio will be slightly bigger, but even then, their overall exposure will be about half a per cent of the loan assets of India's banking system. Typically, an MFI does not give loans beyond Rs 50,000 to a single borrower and the average loan amount disbursed per account by NBFC-MFIs is Rs 16,194.

Clearly, MFIs do not meet the funding requirements of small entrepreneurs who want more than Rs 50,000 and up to a few lakhs. Commercial banks too are reluctant to have business relationships with this segment of borrowers. There are 57.7 million small business units and only 4 per cent of them are able to access institutional finance. How does one solve the funding gap?

The government led by the Bharatiya Janata Party plans to set up Mudra Bank to take care of this. Mudra Bank will have a corpus of Rs 200 billion to refinance all types of MFIs—both non-profit and for-profit MFIs. It will also have a credit guarantee corpus of Rs 30 billion.

Bangladesh has a similar entity for financing microcredit—the Palli Karma-Sahayak Foundation (PKSF). Established in 1990 by the Government of Bangladesh as a not-for-profit company, the principal objective of PKSF is to provide funds to various organizations for their microcredit programmes that finance the poor who have no land or any credible material possession. Access to resources creates employment opportunities and enhances their livelihood. PKSF provides assistance to the poor through different non-government, semi-government and government organizations; voluntary agencies and societies; local government bodies; institutions; groups and individuals, which are called partner organizations.

The latest data available for PKSF relate to the fiscal year 2013 when the number of rural borrowers stood at 4.29 million, accounting for 73 per cent of the borrowers who received assistance from PKSF. Around that time, the average loan size was to the tune of Bangladeshi taka 16,325.

Even though Mudra Bank will be a refinance agency, its scope of work will be much larger than Bangladesh's PKSF. Going by the plans, it will be a statutory body responsible for regulating and refinancing all MFIs that are in the business of lending to micro and small businesses engaged in manufacturing, trading and services activities. It will lay down policy guidelines for micro and small enterprise financing business, register MFI entities and regulate them. Besides, it will also rate MFIs, formulate a code of conduct for the industry to ensure client protection principles and methods of recovery, promote right technology solutions for the last mile, and run a credit guarantee scheme for providing guarantees to the loans that are being extended to microenterprises.

Currently, MFIs are primarily dependent on commercial banks for money, and resources are not cheap. Banks are required to channel 40 per cent of their loans to the so-called priority sector, consisting of agriculture and other small loans, and typically, they give money to MFIs to meet such targets. The MFIs get such loans at 13–14 per cent and lend them at 23–24 per cent, keeping a 10 per cent margin to take care of their operating cost and profit. Mudra Bank is expected to offer refinance at a much cheaper rate and to that extent, the cost of money will come down for small borrowers.

However, do we need yet another refinance agency in the Indian financial system? Quite a few such agencies already exist and none of them can claim to be a success by any yardstick. One is the National Housing Bank (NHB), a refinance agency in the home loan market. Set up in July 1988 by an Act of Parliament, NHB refinances home loans and regulates activities of housing finance companies. The National Bank for Agriculture and Rural Development (NABARD) and the Small Industries Development Bank of India (SIDBI) are also in the business of refinancing. NABARD was set up in July 1982 by a law to promote sustainable and equitable agriculture and rural prosperity through credit support, related services, institutional development and other innovative initiatives. The objective of SIDBI, set up in April 1990 through another law, is to promote, finance and develop the micro, small and medium businesses sector.

Had NABARD and SIDBI been successful in their missions, Finance Minister Arun Jaitley would not have thought about Mudra Bank, which, it seems, will take over some of the refinancing activities of these two institutions and channel the money in a more focused way.

We also need to ponder on whether we need shadow banks to finance micro, small and medium enterprises, while the global trend is to discourage shadow banking and use the main-line banking system to meet the financing needs of all segments. Precisely for this reason, the Reserve Bank of India wants to set up small-finance banks and, given a choice, most existing MFIs will migrate to small banking.

It doesn't make sense to create yet another refinance agency, and positioning it as a regulator leads to conflict of interest, with the same entity lending and overseeing regulations. Over fifty million unfunded small entrepreneurs need funds at a reasonable cost and the best way to meet their need is to give permits to probably fifty small banks and not create yet another refinance agency.

THE GREAT INDIAN FINANCIAL INCLUSION CIRCUS

31 August 2014

For about a million public-sector bank employees, the past fortnight has been extremely hectic. Senior executives could hardly sleep; they were busy at videoconferences with colleagues in every state and even district while junior employees were literally on the street, chasing prospective depositors—something never seen in the history of Indian banking. They were put on notice on Independence Day when Prime Minister Narendra Modi announced the Pradhan Mantri Jan-Dhan Yojana as a national mission on financial inclusion and fixed 28 August as the launch date.

In his address, Modi spoke about the ambitious project to offer banking facilities to all households in India in order to complement the Bharatiya Janata Party–led National Democratic Alliance government's development philosophy of *Sabka Sath, Sabka Vikas*; he followed it up with a personal letter to all senior bankers. He wrote, 'We need to enrol over seven crore households and open their accounts. This is a national priority and we must rise to meet this challenge. There is an urgency to this exercise as all other development activities are hindered by this single disability . . . I will myself recognize the achievements of the best-performing branches.'

One cannot find fault with Modi's earnestness. People in remote villages drink American fizzy drinks like Coke and Pepsi and carry mobile telephones in their pockets, but they are pariahs when it comes to banking; India's banks do not find doing business with them profitable. According to a 2012 working paper of the World Bank, only 35 per cent of India's adult population has access to formal banking.

So, what's the Pradhan Mantri Jan-Dhan Yojana all about? It aims at bringing at least seventy-five million unbanked families into India's banking system by opening two bank accounts per household in rural and urban pockets. All such accounts are being linked to the RuPay debit card, a domestic card network. Every individual who opens a bank account becomes eligible to receive an accident insurance cover of up to Rs 100,000 and once the bank account has been active for six months and linked to the account holder's Aadhaar identity number, he or she would become eligible for an overdraft of up to Rs 5000.

Last Thursday, the government rolled out the programme, claiming that about fifteen million accounts were opened, exceeding the first day's target of ten million. An excited Modi shortened the deadline for achieving the target of seventy-five million new accounts to 26 January from 15 August 2015. He also topped up each account with a life insurance cover of Rs 30,000, adding to the Rs 100,000 accidental insurance benefit. 'Never before in economic history were fifteen million bank accounts opened on a single day,' Modi said. Many Union ministers and at least twenty chief ministers simultaneously launched the scheme in the states. Information and Broadcasting Minister Prakash Javadekar launched it in Pune, Law Minister Ravi Shankar Prasad in Chennai, External Affairs Minister Sushma Swaraj in Bhopal, Home Minister Rajnath Singh in Lucknow and Human Resource Development minister Smriti Irani in Surat. Nirmala Sitharaman, minister of state for finance, even cancelled a visit to Myanmar to be part of the launch.

I happened to be present at Minority Affairs Minister Najma Heptulla's launch function in Kolkata. Forty-odd financially included persons, who opened accounts on that day, walked into a five-star hotel for the first time in their lives and were treated to tea and cookies after Heptulla handed over to them a RuPay debit card and a passbook which says, Mera Khata–Bhagya Vidhata. It didn't take much time to find out that for all of them, it was not their first bank account. Clearly, the banks wanted to meet the target at any cost. A retired banker even compared this programme to the late Sanjay Gandhi's compulsory sterilization drive in 1975. At that time, the health department in various states forced many to undergo sterilization more than once to meet their targets. The bankers followed a similar path—beg, borrow or steal, get a human being to open a bank account; it doesn't matter whether the person was already financially included.

Should we blame Modi for the great Indian financial inclusion circus? To be fair to him, he has resorted to inclusion at gunpoint out of sheer frustration. Lazy bankers have been refusing to expand their services, citing high transaction and technology cost for going rural, while they are sanguine about thousands of crores in loans, given to corporate borrowers, turning bad. For the first time, in January 2006, the Reserve Bank of India had allowed banks to appoint banking correspondents and address the so-called last-mile problem in providing banking services to the masses, but nothing much has happened except for opening millions of so-called no-frills accounts. By December 2013, banking connectivity had been extended to 3,28,679 villages from 67,694 in March 2010, and 229 million basic accounts have been opened, but how many of them are operational?

Financial inclusion is the process of ensuring access to financial services and timely and adequate credit to weaker sections and low-income groups at an affordable cost. Merely opening a bank account doesn't ensure that. Unlike Sanjay Gandhi's sterilization programme or the government's Pulse Polio Immunization initiative, financial inclusion cannot be achieved only by meeting the target numbers.

Pushed to the wall, banks will hit the target by doling out passbooks indiscriminately to anybody and everybody, including those who already have bank accounts. The government must make the bankers accountable and, at the same time, ensure that financial inclusion is supported by inclusion in infrastructure, education and other socio-economic areas. Finally, we need many more banks. Until now, licences for new domestic banks have been a once-a-decade affair.

A PAPER TIGER CALLED BANKS BOARD BUREAU

27 February 2017

On 17 February, Sunil Mehta, a former country head of AIG in India, and T.C.A. Ranganathan, former chairman-cum-managing director of Exim Bank, were appointed non-executive chairman of Punjab National Bank and Indian Overseas Bank (IOB), respectively. The Banks Board Bureau had recommended both.

This should have made the bureau chairman, Vinod Rai, and its members—Anil K. Khandelwal, H.N. Sinor and Roopa Kudva—happy. One would have expected its latest meeting in Mumbai last week to be full of excitement. However, that wasn't the case. These four bring to the table unique skills and expertise and huge experience, but they could be a frustrated bunch as they cannot do what they want to do.

Rai, a former finance secretary, was also India's chief auditor. Khandelwal, an HR expert, headed Bank of Baroda; Sinor, a former joint managing director of ICICI Bank Ltd, headed two national lobbies of banks and mutual funds; and Kudva, a former managing director of the rating company Crisil Ltd heads Omidyar Network India Advisors, a US-based philanthropic investment firm.

Along with the two chairmen, the government also cleared the names of nine executive directors in public-sector banks (PSBs). In at least one case, one general manager whom the Banks Board Bureau had recommended for the executive director's post in a Kolkata-based bank, got his posting at a bank in Mumbai.

Clearly, the bureau can recommend names, but when it comes to the postings of top executives, it doesn't have the final say. Even its recommendations are not sacrosanct. Last year, the bureau had identified Mukesh Kumar Jain, an executive director of Punjab and Sind Bank, to head IOB. It was cleared by the Central Vigilance Commission, but Jain didn't get the job, as a finance ministry division was not comfortable with the choice. The appointment was referred to the department of personnel and training; once again, the

CVC cleared it after a forensic audit, but the ministry has not cleared it as yet.

IOB, with one-third of its loan book being stressed, has been without a regular managing director and CEO for many months now. Its last MD and CEO, R. Koteeswaran, retired on 30 June 2016. IOB's executive director R. Subramania Kumar has been holding the charge of MD and CEO since November.

Instead of taking the bureau's recommendations seriously and referring them to the Appointments Committee of the Cabinet (ACC) for approval, they are all scrutinized de novo by the finance ministry.

Apart from the selection and appointment of board of directors in PSBs, the bureau is also mandated to advise the government on the extension of tenure and termination of services of the board of directors. However, when Sushil Muhnot, a former chairman and managing director of Bank of Maharashtra, was fired in September 2016—four days ahead of his scheduled retirement—for allegedly occupying two houses, the bureau was not consulted.

Even these could be minor irritants. The bigger problem is it doesn't have any say on the resolution of stressed assets, consolidation among the PSBs, their governance, and charting out the roadmap for a banking investment company, as was envisaged by the P.J. Nayak committee. The report of the committee which reviewed the governance of boards of banks in India mooted the idea of the bureau. The government has accepted that, but the big names are probably being used to lend credibility to a platform which supposedly drives reforms in India's public-sector banking industry, while in reality, they don't have much on their plate.

The BJP-led government started the work of reforming India's PSBs in real earnest by holding a first-of-its-kind off-site with bank bosses, called Gyan Sangam, in Pune in January 2015. According to Prime Minister Narendra Modi, it's a 'unique initiative' and 'the first step towards catalyzing transformation'. Subsequently, in August 2015, Finance Minister Arun Jaitley announced the grand Indradhanush plan which, among other things, promised to address issues such as high-level appointments, capitalization, stress in the system, and accountability and governance in government-owned banks.

The Banks Board Bureau's first meeting took place on 8 April 2016 at the fourth floor of the Reserve Bank of India office in Byculla, a neighbourhood of South Mumbai that houses the bureau. After the meeting, former minister of state (finance), Jayant Sinha, tweeted, 'Excellent discussions at the Banks Board Bureau meeting today!' tagging two photographs—one of a ribbon cutting by him with Rai, Sinor, Khandelwal, and the other showing all of them plus Kudva and former RBI governor Raghuram Rajan sitting on sofas and deputy governors R. Gandhi and S.S. Mundra standing behind. Gandhi was an ex officio member of the bureau till recently when another deputy governor, N.S. Vishwanathan, replaced him. The other two ex officio members are the secretary, department of financial services, in the ministry of finance, and secretary, department of public enterprises.

In June 2016, the RBI released norms for a 'Scheme for Sustainable Structuring of Stressed Assets', or S4A, for bad loan resolution, and a critical component of that is an overseeing committee, recommended by the bureau. Around the same time, there was also a meeting of bankers, members of the bureau, the Central Vigilance Commission and the Central Bureau of Investigation, to discuss the resolution of stressed assets. The meeting was hosted by the RBI, but it was the bureau's idea.

Ahead of that, the bureau wrote to the finance ministry, seeking a revision in its mandate and suggesting that it should focus on the resolution of stressed assets, consolidation, capital raising of PSBs and address the governance issues. The ministry, as is its wont, responded in November, keeping the mandate unchanged. Rai, who had been vocal on these issues at various fora, has stopped talking on these since then.

Its mandate remains the selection and appointment of managing directors and CEOs as well as non-executive chairmen of PSBs, helping banks develop a robust leadership succession plan for critical positions, advising the government on the formulation and enforcement of a code of conduct and ethics for bank executives, and enabling banks to develop business strategies and capital-raising plans, among others. Barring the top-level appointments, all other terms of references are vague, and even for appointments, the bureau does not have the final say, and its relationship with the finance ministry division—which has its representative on the bureau—is rather adversarial.

The Banks Board Bureau also doesn't have any role in choosing the non-official directors on the boards of PSBs who typically constitute one-third of the directors on any PSB board, and most are political appointments. For instance, two BJP leaders—Bharat Dangar and Gopal Krishna Agarwal—are currently on the board of Bank of Baroda, even as both the non-executive chairman and managing director and CEO of the bank have been picked up from the market to professionalize it. Of course, Dangar adorns the board not as the fifty-sixth mayor of the city of Vadodara and as a senior BJP leader, but as an assistant professor in the faculty of technology and engineering of the MS University of Baroda. Similarly, Agarwal is a chartered accountant. The attendance of most non-official directors and even some of the government nominees at board meetings is extremely poor.

Incidentally, one large public-sector bank has four chartered accountants on its board, and another, a larger one, did not have a single chartered accountant till recently and it was finding it difficult to hold meetings of its audit committee, which is typically headed by a chartered accountant.

After much persuasion, the bureau could convince the government to agree to compensate the non-executive chairman of PSBs, but the amount is capped at Rs 10,00,000, inclusive of fees for attending board meetings. This is not comparable with what the chairman of a private bank gets.

In its efforts to stay relevant, the bureau has recently sent a proposal to the finance ministry seeking overhauling of the compensation package for the executives of PSBs. The proposal includes stock options, performance-related bonus and a fast-track promotion policy. One would need to see how long the government takes to act on it, if at all.

If the government has any reform agenda for the public-sector banking system, laden with bad assets and starved of capital, talent and governance, the Banks Board Bureau could be an ideal vehicle to drive it. If it doesn't, the bureau will become increasingly irrelevant. Anyway, none of the members seem to know how long their own tenure will be!

Another way of looking at it could be that the members of the bureau have taken themselves more seriously than they should have.

Postscript

Since this column was published, Sinor tendered his resignation, but he was persuaded to withdraw it; Kudva has resigned.

CAN ONLY LOVE FOR OUR POSTMAN ENSURE SUCCESS FOR INDIA POST PAYMENTS BANK?

12 December 2016

People have been waiting eagerly for the launch of the India Post Payments Bank, or IPPB, the largest among the eight that are likely to start operations over the next few months. Eleven entities received the Reserve Bank of India's in-principle approval for floating payments banks but three of them have left the field.

Originally, the Department of Posts, or DoP, which has been running the post office savings bank, wanted to set up a universal bank. It had even applied for a licence. The proposal was discussed at the Public Investment Board, which examines the investment plans of various ministries worth at least Rs 1 billion, and it advised DoP to set up a 'differentiated bank'.

Accordingly, DoP applied to the RBI, seeking a licence for a payments bank and got an in-principle approval on 7 September 2015. The bank has to be made operational by March 2017, but it seems the government wants it to be launched in January. This makes eminent sense in the wake of the demonetization drive—India's financial sector is witnessing turbulence and the payments space is waiting to be grabbed with new ideas and innovations to give a big push towards a cashless economy.

IPPB will start with a Rs 4-billion equity capital and a Rs 4-billion grant from the government to set up a technology network in rural India. Incidentally, India Post, which is run by DoP, is not converting itself into a bank even as there have been many instances globally of post offices transforming themselves into banks. For instance, Germany's Deutsche Postbank, originally a postal bank, is currently a private retail bank. In Japan, a large bank is run by its postal service, but this is likely to be privatized next year.

Under the present scheme, there will be no conversion of any of the current activities of India Post for the payments bank. While the postal savings bank arm of DoP will continue its business, IPPB will come up as a new bank ostensibly for providing payments services to the masses in the hinterland. Indeed, India Post and IPPB will primarily cater to the same group of customers, but the customers will have a choice—whether to continue to bank with India Post or go to IPPB for their savings deposits. Of course, the limit for a savings deposits in a payments bank is capped at Rs 1,00,000.

IPPB is entirely owned by the Government of India and will be run independently by a professional management even as DoP plays the role of a mentor.

Too Many Suitors

A *Mint* report of 12 January 2016 said IPPB was the 'hottest game in town' and that fifty entities, including International Finance Corporation, Barclays Bank, Deutsche Bank AG, Citibank NA and several state-owned banks, have sent proposals to DoP for different kinds of partnerships. Going by the report, banks, insurance firms and asset management companies have been approaching IPPB to form equity partnerships, joint ventures and many other mutually beneficial arrangements.

None should be surprised by the enthusiasm that IPPB is generating. After all, DoP has a network of 1,54,939 post offices, the largest such network in the world. Its beginning can be traced back to 1727 when the first post office was set up in Kolkata. (The current postal system came into existence with the Indian Post Office Act of 1854.) As of 31 March 2015, 90 per cent of the post offices were located in rural India—on an average, 8354 people are served by one post office, which covers 21.22 sq. km.

IPPB has tremendous possibilities as it can bring millions of individuals and small businesses into the formal banking channel by offering savings accounts of up to Rs 100,000 and current accounts with a special focus on micro, small and medium enterprises, small merchants, village panchayats, self-help groups, etc. It can also be the vehicle for the direct benefits transfer of social security payments of various ministries, and pay utility bills, besides taking care of payments of various central and state governments and municipalities as well as colleges, universities and other educational institutions.

It can also play a major role in remittances—both domestic and cross-border—with a special focus on migrant labourers and low-income households, and finally, distribute third-party financial products such as insurance, mutual funds, pension and credit products.

The post office savings bank has a customer base of at least 330 million and the outstanding balance under all post office schemes were at least Rs 6.19 trillion (in March 2015). Clearly, with its network, it can give India's largest lender, the State Bank of India—which, after the merger of all its associate banks with itself, will become one of the top fifty banks globally in terms of assets—a run for its money.

Technology Is Key

The key to the success of IPPB will be its business plan and if that's in place, technology. In October 2009, DoP awarded a forty-five-month information technology modernization contract to Accenture to design a new enterprise IT architecture and migrate DoP to a more efficient, reliable and user-friendly IT system. Tata Consultancy Services Ltd (TCS) bagged the contract for an end-to-end IT modernization programme to equip India Post with modern technologies and systems, and enable it to offer more services to a larger set of customers in an effective manner. Infosys Ltd was employed to put in place the core banking solution as well as construct a rural connectivity network.

The India Post website says that in November 2012, the government approved a Rs 49.09-billion IT modernization project for DoP—in order to transform DoP into a technology-driven department. While Accenture came in early, TCS and Infosys were awarded the projects in 2013.

I understand that till now none of the projects have been completed. There have been glitches galore in the core banking solution while the rural network is only partially done even as the back-end work of TCS remains incomplete. There have been disputes and disagreements with the service providers, and in a few instances, even penalty provisions for delayed delivery have been invoked.

The 2015 annual report of India Post says the entire project is in implementation phase and also outlines the achievements made so far, which include computerization of the north-eastern region, establishment of a data centre and a disaster recovery centre, and networking 27,736 departmental post offices, rolling out core banking solution in more than 17,000 post offices, and setting up 500 ATMs.

Clearly, not even half of the technology work has been done. So, how will IPPB revolutionize India's payments system? At the initial stage, EY helped DoP prepare the project report for the bank, based on which the in-principle licence was given. Now, Deloitte Touche Tohmatsu India LLP is advising IPPB for setting up the bank. According to Communications and Information Technology Minister Ravi Shankar Prasad, IPPB will have 650 branches. They will be located at all district headquarters across India and connected to 1,55,000 post offices.

The Hub-and-Spoke Model

This is a typical hub-and-spoke model with one major difference—the IPPB branches or control offices will be the back office while the post office branches which, for all practical purposes, will play the role of banking correspondents for IPPB, will be its front office. Every post office branch will host an IPPB desk to source business.

To make this model successful, it needs to have the right technology. I understand that DoP floated a request for proposal (RFP) to invite bids from various companies, in July. For any large, complex project, an RFP is considered to be the heart and soul of the procurement. If the software firms are to be believed, there were a few thousand queries by the initial bidders, but only one entity, Polaris Financial Technology Ltd, made a bid; however, it got cancelled. A fresh RFP has been recently floated, but I am not aware how many bidders it has attracted. The cost of the project could be as much as Rs 6 billion.

Typically, it takes at least a couple of months to evaluate the bids and then another six months to implement the project. If IPPB wants to launch its payments bank in January, how will it get the technology platform? Certainly, it cannot use the unfinished technology architecture of the DoP. The only option left before it is to tie up with a bank for the time being and use its IT infrastructure till its own IT backbone is in place. Only State Bank of India has the capability to support IPPB, but will the nation's largest lender extend a helping hand? I doubt it, as IPPB will directly compete with State Bank.

Probably, IPPB will explore a tie-up with Punjab National Bank, which is mostly owned by the government. It is large and is based in Delhi. If indeed such an arrangement is worked out to launch the bank even before its IT infrastructure is ready, this will be a unique instance of a bank launch in India.

In the fiscal year 2015, India Post generated Rs 116.36 billion in revenue, 8 per cent higher than in the previous year, and its total gross expenditure was to the tune of Rs 18,557—11.6 per cent higher than in 2014. Post-recoveries, the deficit was Rs 62.59 billion, 14 per cent higher than in the previous year. A look at the average cost and average revenue of the most popular eighteen items sold by India Post reveals that only two of them are profitable—competition post card and letter—and all the others, including the money order business, which charges a hefty fee, are losing money.

IPPB can make a new beginning only if it is run as a business entity and not as a government department. Till now, a CEO has not been appointed (Vinod Rai of the Banks Board Bureau is in the process of identifying one). DoP has asked the public-sector banks to recommend senior executives for responsible positions at IPPB, but I am not sure how the response has been. Meanwhile, the Institute of Banking Personnel Selection has been looking around to recruit around 3000 people.

Even if the business strategy and the right kind of people are in place for the launch, technology will hold the key to the success of a payments bank. With its phenomenal reach across India, IPPB can do wonders—mapping every inch of the country and making every *kirana* store, petrol pump and mandi its banking correspondent—and usher in a revolution in the payments space when the government is pushing hard for a digital economy.

In his Independence Day speech at the Red Fort on 15 August 2016, Prime Minister Narendra Modi said the Post Office is a symbol of our identity. 'If any government representative gets the affection of a common man in India, it is the postman. Everyone loves the postman and the postman also loves everybody . . . We have taken a step to convert our post offices into payments banks. Starting with this, the payments bank will spread the chain of banks in the villages across the country in one go.'

Love for the postman alone cannot make IPPB a success; it needs to do much more.

CHANGE IS IN THE AIR FOR INDIAN BANKING

12 October 2015

About five weeks after the Kolkata-based Bandhan Bank Ltd started its operations, IDFC Bank Ltd had a quiet launch in Mumbai this month. They had fought it out with two dozen contenders, including a few corporate heavyweights, to get the Reserve Bank of India's in-principle approval one and a half years ago. Barring the fact that the bosses of both the new banks—Chandra Shekhar Ghosh, managing director and chief executive of Bandhan Bank, and Rajiv Lall, vice chairman and managing director of IDFC Bank—are non-bankers, they are as different as apples and oranges.

Lall, fifty-eight, an Oxford University graduate in politics, philosophy and economics, did his PhD from Columbia University. Before taking over as MD and CEO of the erstwhile Infrastructure Development Finance Corporation Ltd in 2005, he was heading the Asian economic research wing of Morgan Stanley Asia Ltd. In the past, he had worked with the World Bank, Warburg Pincus and Asian Development Bank (ADB), besides teaching at Florida Atlantic University.

Ghosh, fifty-five, is the son of a small sweet shop owner in Agartala, Tripura. After getting an MA in statistics from Dhaka University, he worked with BRAC, a non-governmental development organization in Bangladesh, before setting up Bandhan in West Bengal in 2001. He started out by giving microloans from his own life savings of Rs 200,000.

Bandhan started operations with 2022 doorstep service centres, 501 branches and twenty-five ATMs across India. About one-third of the branches are in rural and unbanked pockets. In the past few weeks, it has ramped up its branch network and added substantially to its legacy customer base of 6.7 million. It will continue to serve the so-called bottom-of-the-pyramid segment and add small and medium entrepreneurs to its loan portfolio while collecting deposits from all, including high-net-worth individuals and corporations. It does not want to dabble in corporate loans, at least during the initial stage.

IDFC, in contrast, is positioning itself essentially as a smart corporate bank that will soon have a consumer banking wing. It started with twenty-three branches, of which eight are in Mumbai, New Delhi, Bengaluru, Kolkata, Chennai, Ahmedabad and Pune, offering corporate and wholesale banking products. The rest of the fifteen branches are in Indore, Hoshangabad, Harda and Khandwa districts of Madhya Pradesh, serving the unserved. The focus is on the ease of doing transactions, using state-of-the-art technology.

In some sense, both are challenger banks and will force the high-street banks to redraw their strategies. Big private banks in India and a few state-owned banks too have taken note of Lall's passion for technology and are on a spree to introduce tech-based new products for customers. Their objective is to take the wind out of IDFC's sails. Similarly, some of the banks have started making serious inroads into rural India to try and check Bandhan's expansion. Under Indian banking norms, a bank needs to have an exposure to the so-called priority sector consisting of farmers, small entrepreneurs and others to the extent of 40 per cent of its loan book. If they cannot lend directly, they can give money to other intermediaries such as microfinance organizations, which, in turn, may lend to this segment. Many banks had been doing this, but now a few of them have also started taking direct exposure to the small borrowers.

We are seeing a new wave of competition in Indian banking, and this will intensify as the turf is being disrupted. Between 1994 and 2014, twelve banks were born, but not all of them have survived. In the past seven weeks, two more have made an appearance, and in the next eighteen months, we will see twenty-one more—eleven payments banks and ten small-finance banks.

Payments banks can collect deposits of up to Rs 100,000, provide payments and remittance services, and distribute third-party financial products. They won't be able to give loans and issue credit cards, but they can provide debit cards and Internet banking services. The small banks will be subject to all prudential norms like any other commercial bank and they would need to give 75 per cent of their loans to the so-called priority sector, and 50 per cent of the loan portfolio should constitute small loans of up to Rs 250,000. While payments banks will remain confined to their niche, successful small banks can graduate to universal banks after a few years.

The story does not end here. At least four foreign banks, including DBS of Singapore, have approached the RBI for local incorporation. Once they are locally incorporated, they will enjoy the freedom to open more branches and can even buy out weak local banks. The RBI may also allow some of the strong urban cooperative banks to convert themselves into commercial banks. Finally, banking licences—both for universal banks as well as specialized entities such as small banks and payments banks—are expected to be on tap.

So, be prepared to see huge disruptions in the Rs 90-trillion banking industry in Asia's third-largest economy. The payments banks are expected to eat into the fee income of regular banks by offering smart payments channels using mobile telephony, while small banks will fight pitched battles with big banks in different geographies for deposits. Bolstered by a bigger branch network, locally incorporated foreign banks too will lure in depositors; they will also develop sophisticated corporate and personal banking products.

As the competition intensifies, Indian banks will be forced to innovate—not only for growth but also to stay relevant. We have already seen many incremental innovations in the past few months and the pace will gain momentum as newer banks appear. All this will benefit the customer. At the moment, banks are slow in paring their loan rates when the RBI cuts the policy rate and even after they cut their base rate or minimum lending rate, they do not pass on the full benefit to their borrowers, citing different reasons.

A loan rate cut dents profitability, and the banks love their investors more than their customers—any day. This will change soon.

DO WE NEED A RELIANCE JIO IN INDIAN BANKING?

13 March 2017

Given a choice, most branch managers of Indian banks these days would like to attend classes on how to handle angry customers where they will be taught lessons such as 'never argue back', 'kill them with kindness', 'know how to apologize', 'solve their problems', 'be patient', and so on. Millions of bank depositors are upset; they are venting their anger on social media against 'unkind' banks who, they claim, have been 'fleecing' customers by charging them if they exceed the limit on cash transactions at bank branches and are not able to maintain minimum balance in their accounts.

The provocation for their outbursts is the decision of a few private banks to charge customers for cash deposits and withdrawals exceeding four transactions a month. The announcement by State Bank of India to reintroduce after a gap of five years a penalty on non-maintenance of the minimum average balance in savings and current accounts from 1 April 2017, added fuel to fire. A few banks—both private and state-run—have already been stealthily charging customers when balance in their accounts drop below the minimum limit and for visiting branches too many times, but a sudden burst of announcements has made the customers irate.

Are these banks doing something illegal? Are they unethical? The banking code and standards which underline banks' commitment to customers do not prohibit them from charging such fees. The Banking Code and Standards Board of India—an independent and autonomous institution to oversee that the banks adhere to the code in true spirit while delivering their services—makes it mandatory that when a bank increases any fee or charge or introduces a new fee or charge, it must notify it through statements of accounts, email/text message alerts. Such charges should also be displayed at bank branches one month ahead of the revision. This information must also be made available on the banks' websites.

Normally, changes in fees should be made with prospective effect giving a month's notice. However, if any bank makes any change in fees without giving a notice to the customers, it must notify the change within thirty days. If such a change inconveniences a customer, she may within sixty days of the notice, close her account or switch to any other account without paying the revised charge or interest. The code also prohibits the banks from the so-called 'negative option' banking—that is, selling a product to a customer or charging fees, unless she says no to it. Typically, it is done for high-net-worth customers by sending an email with an 'opt out' link, and unless the customer opts out, it is assumed that she is accepting the proposal.

There are two ways of looking at the current development.

If you're a customer, you would say that the banks are desperate to make money this way as they are being forced to bring down their loan rates, and their net interest margin from loan assets is under pressure. On top of that, they need to set aside money to take care of their piling bad loans and that is denting their profits. So, the banks are looking for new avenues to earn.

You will also say that banks are non-transparent and follow unfair trade practices. How can they charge a flat rate for cash transactions over the limits that they set for the customers? For instance, when a customer deposits Rs 20,000, it could be ten notes of Rs 2000 each or forty notes of Rs 500 each or even 200 notes of Rs 100 each. The cost of currency handling is different in each case. Also, the value of the fifth transaction could be Rs 20,000 or Rs 200.

How can there be a uniform rate? Similarly, if a customer doesn't do any transaction at branches for eleven months a year and does ten transactions in one month, isn't it unfair to charge her for six extra transactions?

The bankers would justify the move saying that such fees do not call for widespread protests as only a minuscule segment of the customers is being affected. Four free cash transactions at branches and another four or five at ATMs a month are enough to meet the needs of customers. How many of them would transact more? Probably not more than 1 per cent of the customers. And the fee earned from excess transactions would not even add a percentage point to the fee income of Indian banks which varies between 15 per cent and 30 per cent of the total income.

They will also say that the latest move is being driven partly to influence customer behaviour as well as recover cost (as the cash handling cost has risen post-demonetization) even as it will add a bit to their revenue. If the customers stop visiting bank branches and use credit and debit cards for transactions, banks will of course earn money, but that's from the merchants. Till now, banks have installed about 1.5 million point-of-sale machines across India, but on a stand-alone basis; probably, the merchant-acquiring business is not yet profitable for any Indian bank. Merchant-acquiring business refers to the mechanism of providing necessary infrastructure to merchants and facilitating payments for goods and services through debit and credit cards.

Similarly, the minimum average balance is the threshold limit below which a bank makes loss for keeping a customer. On a Rs 5000 deposit, a bank can't even earn Rs 500 a year (at 10 per cent interest rate on loans) as one-fifth of the money needs to be used for buying government bonds (the return from which is less than loans) and 4 per cent is kept with the Reserve Bank of India as cash reserve ratio on which a bank doesn't earn any interest. At 4 per cent interest on savings account, the cost for the bank roughly works out to Rs 200 for a Rs 5000 deposit. So, the net interest income is Rs 300 (Rs 500 – Rs 200). Now, factor in the operational cost, transactions cost at branches and ATMs, and the cost of sending quarterly statements. The bank is left with nothing if the balance drops below Rs 5000.

I don't have the latest data. In March 2015, the average balance in a savings bank account in State Bank—where one in every four Indians has an account—was Rs 19,347; in the nationalized banks, it was Rs 19,422. In private banks, the average was Rs 37,715 and in the foreign banks, Rs 194,703. The average savings account balance for the Indian banking industry was Rs 20,051. There may not be any drastic change in the figure now.

As of 31 March 2015, there were 125.5 million Pradhan Mantri Jan-Dhan Yojana accounts (launched in August 2014) and this has risen to 278.4 million now (roughly one out of four such accounts is a zero-balance account). If this has created more low-balance savings accounts, the flow of money in November–December following demonetization has probably more than compensated for this. (State Bank is not applying the concept of minimum balance to the Jan-Dhan accounts.)

Remember, the banks also have other obligations such as loans to the weaker segments of the society, or the so-called priority-sector loans—40 per cent of their loan portfolio—where the transaction cost is higher as the loans are relatively smaller. And, of course, there is the burden of bad loans. But for the government's insistence, they might not have so aggressively ventured into certain sectors such as power and infrastructure where many loans have gone bad. Finally, banking is not a corporate social responsibility. Banks are here to make money.

So, there are equally strong arguments both in favour of such moves and against. Globally, savings accounts are treated almost on a par with current accounts (on which banks do not pay any interest) as both are transactional accounts and very little interest is offered on such accounts. Since banks are free to set savings bank interest rate, why can't the Indian banks do that? They can bring down the interest rate on savings accounts and make all transactions free. Those who want to earn higher interest, they can keep their money in fixed deposits. Except for pensioners, most savings bank account holders don't care for interest. And many of them keep small amount in such accounts. For such customers, the transaction cost (if the limits are exceeded) will erode the entire interest income and probably even part of the principal amount.

Whether the banks bring down the savings bank interest or not (and allow any number of transactions), they can impose such charges as long as they are done transparently and are 'reasonable'.

Therein lies the rub. What is reasonable? And who decides what is reasonable?

Only competition can determine that—something which doesn't exist in Indian banking. A handful of banks exploit the customers in a repressive financial system and often this is done by forming a cartel, taking advantage of the weak consumer protection architecture in the Indian financial system. One way of breaking this could be by bringing in more banks of different sizes and profiles (the banking regulator has already started doing this). The other way could be by allowing large industry houses with deep pockets to float banks—of course, with proper checks and balances.

We need a Jio on the Indian banking turf to shake the complacency of the bankers and their habit of taking the customers for granted.

5

Bad, Bad, Bad Loans

In June 2017, Spain's largest lender, Banco Santander SA, announced that it was taking over the struggling Banco Popular Espanol SA for a symbolic €1. Santander also planned a €7-billion ($7.88-billion) rights issue to infuse capital and provide for the bad loans of Popular, the country's sixth-biggest bank.

The European authorities, led by the European Central Bank, were behind the rescue act. Popular had been struggling under a bad loan burden of €37 billion, mostly real-estate related, but Santander felt that the deal would accelerate its growth and profit from 2019 onwards. Analysts also saw an opportunity for Santander in Popular's small- and medium-sized corporate loan portfolio.

Besides, Santander could also sell off Popular's property assets.

The sale, which was put together at the speed of light, did not impact stock markets. In fact, bank stocks rose in Europe on the day it was announced in Brussels by the Single Resolution Board, an agency formed by the European Union to wind down sick banks.

Obviously, there are differences between the state of affairs in Popular and some of India's state-owned banks (Popular was also facing a run on its deposits), but can the Spanish deal be emulated in India? Is this the way forward to tackle rising bad assets in the Indian banking system? Corporate loans have soured for many government-owned banks. But they have their pockets of strength—retail loans, relatively low-cost current and savings accounts, non-core assets and a vast branch network.

How do we solve the bad loan problem? Spain and Italy offer object lessons. Spain believes in swift action, while Italy allows the problem to fester for years. Should we go the Spain way or continue with our Band-Aid approach?

A new ordinance has bestowed powers on the Reserve Bank of India to force banks to resolve matters in a time-bound manner by moving the insolvency court, forming multiple oversight committees and encouraging banks to take deep haircuts.

As I write this, there is no clarity on how the holes in the balance sheets of Indian public banks will be filled in the aftermath of the clean-up drive although the RBI has been continuously harping on the need to recapitalize the state-owned banks by the government. And while all efforts are on to solve the stock of bad loans, how do we prevent the recurrence of such a mess in future?

The columns in this chapter try to raise some key questions on how the Indian banking system got into this mess; they attempt to provide answers and catch the trend over a period of time even as the quality of assets in the banking system has gone from bad to worse between April 2009—when I first flagged off the issue—and 2017. In fact, from 2009 onwards, I have repeatedly been writing on how the banks have been in a denial mode despite the steady rise of bad loans in their portfolio and erosion in profitability.

How bad is the bad loan scene? There is a Rashomon-like quality to the narrative—with each character having a slightly different story to tell. Every story lends a fresh perspective to what happened, adding new layers of truth.

It all depends on the point of view. Gross bad loans of Indian banks in March 2017 accounted for 9.6 per cent of their loan portfolio. This is one way of looking at the problem, but it does not tell us the full story. To this, one needs to add the loans that have been restructured under different schemes and the many large accounts that are vulnerable as borrowers are overleveraged and not in a position to service loans regularly. We also need to add loans that have been written off. Unlike elsewhere, in India, such loans are removed from banks' balance sheets but are parked at the branch level. As and when some parts of the loans are recovered, they are added back. If such written-off loans are added to the pile, the overall stressed assets could be as much as 20 per cent of the banks' loans.

The banks' exposure to large corporations and infrastructure sector has been the most affected. In this segment, bad loans could be as much as 35–40 per cent.

Needless to say that most private banks are much better off than the state-owned lenders.

Finally, bad loans as a percentage of the overall loan portfolios of banks do not explain the enormity of the problem. We need to look at the bad loans against the backdrop of the net worth or capital and reserves of the banks. In March 2017, for the industry, it was close to 50 per cent, and for private banks, around 13 per cent. However, the average bad loans of the government-owned banks are 75.53 per cent of their net worth. At least in the case of seven of them, they far exceed the net worth.

Taken together, these columns chronicle the story of India's bad-loan crisis, one of the most significant threats to the country's economic well-being. There are also two interesting case studies—Kingfisher Airline and the Amtek Auto Group. They explain how a loan turns bad and where the buck stops.

LOAN RECAST: THE RESERVE BANK'S BIGGEST GAMBLE

5 April 2009

In June 2008, Indian public-sector banks that account for 73 per cent of the country's banking assets cleared some 43 million applications from farmers to waive and recast Rs 653.18 billion of loans. The blueprint for the loan waiver, the biggest undertaken in India, was drafted by the then finance minister P. Chidambaram in the Union Budget for fiscal 2008–09. About 36.9 million small and marginal farmers received a waiver of all their debts; 5.97 million had 25 per cent of their loans written off.

Eight months down the line, in March 2009, the banking industry once again had to sift through millions of applications from borrowers for yet another loan recast. This time, the initiative was taken by the central bank to shield companies as well as individual borrowers from the impact of the economic downturn.

The deadline for filing applications for the loan recast was 31 March, and banks need to settle such cases within three months. By a conservative industry estimate, between 3 per cent and 4 per cent of the total loan assets of Indian banks is likely to be recast. Since the outstanding loan portfolio of the industry, as of 13 March, was Rs 26.9 trillion, about Rs 800 billion to Rs 1.07 trillion worth of loans will be recast.

This will make it the biggest loan recast ever undertaken by the Indian banking system. Under normal circumstances, a loan becomes sticky when the borrower, be it a company or an individual, fails to pay interest on it for ninety days. Once a loan turns sticky, banks are required to provide for it in their balance sheets, and the amount set aside depends on the nature and length of the default.

As the global credit crisis deepened and spilled over into the real economy, including India's, after the collapse of Lehman Brothers in mid-September 2008, the Reserve Bank of India allowed banks to recast all loans, including their exposure to commercial real estate. In fact, banks were allowed to recast loans not once but twice before

30 June except for those given for commercial real estate, capital-market-related activities such as buying shares, and personal loans.

While banks can recast on their own all small loans given to small and medium enterprises and individual borrowers, the relatively larger loans of Rs 100 million and above need to be referred to the corporate debt restructuring (CDR) cell, a mechanism that was put in place in 2001 when some large companies, particularly in the steel sector, got into trouble following a sharp drop in demand and prices.

At the CDR cell, the recast of any loan needs the support of 60 per cent of creditors by number and 75 per cent of creditors by value. Till fiscal 2008, 219 cases were referred to this cell, involving Rs 947.35 billion of debt. The cell rejected twenty-nine cases while sixteen were pending. In other words, 174 firms got Rs 847.14 billion of debt restructured at the forum, and forty-three of them actually cleared their dues to banks.

With increased sales and profitability in the past few years till fiscal 2008, on the back of an economy growing at about 9 per cent annually, those companies that had got their loans restructured at CDR were able to clear their bank dues aggressively. There was also a dramatic improvement in the quality of banks' assets, with the average net non-performing assets of Indian banks dropping to 1 per cent of their loan books in 2008 (gross NPAs 2.3 per cent).

In fiscal 2008, only ten cases were referred to the CDR cell, involving Rs 30.45 billion. A slowing economy and a slump in consumer demand took their toll on the health of companies. In 2008–09, thirty-three cases were referred to the CDR cell, involving Rs 76.72 billion. While these cases are being dealt with in the cell, in which chief executive officers of top Indian banks are members, individually, banks are dealing with millions of borrowers, and in some cases, their exposure could be as little as a few thousand rupees.

There are many ways to recast a loan. It can be done by giving a fresh loan to tide over the current cash flow problem (for a company) or a moratorium on payment (for a home loan or auto loan in cases where the borrower has lost his or her job). Banks can also cut interest rates. For the time being, it is a win-win situation for both the banking industry as well as the borrowers because there will not be any deterioration in the quality of assets of the banks, and borrowers will get time to repay the loans.

There are, however, critics of such a massive recast. According to them, the entire exercise is nothing but an attempt to postpone the inevitable—cosmetic surgery that will help banks protect their balance sheets and profitability for a while. Ultimately, the banks' bad assets will grow as the RBI cannot ask them to recast loans for a third time. This will force the rating agencies to downgrade Indian banks.

This can actually happen if the economic downturn continues. This is a gamble the RBI had to take because it had no choice. If the economy starts looking up in the second half of 2009–10, both banks and borrowers will be spared a major embarrassment.

ARE INDIAN BANKS HEADING FOR A CRISIS?

6 September 2012

A recent report by Credit Suisse Group AG pointed out that exposure to ten large industrial groups constitutes 13 per cent of the entire Indian banking system's loan assets. This means the concentration risk for the Indian banking system is rising.

It's not alarming if seen in isolation. If one looks at the other side of the story—the growing bad assets of banks—the system's vulnerability becomes apparent. The bad assets of Indian banks grew by 46 per cent in the fiscal year that ended in March 2012, nearly three times the pace of their loan books (17 per cent). Add to this the restructured assets, and you know how grave the situation is.

As of 31 March, gross non-performing assets of the banking system amounted to Rs 1.37 trillion and restructured assets Rs 2.18 trillion. If all restructured assets turn bad, then the gross NPAs as a percentage of loan assets jump from 2.94 per cent to 7.61 per cent. This will not happen. By the RBI's estimate, about 20 per cent of restructured assets generally turn bad. If that really happens, the gross NPA ratio rises to 3.87 per cent; and if 30 per cent of the restructured assets turn bad, it reaches 4.34 per cent. This is bad news.

There has been a secular decline in Indian banks' bad assets since the fiscal year 1997 when they amounted to 15.7 per cent of the loans. The percentage of bad assets declined to 2.4 per cent in 2008. Since then, it has been rising—to 2.45 per cent in 2009, 2.51 per cent in 2010, and 2.94 per cent in 2012.

In absolute terms, banks' bad assets have doubled in three years between 2009 and 2012—from Rs 682.16 billion to Rs 1.37 trillion. During this period, the quantum of restructured assets has nearly trebled, from Rs 759.46 billion to Rs 2.18 trillion. And both the bad assets as well as the restructured assets rose even further in the June quarter.

I don't have the restructured asset figures. The gross NPAs of listed banks rose from Rs 1.32 trillion in March to Rs 1.49 trillion in June. This means that for the entire industry, gross NPAs would have crossed Rs 1.5 trillion, and this figure does not include the bad assets of unlisted private banks and foreign banks.

In percentage terms, at least four banks now have more than 4 per cent gross NPAs, led by State Bank of India (4.99 per cent, or Rs 471.56 billion, up from 3.52 per cent and Rs 277.68 billion a year ago).

Bad assets in the coal, iron and steel, mining, construction, textiles and aviation sectors have been on the rise. Bankers are seeing stress in telecom and power sectors too, but the gross NPA level in these two sectors is around 0.5 per cent only. This means the bad assets of Indian banks can rise further as banks have hefty exposures to telecom and power, and neither of these sectors is in the best of health at this point in time.

The biggest beneficiaries of loan restructuring are large industrial houses in the manufacturing sector—8.24 per cent of loans given to such industries have been recast. In the services sector, the comparable figure is 3.99 per cent, and in agriculture, 1.45 per cent. This makes it clear that small borrowers affected by the economic slowdown have not got a respite from loan servicing, but the large industrial houses have got one. It's a win-win situation for both borrowers and banks; the banks need to set aside very little money for restructured loans, and to that extent their profitability is not hit by the provisions needed for bad loans.

Of course, net NPAs, or bad assets after provisions, are not very high. At end-June, for listed banks they were close to Rs 720 billion, and only one bank (Central Bank of India) had more than 3 per cent net NPAs. But this is a small consolation. As banks need to set aside money to bring down their net NPAs, the growth in their capital gets stunted and that affects their ability to expand loan assets. Besides, as they need to provide for bad assets to bring them down, their ability to price their loans competitively also gets affected.

Public-sector banks account for about 70 per cent of the Indian banking industry, but when it comes to restructured assets, their share could be at least 90 per cent. Consider these figures: while the entire banking industry has restructured 4.68 per cent of loans till March 2012, public-sector banks have recast 5.73 per cent of their loans. The comparative figure for private banks is 1.61 per cent, and foreign banks, 0.22 per cent.

In the past three years, the restructured loans for public-sector banks have grown at a compounded annual growth rate of close to 48 per cent while their loan books have grown at 19.5 per cent. For private banks, credit has grown at close to 20 per cent while restructured loans have grown at 8.12 per cent.

Why are public-sector banks more vulnerable than their peers in the private sector? There are several reasons. Since many of them have large balance sheets, their ability to lend to different industries is more than that of most private banks. Their credit appraisal process seems to be weaker than their counterparts' in the private sector; they do not pay market-related salaries and hence cannot attract people with the requisite expertise. Finally, when it comes to giving loans, they are also susceptible to pressure from politicians and bureaucrats.

Indeed, loan recasts are a global phenomenon, pioneered by the Bank of England through the so-called London Approach in the 1970s, which was modified in the 1990s. The objective is prevention of liquidation of companies hurt by external developments, with the pain shared equally by the companies and their bankers. But the Indian context is different. There is no bankruptcy law here and the banking system seems to be suffering more than the borrowers themselves.

ARE BANKS IN A DENIAL MODE?

9 September 2012

Anil Ambani is looking to sell the stake that Reliance Communications Ltd (R-Com) has in Reliance Infrastructure Ltd and list R-Com's undersea cable unit. The chairman of India's second-largest mobile carrier (in terms of subscribers) has said the entire proceeds would be used to repay debt. In a recent interview, Pratip Chaudhuri, chairman of State Bank of India, said he was seeing stress in the power, steel, metal, aluminium and fertilizer sectors. Chaudhuri suggested that the promoters of stressed companies should be ready to cede part ownership.

Ambani's intended action and Chaudhuri's observation form a theme—many Indian corporations are in trouble and some say the situation is as bad as it was in the late 1990s when many big conglomerates defaulted on bank loans, leading to large-scale loan restructuring. The steel makers were the most affected then. The Asian currency crisis in 1997–98 and the collapse of the Soviet Union saddled the industry with excess capacity and low demand, leading to the restructuring.

However, the banks seem to be in a denial mode. Ask any bank chairman about the state of affairs and the standard reply is: such things happen in a slowing economy and it cannot get worse. Whatever the reasons may be, the fact is that too many sectors and companies are in stress and that's not good news for the banking system.

R-Com had Rs 356.48 billion of debt on its books as of June. Going by a 2 August report by Credit Suisse, Anil Ambani's Reliance Group had Rs 867 billion of debt by the end of fiscal 2012, up from Rs 261 billion in 2007. The report mentioned how banks' exposure to a group of ten conglomerates had increased from Rs 993 billion to Rs 5.4 trillion between 2007 and 2012 at a compounded annual growth rate of 40 per cent while the banking system's overall loans grew at 20 per cent.

This isn't the full story, though, as many industrial houses have borrowed overseas. One investment banker told me that one large conglomerate had taken bridge loans of at least $350 million from a few foreign banks for two of its group companies, which they are expected to pay back by selling bonds, but it's not easy to raise money through bond sales. Another telecom company of a large industrial group already has Rs 230 billion of debt on its books and may need another Rs 100–120 billion for spectrum licence. Banks will be only too happy to lend although the company may not find it easy to pay back.

Look at Indian companies' interest coverage ratio—calculated by dividing a company's earnings before interest and taxes for a particular period by its interest expenses. The lower the ratio, the more the company is burdened by debt. A lower interest coverage ratio indicates that the company is not generating sufficient revenue to meet interest expenses.

A study by the rating agency Crisil Ltd shows the interest coverage ratios of Indian companies for the fiscal year that ended in March 2012 at a three-year low, marginally higher than what was seen in fiscal 2009 after the collapse of Lehman Brothers. The drop in the interest coverage ratio is the fallout of a combination of shrinking earnings and rising interest cost. To fight persistently high inflation, India's central bank hiked its policy rate thirteen times in the past two years until April when it cut the rate by half a percentage point, but banks have not yet pared their loan rates for all borrowers.

While there are cash-rich companies such as Coal India Ltd, Reliance Industries Ltd, Infosys Ltd and a few others that have been looking for acquisitions to make use of their money, many have been paying the price for mindless expansion into diverse fields. The stock market is punishing some of them severely. Theoretically, one can now buy publisher Deccan Chronicle Holdings Ltd for Rs 2.68 billion. Similarly, the market cap of OnMobile Global Ltd, a mobile value-added services company, is Rs 3.94 billion, and Kingfisher Airlines Ltd's is Rs 7.65 billion.

The banks prefer to restructure loans that are on the verge of turning bad and not write them off, as a write-off will hit their balance sheets. If they seriously want to get rid of the bad apples, some of the banks will see their quarterly profits being wiped out. Since bank chief executive officers won't be there forever, the best way to tackle such a situation is to be in a denial mode and keep making profits till the next CEO comes in with a broom and launches a clean-up operation. Ironically, the new CEO too leaves behind the same legacy for his successor when he retires.

HOW MANY BANKS ARE SWIMMING NAKED?

30 May 2016

On 2 October 2014, Prime Minister Narendra Modi launched Swachh Bharat Abhiyan—India's biggest-ever cleanliness drive. Around three million government employees and students of schools and colleges participated in the event to clean the streets, roads and other infrastructure.

A year later, Raghuram Rajan, governor of India's central bank, steered a similar drive to clean up the balance sheets of the country's commercial banks. In the five months between August and December 2015, the Reserve Bank of India inspected their loan portfolios with a toothcomb and asked them to make provisions for three types of assets: non-performing assets that were earlier not recognized by them; loans given to various projects where the dates of commencement of commercial operations have passed, but the projects have not yet taken off; and loans which have been restructured. The banks were given the freedom to make provisions in two phases for the December and March quarters of fiscal year 2016, at least 50 per cent each.

Here is the result of this:

Barring one, Dhanlaxmi Bank Ltd, all listed banks in India had announced their earnings for fiscal 2016. In the March quarter, fifteen out of twenty-five public-sector banks announced net losses. As a group, the public-sector banks posted Rs 234.93-billion loss against a net profit of Rs 85 billion in the quarter of the previous year. Not a single private-sector bank posted a loss in the quarter even as their collective net profit dropped by 14 per cent—from Rs 102.54 billion to Rs 88.07 billion. Comparable data for India's newest bank, IDFC Bank, were not available. Overall, thirty-eight listed banks posted a loss of Rs 146.86 billion against a net profit of Rs 187.54 billion in the 2015 March quarter.

Punjab National Bank led the pack of loss-making lenders with a Rs 53.67-billion net loss in the March quarter, followed by Canara

Bank (Rs 39.05 billion), Bank of India (Rs 35.87 billion), Bank of Baroda (Rs 32.30 billion), Syndicate Bank (Rs 21.58 billion), IDBI Bank Ltd (Rs 17.36 billion) and UCO Bank (Rs 17.15 billion). The loss would have been higher for many of them had they not got the benefit of tax write-backs.

Many of the public-sector banks have posted losses for two successive quarters, and as a result, thirteen of them ended the fiscal year with net losses; nine of them have reported profits, but their earnings in the year that ended on 31 March are lower than what they had recorded in the previous fiscal. Only three state-run banks reported a rise in net profits. Bank of India's annual loss has been Rs 60.89 billion and that of Bank of Baroda, Rs 53.96 billion. Among the private banks, barring three, all have posted higher net profits in 2016 compared to the previous year.

The reason behind the hefty losses for many and a sharp drop in profits for others is higher provisions—the money they had to set aside to take care of their NPAs or bad loans. Data show that the pile of provisions made by the banking system has risen by 87 per cent in 2016—from Rs 936.98 billion to Rs 1.75 trillion. Both private and public banks have been aggressive in making provisions, and yet, most private banks were able to make decent profits because they continued to earn higher interest income as well as fee income—something which their rivals in the public sector have not been able to do. I am dealing with that issue a little later in the piece.

The gross bad loans of these thirty-eight listed banks rose by 95 per cent in one year—from Rs 3.09 trillion to Rs 5.8 trillion. Of this, in the March quarter alone, bad loans rose by almost Rs 1.5 trillion, after adding close to Rs 1 trillion worth of bad assets in the December 2016 quarter. The public-sector banks account for around 90 per cent of the bad loans, although their market share of banking assets is around 70 per cent. State Bank of India's gross bad loan is close to Rs 1 trillion. Punjab National Bank comes a distant second at Rs 558.18 billion, followed by Bank of India at Rs 498.79 billion and Bank of Baroda at Rs 405.21 billion.

After setting aside the money, the net bad loans for this set of listed banks more than doubled in 2016—from Rs 1.67 trillion in fiscal 2015 to Rs 3.38 trillion. Here too, the public sector banks' share is more than 90 per cent.

In percentage terms, for many public-sector banks, the gross bad loans more than doubled during the year. For UCO Bank, it rose from 6.76 per cent to 15.43 per cent; that of Bank of India, from 5.39 per cent to 13.07 per cent; and Bank of Baroda—from 3.72 per cent to 9.99 per cent.

Overall, fourteen out of twenty-five public-sector banks now have gross bad loans of at least 9 per cent and a maximum of 17.4 per cent.

Among private banks, ICICI Bank Ltd is the only entity which has more than 5 per cent gross bad loans (5.82 per cent). After making provisions, fifteen state-owned banks have at least 5 per cent and a maximum of 11.89 per cent net bad loans. In the pack of private banks, three have between 2.35 per cent and 2.98 per cent net NPAs.

Even after declaring bad assets and providing for them, the private banks could make profits because most of them continued to lend money and earn interest income besides fee income. This is not the case with the public-sector banks.

In the March quarter, the public-sector banks' net interest income actually dropped by 2 per cent from a year earlier while the private banks' net interest income rose by 21 per cent. For 2015–16, the net interest income of public-sector banks rose only marginally—from Rs 1.9 trillion to Rs 1.94 trillion—while private banks posted 21 per cent growth in their net interest income in the entire year.

This is the most worrying aspect of bank earnings in fiscal 2016. Scared of piling up bad assets, many public-sector banks have stopped giving loans and started shrinking their balance sheets. While collectively, the loan book of thirteen listed private banks has grown by 22.40 per cent in 2016, that of twenty-five public-sector banks has grown by 2.73 per cent and at least eight state-owned banks have shrunk their loan books. UCO Bank's loan portfolio has shrunk by 15 per cent and that of Bank of Baroda, by more than 10 per cent. Bank of India, Indian Overseas Bank and a few others feature in this list.

Once a bank decides not to give fresh loans fearing rise in bad assets, its interest income shrinks and that hits its profitability and ability to provide for bad assets.

Even though both the government and the RBI have put up a brave front and claim that all is well on the capital front, quite a few Indian banks will soon face the music. Since they are not making profits that could be ploughed back to bolster their net worth, they will not have enough capital to be able to lend. As of 31 March, twenty-five listed public-sector banks had Rs 55.4 trillion of loans on their books, and about 10 per cent of the amount, about Rs 5.3 trillion, are gross bad assets. Once we add the restructured loans and those loans that had been written off, the total stressed assets could be at least 20 per cent.

The key question here is: is the worst over for Indian banks?

State Bank of India's boss, Arundhati Bhattacharya, has given us a clue to interpret the status. Announcing the bank's earnings last week, she said her bank has identified and kept Rs 313.52 billion worth of risky loans on a 'special watch'.

As much as 70 per cent of these loans could end up becoming bad, but if the economy improves, then only 30 per cent could turn bad.

Many have been taking heart from the fact that the Indian banking system had gone through a worse period in the early 1990s when the bad assets were even higher. If it could pull it off then, why worry now? Looking back at the early 1990s will surely make us feel courageous, but it may not be an ideal comparison. The risk is far higher now, as the banks' exposure to loans is much more than what it was in the early 1990s, with the reserve requirements steadily coming down.

For example, in 1992 and early 1993, Indian banks' mandatory bond-buying, or the statutory liquidity ratio, was 38.5 per cent, which came down to 31.5 per cent in 1994. Similarly, banks' cash reserve ratio, or the portion of deposits that the commercial banks are required to keep with the RBI, was 14.5 per cent in 1993 which rose to 15 per cent in 1994. Currently, banks have 21.25 per cent SLR and 4 per cent CRR.

This means that banks could not lend more than 47 per cent of its deposits in 1992, but now it can lend as much as 74.75 per cent. So, even if the bad loans do not cross the early 1990s level in percentage terms, the risk to banks' balance sheets is far higher today as a much larger portion of their resources is being used to give loans. Fears of a collapse are certainly exaggerated as these banks are backed by the government, but living in a denial mode may not be wise. Many state-run banks are swimming naked now.

BANKS ARE STRESSED: WHAT DO WE DO?

11 July 2016

A day after the Reserve Bank of India released its biannual Financial Stability Report, outlining the 'significant challenges' being faced by Indian banks, thirty-one out of thirty-three big banks in the US cleared the final round of the Federal Reserve's annual stress tests, signifying the resilience of the US financial system.

Only one of the largest banks of the US—Morgan Stanley—got a conditional passing grade, while two others, Deutsche Bank AG and Santander Bank NA, both US subsidiaries of European banks, failed. In the previous year too, the duo did not qualify.

The stress tests essentially gauge whether the banks in the US with at least $50 billion in assets each have enough capital, management bandwidth and other safeguards to survive a financial crisis.

Ahead of the stress tests results on 29 June, the Fed had said that all big banks would be able to make it through a recession. Since the global financial crisis in the aftermath of the collapse of Lehman Brothers in September 2008, the banks have been directed to create a cushion of large capital against likely losses from a recession or any other developments that shock the market. The 29 June statement has also outlined areas where the Fed expects further improvement next year.

The RBI stress test, on the other hand, indicates that risks to the banking sector increased significantly in the second half of 2015–16, driven by deteriorating asset quality and lower profitability. Indeed, the financial system is resilient, but it could become vulnerable if the macroeconomic conditions deteriorate sharply.

Saddled with bad assets, the banks are expected to remain risk-averse and not lend money to corporations; besides, in the absence of adequate capital, their ability to lend will also be impacted.

Simply put, Indian banks are caught in a vicious cycle: they are not willing to lend for fear of adding to bad assets; this dents their interest income and profitability; and that, in turn, further erodes their ability to lend as they are not able to plough back profits to bolster their capital.

The credit growth of Indian banks slowed to 8.8 per cent in March 2016 from 9.4 per cent in September 2015; the growth in deposits too declined from 9.9 per cent to 8.1 per cent during this period.

The gross non-performing assets as a percentage of advances rose to 7.6 per cent from 5.1 per cent and, overall, the proportion of stressed assets rose to 11.5 per cent from 11.3 per cent. After setting aside money, the net NPAs of banks rose sharply—from 2.8 per cent to 4.6 per cent between September and March. On every parameter, the state-owned banks are in a far worse shape than their private peers.

In March, the top 100 borrowers accounted for almost 28 per cent of credit given to large corporations and a little over 16 per cent of Rs 75.3-trillion bank credit. They also accounted for more than one-fifth of the gross NPAs of the Indian banking system.

The RBI stress test suggests that gross NPAs of the banking system may rise to 9.3 per cent by March 2017 'under a severe stress scenario'. For the state-owned banks, it could be as high as 11 per cent. Higher bad assets will force banks to set aside more money, dent their profitability, and they would need capital infusion to be able to support the demand of loan from the corporate borrowers.

Unlike the US Federal Reserve, which identifies the banks that fail the stress tests, the Indian banking regulator does not expose individual banks and rightly so, as this could lead to a run on a bank, with a large number of depositors rushing to withdraw money simultaneously, due to concerns about the particular bank's solvency. In such a scenario, the money kept by a bank with the RBI in the form of cash reserve ratio as well as government bond-holding—which could be liquidated to generate cash—may not be enough to cover the deposit withdrawals.

The RBI prefers to talk in terms of number of banks at risk and not who they are. For instance, stress tests on banks' credit concentration risks, it says, is significant for eight banks, accounting for a little over 12 per cent of loans and they may end up having capital less than what they require.

Since 2010 when the first signs of stress were seen, the government has pumped in Rs 677.34-billion capital to keep the public-sector banks running. It has agreed to infuse an additional Rs 700 billion even as the state-owned banks will have to raise over Rs 1 trillion from the markets to meet their capital requirements.

Media reports suggest that the finance ministry has already finalized the plan for the first round of capital infusion of around Rs 100 billion. After pumping in Rs 250 billion into twenty-one state-owned banks last fiscal year, the government has committed to offer Rs 250-billion capital to these banks in the current year and another Rs 100 billion each in 2018 and 2019.

For the big US banks and their investors, the annual stress tests are extremely critical as those who pass the grade are entitled to pay dividends and buy back stocks from their shareholders. In the Indian context, such a test still largely remains an academic exercise as the government seems to believe in a perpetual, unconditional bailout theory.

In the thick of the global financial turmoil, the US Treasury announced a Troubled Asset Relief Program, or TARP, of up to $700 billion to save its privately managed banks from the sub-prime mortgage crisis. Most of this amount has been invested, loaned or paid out by the Treasury, and the banks have returned more in the form of interest, dividend and fees.

The Band-Aid approach that India follows will keep the system alive, but one cannot expect a turnaround till such time the government accepts that capital infusion is just one of the tools and it needs to do more to revive the weak banks.

Meanwhile, wary of corporate credit, now the banks are chasing retail loans; the trend will continue till they burn their fingers.

FOUR STATE-OWNED BANKS TO WATCH OUT FOR

20 February 2017

Listed Indian banks' gross bad loans crossed Rs 7 trillion in the December quarter. This is no nasty surprise. In fact, the December *Financial Stability Report* of the Reserve Bank of India warned that gross bad loans of banks might rise further and public-sector banks would be the worst hit. Gross bad loans of the Indian banking industry as a percentage of loans rose to 9.1 per cent in September, from 7.9 per cent in March. If one includes restructured loans, the overall stressed assets to advances ratio was 12.3 per cent in September. In the December quarter, it rose further, even though the pace of growth has slowed at many banks.

While enough is being written on the overall health of the Indian banking system, it may not be a bad idea to sift through data and identify the worst-affected state-owned banks, a few of which are fast losing their relevance in the financial system. For this purpose, I have looked at data over the past six quarters—between September 2015, a quarter before the clean-up drive started, and December 2016.

Between August and December 2015, the RBI inspectors pored over the loan books of all banks as part of a first-of-its-kind asset quality review and asked them to set aside money for three kinds of loans: non-performing assets that they had not recognized yet; loans given to projects where the dates of commencement of commercial operations had passed but the projects had failed to take off; and restructured loans.

The banks had to provide for the first two types of loans in two phases in the December and March quarters of the fiscal year 2016, at least 50 per cent each. For restructured loans, they were asked to set aside or provide for 15 per cent of the loan amount in six quarters, 2.5 per cent each, till March 2017. While we will have to wait till March when the entire clean-up exercise gets over, a few banks have already exposed their vulnerability.

The idea is not to create panic. Indeed, depositors' money is safe with these banks, but besides taking deposits, a bank's primary job is to give loans and support economic growth. A few public-sector banks are no longer capable of doing this.

The first obvious health-check parameter is bad loans.

Indian Overseas Bank (IOB) has the ugliest balance sheet among public-sector banks. Its bad loans were 22.42 per cent of loan assets in December 2016, more than double the 11 per cent in September 2015—just before the first impact of AQR was seen in the banks' balance sheets. UCO Bank's gross NPAs are 17.18 per cent and both United Bank of India's and IDBI Bank's gross NPAs are well over 15 per cent—all have doubled since September 2015.

In absolute terms, during this period, gross NPAs of IOB rose from Rs 194.24 billion to Rs 345.02 billion. For UCO, the rise has been from Rs 122.27 billion to Rs 221.81 billion; and for United Bank of India, from Rs 61.12 billion to Rs 108.45 billion. IDBI Bank's gross NPAs have more than doubled from Rs 147.58 billion to Rs 352.45 billion.

However, this is only half the story. We need to look at the overall stressed assets, including restructured loans, a sizable portion of which is unlikely to be recovered. In December 2016, the stressed assets of IOB were Rs 502.07 billion, UCO Bank Rs 280.28 billion, United Bank of India Rs 210.67 billion and IDBI Bank Rs 605.02 billion. As a percentage of total loan assets, roughly one-third of all loans of United Bank of India (33.07 per cent) and IOB (32.63 per cent) are stressed. For IDBI Bank, this ratio is 27.76 per cent and UCO, 21.71 per cent.

Even this does not reveal the real state of affairs. Banks periodically write off loans, and many such write-offs are the so-called 'technical write-offs', a typical Indian concept whereby a bad loan is taken off the balance sheet of a bank, but parked in a branch and the recovery process continues. Banks get tax benefits on recovered bad loans, and this also depresses their NPA figures. Only after adding the written-off loans to the stressed assets do we get to know how bad a bank's health is.

By making massive provisions, most banks have been able to bring down their net NPAs. In the past six quarters, IOB had provided for Rs 98.04 billion, UCO Rs 87.71 billion, United Bank of India Rs 29.99 billion and IDBI Bank Rs 151.60 billion. With the slowing of fresh bad loans accumulation, the amount of money set aside for bad loans is progressively going down for most banks, but not for these four. Provisioning hits profits and erodes capital.

It may not be easy to make hefty provisions in the coming days as net interest income, or the interest earned on advances minus the cost of deposits, has been coming down for these banks and the so-called 'other income', which includes treasury profit, will take a hit with the rise in bond yields. Yield and prices of bonds move in opposite directions.

The net interest income of IDBI Bank almost halved between September 2015 and December 2016, from Rs 16.12 billion to Rs 8.5 billion. For United Bank of India, the drop is from Rs 6.39 billion to Rs 3.61 billion; UCO, from Rs 14.16 billion to Rs 9.76 billion, while IOB's fall in net interest income is marginally down—from Rs 13.98 billion to Rs 13.35 billion—after it dropped below Rs 13 billion for two successive quarters.

Shrinking Loan Books

What is worrisome is that while bad loans are ballooning, the loan books of three of these four banks have been shrinking. IOB's loan portfolio shrank by 14 per cent between December 2015 and December 2016 (Rs 1.79 trillion to Rs 1.54 trillion) and that of United Bank of India, by over 9 per cent. UCO's loan book has shrunk by 5 per cent, but IDBI Bank has managed to grow by 4 per cent. For IOB and UCO, deposit portfolios too have shrunk, while United Bank of India and IDBI Bank continue to garner fresh deposits. The government's demonetization exercise which forced citizens to return old high-value notes in November–December helped banks grow deposits.

Higher provisions and a drop in interest income have hit their profitability. In the past five quarters since December 2015, IOB has made an accumulated loss of Rs 32.59 billion in addition to a

Rs 5.51-billion loss in September 2015. UCO's loss since December 2015 has been Rs 44.75 billion. United Bank of India has managed to record small profits in four of the five quarters, but still accumulated a Rs 2.5-billion loss, while IDBI Bank's accumulated loss in the past five quarters is Rs 58.78 billion.

Of course, all four banks have the capital to meet the regulatory requirement for now, but that's small consolation. A look at the capital and reserves or net worth of these banks and the pile of bad loans they have accumulated does not inspire much confidence. For IOB, gross NPAs are more than two and a half times its net worth; both UCO and United Bank of India have bad loans at least double their net worth. IDBI Bank's bad loans are 1.3 times its net worth.

If we look at their net worth against the backdrop of the stressed assets they have piled up, the scene is much worse. Both United Bank of India and IOB's stressed assets are almost four times their net worth; for UCO, it is close to three times; and for IDBI Bank, over two times. Even net NPAs of IOB, United Bank of India and UCO are higher than their net worth.

To be sure, apart from this quartet, quite a few other public-sector banks are stressed and their return on assets and equity is in the negative zone. Bank of India and Oriental Bank of Commerce have seen marginal growth in deposits in the past one year; both of them as well as Central Bank of India, Bank of Maharashtra and Dena Bank have shrunk their loan books. Before posting small profits in the past two quarters, Bank of India had posted more than Rs 60-billion loss in four successive quarters. Central Bank of India recorded Rs 35.82-billion loss in the past five quarters.

For Allahabad Bank, the accumulated loss is Rs 14.92 billion (in three out of five quarters) and Dena Bank Rs 12.78 billion (four out of five quarters). Stressed loans are one-fourth of Dena Bank's loan book. Punjab National Bank and Andhra Bank also have deep pockets of stress. Even a relatively strong Bank of Baroda posted Rs 65.72-billion loss in the December 2015 and March 2016 quarters and its collective net profit in the next three quarters could make good roughly 20 per cent of the losses. Its stressed loans are one-fifth of its overall loan book, which has shrunk by almost 9 per cent in the past one year, and deposits haven't grown at all.

While for a few well-capitalized banks, consolidation in balance sheet could be a strategic decision, for most, it betrays their vulnerability. They are too stressed on most parameters and, by not giving fresh loans (or giving very selectively only to prevent old loans from going bad—the so-called 'evergreening'), they are increasingly finding it difficult to justify why they should be around.

Still, large-scale capital infusion in individual banks, consolidation or culling or even creation of a bad bank is unlikely to happen soon. The government will get out of the denial mode when it sees the investment demand picking up in a big way, corporate borrowers scrambling for credit, and the banking system not able to support India's growth.

Meanwhile, bank stocks continue to rise. In the past one year till last Friday, IDBI Bank stock has risen by 55 per cent, United Bank 36 per cent, UCO 13 per cent and IOB 11 per cent. Perhaps the market knows more than what meets the eye.

NPA ORDINANCE: THE LAST ACT OF BAD LOAN RESOLUTION?

(Part I)

8 May 2017

Over the next fortnight, many state-owned banks, led by State Bank of India, are expected to aggressively push for deep restructuring of some of the large bad assets such as Essar Steel Ltd (Rs 450 billion) and Bhushan Steel Ltd (Rs 470 billion), among others. These will be taken up at the executive committee meetings of individual banks and also at the forum of lenders. On the table are plans for extension of the tenure of repayment of loans, reduction in interest rates, pledge of shares as well as personal guarantees by the promoters of distressed companies, and conversion of unsustainable debt into preference shares/low coupon debentures, and other covenants.

Behind the sudden rush is an ordinance signed by the President of India last Thursday amending the Banking Regulation Act, thereby giving powers to the Reserve Bank of India to push the banks hard to deal with the bad assets. The banking regulator is also being authorized to invoke the Insolvency and Bankruptcy Code against loan defaulters.

If the reaction of the stock market is anything to go by, the ordinance did not match the hype that was created in the media in the run-up to its promulgation. Are the new proposals adequate to clean up the banking system in the world's fastest-growing major economy?

Between 2001 and now, there have been quite a few schemes such as corporate debt restructuring (CDR), strategic debt restructuring (SDR) and Scheme for Sustainable Structuring of Stressed Assets (S4A) to address the problem of rising bad loans in India, but none of them have succeeded. The listed Indian banks had Rs 7.2 trillion worth gross bad loans in December and this is expected to cross

Rs 8 trillion in March. At least another Rs 2.1 trillion are the so-called special mention accounts, or SMA-1and SMA-2.

The SMA-2 category refers to those accounts where the principal or interest payment is overdue for sixty-one to ninety days. This is the third stage in an account's progress to becoming a non-performing asset, or NPA, after SMA-0 (where the principal or interest payment is not overdue for more than thirty days, but the account shows signs of incipient stress) and SMA-1 (where the principal or interest payment is overdue for thirty-one to sixty days).

The Videocon group (Rs 330 billion), Essar Power Ltd (Rs 110 billion), Jaiprakash Associates Ltd (Rs 229.60 billion), Jaiprakash Power Ventures Ltd (Rs 147 billion), JP Infrastructure Ltd (Rs 100 billion), Naveen Jindal's Jindal Steel Ltd (Rs 460 billion) and Anil Ambani's Reliance Communications Ltd (Rs 420 billion) are some of the corporations that fall into this bracket. Depending on their cash flow and repayment of banks dues, they shift between the two buckets—SMA-1 and SMA-2; for the banking system, they are stressed but performing assets.

The finance minister has pegged the stressed asset volume at Rs 9.6 trillion, but I presume this figure does not include the cases which are under SDR where the banks continue to classify them as standard assets for eighteen months. Under SDR, a consortium of lenders could convert part of their loan exposure in a stressed company into equity, and own at least 51 per cent of it. They can also change the management of companies that were not able to service the bank loans. We have hardly seen a change in management in companies that have undergone strategic debt restructuring.

The stressed companies being tackled on the SDR platform for which new investors are yet to be identified could be worth around Rs 1 trillion. There are overleveraged promoters who have very little skin in the game as they have taken vanilla loans from one set of banks for the holding company and, at the same time, loans against pledge of shares of their operating companies from another set of banks and NBFCs in order to minimize their own contribution. Similarly, there are banks which have been evergreening certain loans—giving fresh loans to the borrowers to pay off the old ones. This is why one particular account could be in the category of SMA-1 or SMA-2 or even a non-performing asset for one bank and a regular asset for another.

Key Takeaways

The two key takeaways from the latest move to clean up banks' sheets are: bank executives are expected to be protected from the glare of the investigative agencies—Central Bureau of Investigation and Central Vigilance Commission—and India's chief auditor, the Comptroller and Auditor General, while taking a deep haircut to resolve some of the bad assets. This is not explicitly stated in the ordinance, but this will be done by making the oversight committees, or OCs, responsible for such resolutions. Currently, there is only one two-member OC—consisting of former State Bank of India chairman Janki Ballabh and former chief vigilance commissioner Pradeep Kumar. Work is under way to amend the Prevention of Corruption Act and once this is done, the formal shield for the bankers from such investigations will be in place.

Bad loan resolution will now happen in a time-bound manner. If the banks show reluctance, the RBI will force them to act. Frankly, there haven't been enough incentives for the banks to act on war footing against bad loans. Once a loan becomes an NPA, a bank is required to set aside money or provide for 15 per cent of the loan amount in the first year, an additional 10 per cent in the second year, 15 per cent in the third year, and finally the rest 60 per cent in the fourth year. For a bank chief, making such provisions is easier than taking a 40–60 per cent haircut at one go. On the one hand, such deep haircuts can attract the attention of investigative agencies, and on the other, higher provisions—following a deep haircut—erode bank's profits and capital.

This is why the bankers' lobby, Indian Banks' Association, has been asking for staggering such provisions over a period of eight quarters, but the banking regulator doesn't have much sympathy for this. However, to hasten the process of resolution, it is saying that 60 per cent of creditor by value and 50 per cent by number of the lenders will now be the basis of any action for bad loan clean-up. Till now, any such decision needed to be backed by 75 per cent by value and 60 per cent by number of lenders.

This is expected to speed up the process. One of the key reasons why there has been enormous delay in resolving the bad assets is the bankers' refusal to reach a consensus on such deals. A case in point is the Russian oil major Rosneft's plan to acquire Essar Oil for $12.9 billion. Rosneft plans to acquire a 49 per cent stake, and another 49 per cent stake will be shared between commodities trader, the Netherlands-based Trafigura, and the Russian private investment group, United Capital Partners. Once the deal is done, armed with the cash, Essar group will be able to service bank loans in a much more efficient way, but some of the banks which have exposure to the group have not yet given their approval to the deal.

Many are questioning the direct involvement of the banking regulator in the bad asset resolution process. Should the regulator do this? Isn't there a conflict of interest? If this is done, what prevents the RBI from directing the banks where to lend, and thereby return to the directed lending regime?

While there is merit in such a debate, we must remember that this is an extraordinary situation which calls for extraordinary measures. The overall stressed assets of the banking system at this point could be as much as Rs 12 trillion, more than 8 per cent of India's gross domestic product. This is less than 15 per cent of bank credit, but since bad loans in other sectors such as retail and agriculture are much lower, around 40 per cent of the industrial credit given by Indian banks could have gone sour. We cannot remain in a denial mode.

The RBI could have done this on its own as the RBI Act empowers the central bank to direct banks, but it has taken the ordinance route probably for the demonstrative effect—to tell the world that both the RBI and the Government of India are on the same page when it comes to cleaning up the banking system.

While an aggressive banking regulator will force the banks to clean up their books, who will fill in the big holes in their balance sheets? Deep restructuring of loans will lead to massive provisions and that will wipe out many banks' capital. The ordinance marks the beginning of a new clean-up drive, but it can only be successful if the government is willing to pump in fresh capital. Or else, quite a few banks will go belly up. Of course, if the government has something up its sleeve for mergers and consolidation of banks, that's a different story.

Postscript

While both the regulator and the majority owner are determined to clean up the banking system—and rightly so—the government is showing no laxity in tightening the screw around top loan defaulters that are suspected of wrongdoings. The Serious Fraud Investigation Office (SFIO) of the central government is probing into the affairs of Bhushan Steel Ltd and Bhushan Power and Steel Ltd. In the last week of April, a senior executive of SFIO, a part of the Ministry of Corporate Affairs, wrote to the chiefs of all banks, asking for information on the bank accounts of all group companies and their directors—some forty-nine of them.

The SFIO wants a copy of the account opening form, the KYC (know your customers) documents submitted by them, and the statement of accounts of the past ten years, under Section 65B of the Indian Evidence Act, 1872. It also wants the details of Demat accounts, linked to the bank accounts, statement of holdings as well as details of all transactions. Besides, it has asked for details of credit cards issued to any of the directors, their family members and senior executives of the companies under investigation, and details of their loan accounts.

The banks have been directed to submit all documents—as per the provisions laid down by Section 2(A) of the Banker's Book of Evidence Act, 1891, within seven days. The list of forty-nine group companies and their directors also include their PAN numbers. I presume, the banks have already responded and the investigation is going on full steam.

NPA ORDINANCE: THE LAST ACT OF BAD LOAN RESOLUTION?

(Part II)

15 May 2017

Former Reserve Bank of India deputy governor Subir Gokarn once said that banks' non-performing assets are like cancer—if not treated at an early stage, the patient will die.

Viral Acharya, the RBI's current deputy governor in charge of monetary policy, has used another simile to illustrate the same point—a bank not keeping adequate capital to absorb losses arising out of bad loans is like allowing a person who has slipped off the terrace of a skyscraper to fall and die.

The latest move of empowering the RBI to directly intervene in the resolution process is expected to speed up the exercise, but some of the banks will 'slip off the terrace of a skyscraper and die' unless the government keeps the parachute ready in the form of fresh capital infusion. Of course, the banks can generate some capital by revaluing their fixed assets innovatively, but that will not be enough to keep them alive.

For quite some time, the RBI has been tightening the noose around those banks which are refusing to see the writing on the wall. Apart from a series of resolution schemes to clean up the bad assets, in the five months between August and December 2015, the banking regulator conducted a first-of-its-kind asset quality review and asked them to set aside money for three kinds of loans: NPAs that they had not recognized yet; loans given to projects where the dates of commencement of commercial operations had passed but the projects had failed to take off; and restructured loans.

The banks had to provide for the first two types of loans in two phases in the December and March quarters of fiscal year 2016, of at least 50 per cent each. For restructured loans, they were asked to make 15 per cent provision in six quarters, of 2.5 per cent each, till March 2017. As and when all banks announce their March quarter earnings, clarity will emerge on the enormity of the bad loan problem.

Meanwhile, the RBI has done three things in the run-up to the banks' March quarter earnings. It has revised and tightened more-than-a-decade-old prompt corrective action, or PCA structure; encouraged banks to make provisions at higher rates for the advances given to the stressed sectors of Indian economy; and asked banks to make suitable disclosures in case there are any material divergences in banks' asset classification and provisioning to that of the RBI norm in the 'Notes to Accounts' of their upcoming annual financial statements.

Are these enough? Definitely not, and this is why the Banking Regulation Act has been amended through an ordinance and the RBI has been given more powers to direct banks and speed up the process, since without a healthy banking system, the economy cannot run at full throttle.

In 2004, the PCA norms had stipulated that if a bank's net NPAs crossed 10 per cent but by less than 15 per cent, there would be a special drive to reduce NPAs; the loan policy would be reviewed and steps would be taken to strengthen credit appraisal skills, among other things. For net NPAs of 15 per cent and above, in addition to these, banks' boards would be called for discussion on a corrective plan of action.

The latest PCA framework talks about three risk thresholds for net NPAs: 6 per cent to less than 9 per cent; 9 per cent to less than 12 per cent; and 12 per cent and above. Apart from the bad assets, capital, return on assets and the leverage ratios are other benchmarks for a bank's health check. Depending on the scale of deterioration in a bank's health, the RBI can take actions, varying between a clampdown on branch expansion to higher provisions, removal of the management and even superseding the board.

Tightening of the PCA norms has been long overdue. Between 2001 and 2005, the average net NPAs of the banking system were

4.2 per cent, less than now. Besides, since the reserve requirements such as cash reserve ratio (part of deposits kept with the RBI) and the statutory liquidity ratio (mandatory bond buying) were far higher then, in absolute terms, banks' bad assets were much lower. Indian Overseas Bank, United Bank of India and Dhanlaxmi Bank Ltd, and IDBI Bank Ltd have already come under the ambit of the PCA; once the March quarter earnings are out, a few more banks could come under it. In the December quarter, at least eleven banks had more than 9 per cent net NPAs, including three State Bank of India associates which have since been merged with it.

The Stressed Telecom Sector

The banks have also been asked to make higher provisions for standard advances given to the stressed sectors of the economy, following a board-approved policy which must be reviewed every quarter. The RBI is particularly worried about the telecom sector—which is undergoing severe stress—and has asked banks to review the segment latest by 30 June and consider making higher provisions for standard assets in this sector. Under current rules, most standard assets attract a provision of 0.4 per cent. The few exceptions include credit to commercial real estate (1 per cent provision) and residential real estate (0.75 per cent).

However, the regulator hasn't specified the extent of higher provisioning for standard loans to the telecom and other stressed sectors. Leaving it to the discretion of individual bank boards, the regulator may see different levels of provisioning for the same sector by different banks. After all, their risk management system is not uniform and that's why some banks have more NPAs than others.

In fact, the telecom sector is stressed. The Indian banking sector's exposure to the telcos is around Rs 1 trillion and the industry's overall indebtedness is close to Rs 5 trillion. Besides, the telcos need to pay around Rs 3 trillion to the government for sharing revenue on the allocation of spectrum. The rating agencies have been downgrading the outlook of many telcos. Intense competition is denting their revenue and the interest coverage ratio—calculated by dividing a company's earnings before interest and taxes (EBIT) by its interest expenses—for the sector has dropped below 1. Interest coverage ratio of 1.5 or lower questions a company's ability to meet interest expenses. The aggregate revenue of the telecom sector was Rs 1.8 trillion in 2016 against an overall liability of Rs 8 trillion.

Power Sector in Poor Light

The power segment is probably in an equally bad, if not, worse shape. There are coal-based projects worth 15,200 megawatt (MW) which have been completed, but do not have the power purchase agreements (PPAs) and hence are not eligible for fuel-supply agreements. The cost of imported coal hits their profitability. Another set of coal-based power projects—for 13,700 MW—have been at various stages of construction. Indeed, captive coal blocks bring down the cost of operations but deprecation in currency (these power plants were planned in 2010–11 when the rupee–dollar exchange rate was 44/45 vs 64/65 now), and the time overrun have made them unviable.

Besides, there are stranded gas-based power plants to produce 15,000 MW and hydropower for 2000 MW.

The UDAY Scheme (Ujwal Discom Assurance Yojana) announced in November 2015 by the central government for the stressed electricity distribution companies (discoms) envisaged taking over 75 per cent of the debt of the discoms by Indian states. The plan has been to bring down the interest cost and push up the revenue by raising the tariff. However, there seems to be no light at the end of the tunnel for the power plants. Indeed, they have saved on interest costs but many discoms are facing regulatory hurdles for increasing the tariff, and the aggregate technical and commercial losses have risen.

The EPC Segment

The engineering, procurement and construction (EPC) segment where over Rs 1 trillion bank loans have been stuck is also not showing any signs of improvement. In August 2016, the Cabinet Committee on Economic Affairs, headed by Prime Minister Narendra Modi, approved a series of initiatives to revive the construction sector.

The National Institution for Transforming India, or NITI Aayog, quickly followed that up to address the delayed payment or non-payment by the government departments and public-sector undertakings after completion of projects. Typically, all these projects are fraught with disputes which delay payments. It was decided that 75 per cent of the payments to contractors must be released against bank guarantees where the arbitration awards have gone in their favour but are being challenged. The payment will flow into an escrow account and the lenders' dues will be cleared on priority. However, no progress is seen as yet.

Steady Steel

The only segment which is seeing substantial improvement is steel where banks' exposure is to the tune of around Rs 3.3 trillion. Steel companies' earnings, or EBIT, has doubled following the anti-dumping measure by the government in the shape of a minimum import price, coupled with availability of raw material, following regular auctions by iron ore miners. The government's decision to prefer domestically manufactured iron and steel products will also help the steel producers even as the demand is set to rise for various upcoming projects of Indian Railways, the dedicated freight corridor, regional airports, smart cities, and the mushrooming of affordable housing projects, among others.

Simply put, it is unfair to blame the bankers alone for the current mess. We need to sensitize the bankers on risk management and monitoring of projects as much as we need to address the core issues in real economy to avoid the nightmare of certain banks being buried under the pile of bad loans. The steps taken by the steel ministry to revive the sector can be emulated by others. For instance, many of the old power plants of NTPC Ltd have served their lives and they need to be decommissioned. It will take a while for the new plants to come up and their tariff will be relatively higher. NTPC Vidyut Vyapar Nigam Ltd, NTPC's trading arm, can buy from the 15,200-MW power projects that do not have PPAs. The blended cost—the cost of power purchased from these plants and NTPC's new-generation plants—will be less and bring down the cost for the discoms.

FINALLY, THE RBI CRACKS THE DA VINCI CODE OF INDIAN BANKING

29 May 2017

For many Indian banks, keeping asset quality impeccable at any cost is the Holy Grail to satisfying investors and pushing up their valuations. From now on, they will find it difficult. India's banking regulator seems to have cracked the da Vinci code of lending in the world's fastest-growing major economy.

Early this month, Yes Bank Ltd's annual report for the fiscal year 2015–16 showed that the lender's assessment of bad loans in the previous fiscal year was very different from that of the Reserve Bank of India. For 2016, Yes Bank had disclosed gross non-performing assets of Rs 7489 million, but the RBI's assessment of the bank's correct level of gross NPAs was, hold your breath, more than six times higher—Rs 49,256 million. Had Yes Bank assessed the quality of its loan assets the way the RBI would have liked it to, its 0.8 per cent gross NPAs would have been 6 per cent.

As a result of this divergence, the difference in provisioning for the year stands at Rs 8.58 billion. This would have pared the bank's net profit by 22 per cent.

As far as the net NPAs are concerned, there has been a divergence of Rs 33.19 billion between Yes Bank's reported figure and the RBI's assessment.

There has been a divergence between the RBI assessment and the actual reporting of bad loans by at least two other private-sector lenders—ICICI Bank Ltd and Axis Bank Ltd. At ICICI Bank, the difference in gross NPAs was to the tune of Rs 51.05 billion, leading to an additional provisioning of Rs 10.71 billion in 2016.

At Axis Bank, the banking regulator had found a gross NPA divergence of Rs 94.78 billion, raising its bad loans in the last fiscal year to Rs 155.66 billion.

If we assume that the regulator's assessment is correct, then Axis Bank's gross NPAs in 2016 would have made up 4.5 per cent of its loan book against the reported 1.78 per cent. At ICICI Bank, gross NPAs would have been 7 per cent against 5.85 per cent.

In the fiscal year 2016–17, Yes Bank reported 1.51per cent gross NPAs; Axis Bank 5.52 per cent and ICICI Bank 8.74 per cent. To what extent they would rise following the RBI's inspection of their loan books is anybody's guess at this point.

Probably, these three banks are no exceptions. Such divergence between the RBI's assessment of the loan books and banks' recognition of bad assets may come to light at a few other banks, including government-owned ones, when they make public their annual reports although the quantum of 'under-reporting' may vary.

The genesis of this is an RBI notification on 18 April which says: 'There have been instances of material divergences in banks' asset classification and provisioning from the RBI norms, thereby leading to the published financial statements not depicting a true and fair view of the financial position of the bank.' The regulator advised the banks to make adequate disclosures of such divergences in the notes to accounts of their annual financial statements.

The RBI inspectors found these when they took a close look at the loan books of all banks in the second half of 2015 under the so-called 'asset quality review', a first-of-its-kind review to force the banks to clean up their balance sheets.

Under the regulatory norms, when a borrower is not able to service a loan for three months, it becomes an NPA and the lender needs to set aside money or provide for it. Then, why should there be any divergence?

Well, it's not always that simple; under certain circumstances, one can take a 'view' on whether a particular loan is good or bad. For instance, when the principal or interest payment for a particular loan is overdue between sixty-one and ninety days (and not exceeding ninety days), this is called a 'special mention account-2', or SMA-2. If a loan exposure continues to be in this category for months, a prudent banker would prefer to classify it as an NPA even though technically, it can continue to be treated as a standard asset.

Then, there are complexities for some of the restructured infrastructure loans. There have been cases where banks have given the borrowers more time, depending on the date of commencement of commercial operations. Many such loans have been restructured twice and continue to be tagged as standard assets in the banks' books. Often, the date of commencement of commercial operations is subject to interpretation and the RBI may not be comfortable with such cases.

Financial Innovations

The real issue lies elsewhere. While conducting the AQR, the RBI inspectors had found many instances of the same loan exposure being classified as bad by one bank, but good by another. How does this happen? Well, this is a kind of financial innovation which some of the Indian banks are quite good at. They disburse working capital loans to the stressed companies which help them service their term loans; they also disburse fresh loans already sanctioned—again to help the borrowers pay back the loan instalments. There are also instances of banks giving new loans to other group companies of stressed borrowers for the same purpose. I know of quite a few such instances, but I am not suggesting that these three banks have resorted to such practices, technically called 'evergreening'.

There have been many instances where the auditors of a bank do not agree with the management point of view on certain loan accounts and they make their displeasure public in the notes to the accounts.

Now, we are seeing the divergence between the bank management's treatment of a loan account (endorsed by its auditors) and that of the banking regulator's.

Interestingly, the RBI has refrained from taking any action against such banks and left it to the market to punish them. By disclosing the divergences, the banks run reputation risks, but what about the auditors? Both the banks and their auditors are under the RBI's watch now and they will not be able to continue with such practices for long.

LIFE AFTER KINGFISHER FOR INDIAN BANKS

5 April 2016

The person who did this act on the Indian banking system and others who may be planning further such acts are evil people. They don't represent the business community; they don't represent a legitimate group of promoters. They are flat bank defaulters. The only thing they can think about is default. As a nation of good folks, we are going to hunt them down; and we are going to find them, and we will bring them to justice.

The search is under way for those who are behind these defaults—the rogue promoters as well as the bankers who facilitate the loans that go bad. We will direct the full resources of our intelligence and law enforcement communities to find those responsible and bring them to justice. We will make no distinction between the promoters who committed these acts and those who facilitated them.

God bless India.

Given a choice, the Indian government, politicians of different hues as well as a part of the media would have loved to address the nation this way after UB Group chairman Vijay Mallya, whose grounded Kingfisher Airlines Ltd has not returned some Rs 91 billion to a consortium of banks led by State Bank of India, left for the UK on 2 March.

I will not be surprised if Mallya says he is afraid of coming back to India as he runs the risk of being lynched by a mob. Bankers too are scurrying for cover as everybody is questioning their expertise and integrity.

I don't have great admiration for Mallya. Only once I came close to saying hello to him at his Mumbai office, but the meeting, arranged by his communication executive, never took place. I left after waiting for close to two hours. I cannot comment on other allegations against Mallya, but punctuality has certainly never been his virtue.

While none can question the efforts of getting Mallya back to India and recovering the money from him since he had offered a personal guarantee to the banks when the loan was restructured, the collective rhetoric against defaulters and public-sector bankers could end up killing the industry as well as the banks. As we are painting everybody with the same brush, it is blurring the distinction between the bad and the ugly among the borrowers, and fast diminishing bankers' appetite for risk.

The multibillion-dollar Eurotunnel, the undersea rail link between Britain and France, has been a nightmare for lenders because of cost overruns that forced massive debt restructuring in 2007. Globally, business failures and commercial decisions going wrong are a reality, but can we criminalize business failures? If we do so, banks will stop lending to the industry and the government's efforts to push up the contribution of manufacturing to India's economy from the current level will limp.

Venture capital can support start-ups, but we need bank loans if big projects are to take off. Indeed, we can shift the focus and decide to become an agrarian economy, but even that won't solve the problem as farm loan waivers will always remain a threat to the banking system's health and credit culture.

So, what's the way forward?

In developed markets, the banking system typically meets the need of the retail borrowers while the corporate bond market takes care of the money that large industrial houses require, and the creation of infrastructure is the responsibility of the government. In India, the banks are expected to do all.

Till the late 1990s, banks had mostly focused on giving working capital loans. Sensing an opportunity, they got into retail financing early this century even as the death of the development finance institutions such as the Industrial Credit and Investment Corporation of India (ICICI) and Industrial Development Bank of India pushed the banks into project financing. They love displaying the tag of a universal bank which can do everything under the sun, but the bankers never developed the skill for appraisal of projects and monitoring them.

Project Appraisals

For project appraisals, they typically depend on chartered accountants, external valuers, the so-called lenders' engineers or the agency involved in technical due diligence and risk assessment of projects, and investment banks such as SBI Capital Markets. Since the investment banks are appointed by the borrowers, they often end up selling many not-so-credit-worthy projects to the banking community.

Since the public-sector banks can neither develop project appraisal skills overnight nor pay top dollars to attract talent from the market, it's time they set up a project appraisal agency for doing this job. In 1987, ICICI, Unit Trust of India and a few other financial institutions had set up India's first credit rating agency, Crisil Ltd. Almost three decades later, a similar structure can be replicated for a different purpose.

State Bank of India can take the lead and a few others can chip in with equities and set up such an agency. It must be run by competent professionals who understand the risks and rewards of giving money to different sectors. The bankers should have nothing to do with such an institution, barring setting this up and outsourcing project appraisals to it.

Indeed, external developments such as delays in getting regulatory clearances will lead to time and cost overruns and jeopardize the viability of certain projects, but to some extent, such an agency will put a lid on the fresh creation of bad loans. However, what should be done with the stock of bad assets?

For the listed banks, the rise in bad assets has been close to a trillion rupees in the December quarter—from Rs 3.4 trillion to Rs 4.38 trillion. After provisions, net non-performing assets, or NPAs, of the banking industry in the December quarter crossed Rs 2.5 trillion, and the state-run banks account for more than 90 per cent of this. According to a Reserve Bank of India estimate, in the September quarter, the combination of recognized NPAs, restructured assets as well as written-off assets was to the tune of

17 per cent for public-sector banks and 14.1 per cent for the industry. I bet both will rise further in the March quarter as banks continue their clean-up drive, goaded by the regulator.

Over the past fortnight, Finance Minister Arun Jaitley has reiterated that the banks must endeavour to get back every single penny lent to corporate houses. In a rare advisory last Friday, the government—the majority owner of the public-sector banks—instructed the lenders to start invoking personal guarantees of promoters and recover the dues without losing time in case companies have failed to repay the loans. An eminent lawyer himself, Jaitley is well aware of the legal framework within which the banks operate.

Legal Hurdles

There were some 72,500 pending cases in the debt recovery tribunals, or DRTs, in December 2015 involving close to Rs 4 trillion, a little less than the heap of bad assets of listed banks at that time. A quasi-judicial forum to facilitate debt recovery by banks, a DRT is expected to dispose of a case that banks refer to it within 180 days, but each of the thirty-three DRTs operating in India are struggling with 2200 pending cases on average every year.

The Securitization and Reconstruction of Financial Assets and Enforcement of Security Interest (SARFAESI) Act, a 2002 law, empowers banks to attach assets of defaulters, but it is easier said than done as the DRTs are not equipped to handle so many cases even as the defaulters move from such tribunals to high courts and even the Supreme Court to buy time.

In the Mallya case, the banks had moved the DRTs in 2012. There have been at least twenty cases pending and hundreds of hearings and adjournments at different DRTs, high courts and the Supreme Court. The efforts to recover money have been on for four years, but everybody has woken up only now, after Mallya left the country.

And here is how the cases referred to the DRTs swelled in the past five years in tandem with the rise in banks' bad debt. In 2011, the tribunals disposed of 12,122 cases involving Rs 211.55 billion, but there were 54,061 cases pending and the amount involved was to the tune of Rs 1.46 trillion. In 2012, the number of pending cases dropped to 41,205 and the amount involved to Rs 1.31 trillion, but in 2013, the number of cases rose to 47,933 and the money involved increased to Rs 1.79 trillion. In 2014, there were 59,645 cases involving Rs 3.75 trillion. Going by its past record, even if the banks do not move the tribunals with a single fresh case, it will take at least six years to clear the pending cases.

The proposed bankruptcy code will not be able to change the scenario overnight. It is too aggressive even by the standards of the developed markets and it will not be easy to implement unless the government puts in place the right logistics.

Recapitalize and Privatize

Everybody seems to be agitated on bank recapitalization, and rightly so. After all, why should the government continue to use taxpayers' money to keep the public-sector banks alive? Including the Rs 250-billion bank recapitalization announced in the recent budget, the government will end up spending close to Rs 930 billion in the six years since 2010 to keep these banks running. Higher NPAs also prevent banks from paying a higher interest rate to the depositors and lower loan rate to the borrowers, as they struggle to set aside money to provide for bad loans, and that erodes their profitability.

The best solution is, of course, privatization. Instead of pushing for consolidation, the government should decide to bring its stake in public-sector banks to below 50 per cent and stop sending advisories to them. The chances of getting the money back from privately run banks is far more than public banks as they will continue to make the same mistakes and need more money in future.

After the collapse of Lehman Brothers, the US Treasury announced a Troubled Asset Relief Program, or TARP, of up to $700 billion to save its privately managed banks from being submerged in the sub-prime mortgage crisis. Till 14 March, $619 billion has been invested, loaned or paid out by the treasury even as the banks have returned $683 billion in the form of interest, dividend and fees. The treasury has earned some $64.5 billion, or more than 10 per cent return, on its investment. The Indian government cannot expect such returns from its fund infusion in the public-sector banks unless they are privatized.

Since this will not happen anytime soon as the government does not have the stomach to take such a politically sensitive decision, it must address issues such as strengthening the legal system and the bank boards, and building expertise by offering the right incentives on a war-footing.

An aggressive fishing expedition on every defaulter and banks may do more harm than good to the economy unless India has many Walt Disneys who have unique business ideas and can fund their own projects.

WHAT'S NEXT, MR VIJAY MALLYA?

14 March 2016

The Indian banking industry has no dearth of defaulters. Not even the so-called 'wilful defaulters', who have the capacity to pay, but don't or divert loans for other purposes.

So, what's so special about Vijay Mallya, the flamboyant chairman of UB Group, whose grounded Kingfisher Airlines Ltd has not returned some Rs 91 billion to a consortium of banks, led by State Bank of India? Why is there so much noise in the media? This is probably because of Mallya's blatant exhibition of wealth. His sixtieth birthday bash in Goa in December and frequent offerings of gold on previous birthdays at the Venkateswara shrine in Tirupati in Andhra Pradesh, among other things (they are so well known that it is not worth repeating), show the gap between his personal wealth and the indebtedness of his company.

'Limited Liability'

A promoter of a company can have money and still get away with not repaying the banks because of the so-called 'limited liability' concept outlined in the Companies Act. Liability connotes responsibility. The law caps promoters' liability in a joint stock company to the extent of their shareholding in the company even if the firm owes ten times the amount to the banks and goes bankrupt.

The same is applicable to limited liability partnership, or LLP firms, where the liability of the partners is limited to their individual contribution to the capital of the firm. The Companies Act, 2013, has also introduced the concept of a one-person company to encourage entrepreneurship, where the director's liability is limited to the amount subscribed in the share capital.

However, the Companies Act makes the promoter responsible under various sections with regard to civil and criminal liability for fraud, misuse of company's funds and personal gain resulting from misuse of office powers which are delegated by the board. In case of listed companies, more stringent rules apply if a promoter makes a misstatement in the offer document when it goes for listing. The Companies Act, 2013, has increased monetary penalties and imprisonment on directors, including the so-called 'officers in default'—the whole-time directors, the key managerial personnel and every director who is aware of a contravention of law, but never raised any objection at board meetings.

Breach of Contract

So, what does all this mean for the lenders to Kingfisher? Well, banks give loans to companies after signing a contract and any default in repayment is a breach of contract and not a criminal offence. Even wilful default per se is not a crime under the Indian Penal Code. Of course, a wilful defaulter can be prosecuted for criminal misappropriation of funds and/or forgery. The onus in such cases is on the lenders to prove the criminal intent of the borrower.

The Serious Fraud Investigation Office, or SFIO, set up under the new Companies Act, can also get involved in such cases. (It has done so in this particular case.) The SFIO is empowered to initiate an investigation in public interest or on a request from any department of the central or state governments, and if found guilty, the fraudster can be put behind bars for up to ten years.

Personal Guarantee

Mallya cannot get the cover of the limited liability concept—which he claimed to be enjoying in his statement issued late night on 6 March ('All the enquiries conducted have failed to find any evidence of misappropriation of funds by Kingfisher Airlines or myself . . . Absent any fraud, the concept of corporate limited liability cannot be ignored')—because he had given his personal guarantee for the Kingfisher loan. He, in fact, had charged the banks Rs 980 million for offering this guarantee. Once the Reserve Bank of India got wind of this, it asked the banks to recover the money. The amount was initially debited from Kingfisher Airlines' liability to the banks in its 2010–11 profit and loss account, but the next year, the entry was reversed, doing away with the fee.

Since its inception in 2005, Kingfisher had never posted a profit. Its losses zoomed after it acquired low-cost airline Deccan Aviation Ltd in 2007. Between fiscal 2008–09 and September 2012—around the time it was grounded—its accumulated losses reached Rs 80.158 billion. By 31 March 2013, its accumulated losses had zoomed to Rs 160.2346 billion, making its net worth a negative Rs 129.1982 billion.

Globally, more airlines have gone bankrupt than companies in any other sector. Why did the banks take such a large exposure to Kingfisher? It seems their assessment was based more on impressions than facts. Mallya, a member of the Rajya Sabha and who appeared to emulate the flashy lifestyle of Virgin Group's Richard Branson, knew how to convince the bankers. (By the way, Mallya is not particularly fond of the Branson comparison—he would rather have Branson be called the UK's Mallya!) At its peak, Kingfisher was flying sixty-six planes to sixty-eight locations, including eight international destinations, with 374 flights a day, and accounted for 20 per cent of the market.

The Kingfisher debt was first restructured in November 2010 when the bankers' consortium converted Rs 13.55 billion of debt into equity, at a 61.6 per cent premium to the market price of Kingfisher Airlines' stock. Following this, banks owned 23.21 per cent of the airline's equity. The promoter too converted Rs 6.48 billion of debt into equity. Apart from this, the bankers also stretched the period of repayment of loans to nine years with a two-year moratorium, and cut the interest rates and sanctioned a fresh loan.

Business Model

With the price of jet fuel at its peak and a business model in which the focus was more on in-flight experience than on timely arrivals of planes and rationalization of routes, it could not have survived. The fuel price peaked at $147 a barrel in August 2008. The price has dropped to a little over $40 a barrel now, declining close to 73 per cent from its peak. Kingfisher also started flying to international destinations after its acquisition of the low-cost Air Deccan when the economic slowdown had already gripped the world.

A foreign airline could have done the rescue act. Mallya discussed the matter with a couple of them and tried his best to change the law that did not allow a foreign airline to pick up a stake in Kingfisher even as foreign entities were permitted to pick up to 49 per cent, but failed. (Foreign entities could hold a stake in Indian aviation, but foreign airlines could not, which they can now.) By end-2012, it was curtains for Kingfisher Airlines.

The rating company Crisil Ltd downgraded Kingfisher Airlines' credit rating to its lowest 'D' grade, denoting default. Probably, the lenders did a desktop Excel sheet exercise while restructuring the loan and did not probe deep. Incidentally, even in 2008, the company's gearing ratio, or the ratio of its long-term debt to its equity capital, was 3.54 against the industry average of 2.06.

Securities on Offer

Since most airlines lease aircraft, banks do not get planes as primary security for loans given to airlines. So, while doing the restructuring, the banks took a couple of Mallya's properties in Mumbai and Goa, helicopters and shares of group companies United Spirits Ltd and Mangalore Chemicals and Fertilizers Ltd as collaterals. Banks also took a first charge on fixed assets such as coaches that ferry passengers to the tarmac, and tractors, besides a corporate guarantee from United Breweries (Holdings) Ltd, the group holding company, and the Kingfisher brand, which audit firm Grant Thornton India valued at Rs 30 billion.

The sale of properties and shares has generated some money for the banks, but not enough to cover their entire exposure. (Mallya claims that the banks have recovered Rs 12.44 billion from the sale of pledged shares and that another Rs 12.50 billion has been lying with the Karnataka High Court, but bankers are giving a smaller figure.

Kingfisher House in Mumbai, the company's headquarters, is being auctioned, with the reserve price at Rs 1.5 billion.)

The bankers are now training their guns on Mallya's personal assets, which he has in plenty. They have a legitimate claim on the $75 million that Diageo Plc is paying Mallya—a severance package for quitting as chairman of USL—since he had given the personal guarantee. They can also lay claim to all his assets strewn over the US, the UK and other parts of Europe, South Africa and India. But it won't be a cakewalk.

Hounded by investigation agencies, Mallya left India on 2 March, but through his statements and multiple tweets, he claims that he is not absconding.

Three Possibilities

First, Mallya may never come back to India. And if he chooses to live in London, he will not be the first Indian to do so. Lalit Modi, the first chairman and commissioner of the Indian Premier League, has also been accused of alleged financial irregularities like Mallya, and has been living in London since 2010. It will not be easy to extradite Mallya from London unless the bankers are able to prove that he has committed serious criminal offences.

Second, Mallya may come back and decide to fight the legal battle that could go on for years. Even though he had given personal guarantees, getting hold of his personal assets may not be easy as he may have created trusts to manage them. Even after giving a personal guarantee to bankers, one can sell assets or ring-fence them by creating trusts as long as they are not attached by a court order. The obligation of a personal guarantor is more moral than legal till the time it is invoked. Of course, Mallya would need to fight on other fronts too—including charges of money laundering.

Finally, the banking community and Mallya can reach a settlement following which the banks may get back a substantial portion of their loans, but not the entire sum. (In his statement,

Mallya had mentioned about his efforts to reach a one-time settlement with the banks and claimed to have had three meetings.)

Can Mallya be made an example of—similar to Subrata Roy of Sahara India—and sent to Tihar Jail? Probably not, as his approach to the country's court of law is very different from that of Roy's, who has been in Tihar Jail for about two years now, writing books.

A Lesson for All

While we wait and watch how the drama unfolds, the fight between Mallya and the Indian banking system is a lesson both for promoters and bankers. While the promoters will be wary of the fact that crony capitalism cannot always win, the bankers must learn how to assess credit risks. And if indeed some influential ministers had played a key role in ensuring the restructuring of the Kingfisher loan in 2010, as a few bankers say in private, they should also not be spared.

Along with recovering the money, the investigation agencies must also uncover how an airline with Kingfisher's business model could get so much funding from the banking system. Was it Mallya's persuasive power or the banks' naivety in assessing the risks or something more that's not in the public domain?

AMTEK AUTO: BANKS TO BLAME FOR BLOATED DEBT

(Part I)

7 December 2015

The Cabinet approval for the recast of power distribution companies by converting their loans into state government bonds will pare Indian banks' pile of stressed assets—now around 14 per cent of their loan portfolio. Once bank loans to such companies to the tune of about Rs 4.3 trillion get converted into bonds, there will be relief, and banks' stressed assets will come down to around 10 per cent.

However, it's too early to uncork the bottle of champagne as yet. There are a few hurdles that will come in the way of attempts to take the scheme from the drawing board to action. More importantly, there will be many more instances of high-value loans turning bad which have not been accounted for. We can say the banks are hiding or postponing the inevitable or even trying hard to resolve them, depending on whether we are brutally frank, mildly critical or empathize with the bankers—a motley group of smart, super-efficient and inefficient professionals.

One such exposure is the Amtek Auto Group. And it is not small—a debt burden of Rs 211.34 billion in June 2015: a combination of bonds, term loans, working capital loans and external commercial borrowings, or ECBs.

The group is under stress and its latest earnings—a consolidated loss of Rs 9.87 billion for the year that ended on 30 September (for the first time since 2004), against a net profit of Rs 8.4821 billion the previous year—aren't good news for the lenders. Amtek Auto follows the October–September financial year. For the September quarter, its stand-alone loss is Rs 1586.2 million against a net profit of Rs 743.7 million a year ago.

Its total income for the year dropped to Rs 152.134 billion from Rs 157.066 billion a year ago and the bulk of the erosion happened in the September quarter—a fall to Rs 8.338 billion from Rs 10.421 billion a year earlier.

The Delhi-based company, one of the world's largest auto parts makers and suppliers to almost every carmaker in India and many overseas, hit the headlines when it defaulted on repayment of bonds worth Rs 8 billion. But that happened in September, so why one more piece on Amtek?

Well, this is an attempt to put things in perspective—how the banking system is used to whet a typical Indian promoter's appetite for building an empire of related and unrelated businesses across different geographies. The story is probably not new, but since Arvind Dham, the promoter of Amtek Auto, is a first-generation entrepreneur, it's an interesting case study.

I have not sought his version while writing this piece, which is primarily based on research and interaction with the banking community. And of course, the company information is available in the public domain.

A 6 December *Business Today* piece says Dham has chalked out his retirement plans, with his new abode in the Himalayas nearly ready. Dham, who had played cricket with the likes of Kapil Dev, wants to restrict his involvement to an advisory role after the debt crisis is sorted out. No wonder bankers these days see his nephew Gautam Malhotra, in his mid-thirties, managing director of Amtek Auto, driving the discussions at the negotiation table.

A Fairy-tale Rise

Dham's was a fairy-tale rise. After dabbling in the small family business of construction for two years, in 1987 he shifted his focus to auto components, something close to his heart, when Suzuki selected him as one of the vendors for Maruti. Amtek Auto was incorporated in 1988. In 1993, the company started forging operations in Gurgaon, and three years later, in 1996, set up a machining unit there. In 1997, it entered into a joint-venture agreement with Benda Kogyo Japan and formed Benda Amtek Ltd for making flywheel ring gears. That was the beginning of a series of foreign collaborations and acquisitions over the next one and a half decades. The list is a mile long, but let's highlight some of them.

In 1999, it entered into a joint venture with Ateliers de Siccardi and formed Amek Siccardi at Manesar for making crankshafts. Two years later, it acquired auto component manufacturer Wesman Halverscheidt Forgings and took over the Indsil Auto Components Coimbatore (India) Ltd, a fully automated foundry with machining facilities. In 2002, it set up an iron casting facility at Bhiwadi, Rajasthan, and acquired 14.5 per cent in Ahmednagar Forgings Ltd, later ramping up the stake.

Then in 2005, it acquired a 70 per cent stake in Zelter GmbH and the very next year signed an equal-partnership joint venture with a large Canadian company, Magna Powertrain, for making two-piece flex plate assemblies for automotive applications. Another joint venture followed with the same firm.

In the next few years, it set up a high-pressure aluminium die-casting facility and another unit for forging, casting and machining (both in Pune), expanded the capacity of machined auto parts and forging, and acquired a very large, precision automobile machining company, Triplex Keltron Group, Amtek's strongest competitor, running close to 185 different machining lines in various parts of the UK.

It didn't stop there. In 2008, it signed a joint-venture agreement with the leading US railcar maker, American Railcar Industries Inc., and another with FormTech Industries LLC, based in Royal Oak, Michigan, to set up a facility for making Hatebur hot forgings in India and Europe.

The collapse of the US investment bank Lehman Brothers Holding Inc. in September 2008 and the dramatic drop in consumer demand that followed in its aftermath did not dampen Dham's spirit. With equal gusto, he floated joint ventures with the Japanese steel maker Sumitomo Metal Industries Ltd and the Israeli firm Enertec Management Ltd, and expanded capacity at local units at a breakneck speed.

How the Cookie Crumbled

There was super-aggressive growth both in India and overseas, backed by plenty of money available in the form of cash flow from business as well as bank loans. The composition of the business too changed.

Over the past two years, Amtek's international business has grown to 44 per cent of total revenue and 24 per cent of the total EBITDA, or earnings before interest, taxes, depreciation and amortization—a metric used to measure a company's operational profitability—but it has only a 7 per cent share in the total group debt.

If this sounds a bit vague, look at the figures. I don't have the September data. For the nine months ending in June 2015, Amtek Auto had a revenue of Rs 29.40 billion, other Indian entities were Rs 43.05 billion, and the contribution from international business came to Rs 57.14 billion, taking the total to Rs 129.60 billion.

When it comes to EBITDA, in June, Amtek Auto had Rs 7.81 billion, other Indian entities Rs 9.94 billion while the overseas operations' contribution was Rs 5.46 billion. The total was Rs 23.21 billion.

Now comes the most interesting piece of this puzzle: the debt. Amtek Auto had a debt of Rs 99.23 billion in June 2015; its other Indian entities, including Ahmednagar Forging and Castex Technologies (formerly, Amtek India Ltd), a debt of Rs 98.11 billion, and international businesses only Rs 14 billion. Out of the total Rs 211.34-billion debt, international businesses' exposure to lenders was only 7 per cent. Simply put, by using the Indian banking system, Amtek has built its international business. But its lenders do not get the benefit of the cash flows from the international business as they have been ring-fenced. How?

In November 2014, Amtek Global Technologies (AGT), the holding company for international businesses, entered into a credit arrangement with KKR & Co. L. P. under which KKR provided AGT with €235 million of long-term financing. While doing so, KKR restricted Amtek and AGT from making any repayment to its group entities and/or any other payment to the Indian entities. These details were not disclosed to lenders in India, coming to light only when Amtek was facing a cash crunch, leading to delayed payment of interest and principle dues to Indian lenders, beginning April 2015.

On a conservative estimate, if Amtek's loan cost is around 10 per cent, it has to serve at least Rs 21 billion in interest alone. How can Amtek serve this when its EBITDA from domestic operations is less than this, around Rs 17.75 billion?

In the six months between September 2014 and March 2015, Amtek Auto's capital expenditure was Rs 16.23 billion. This investment was done in an environment where capacity utilization at the company had been 35 per cent in forgings and castings, 33 per cent in aluminium castings and 50 per cent in machined auto components.

As of March, Amtek Auto had extended Rs 12.30 billion as loans and advances to related parties, including Rs 6.54 billion to its international subsidiaries (AGT, Amtek Deutschland GmbH, Amtek Investments [UK] Ltd, Amtek Germany Holding GP GmbH and Amtek Precision Engineering Pte Ltd).

In addition, since September 2013, Amtek has acquired three international companies—Asahi Tec, Rege Holding GmbH and Scholz Edelstahl GmbH—with a combined revenue of $710 million and at an estimated value of $227 million.

Auto components may be his first love, but the promoter of Amtek believes in diversification—even if that means getting into new businesses which are totally unrelated to his company's core business. So, we find Rollatainers Ltd, a thinly traded public listed firm that offers complete packaging solutions. The promoters of the Amtek Group hold a 75 per cent stake in this company.

Rollatainers, in turn, owns Barista Coffee Co. Ltd, Mapple Hospitality Pvt. Ltd (hotels and restaurants, with a presence in Delhi, Bengaluru, Jodhpur, Corbett and Bhimtal), franchises in India for Wendy's and Jamie's Italian, Welgrow Hotels Pvt. Ltd (which owns the Italian restaurant chain Sartoria) and Kylin, which operates a range of restaurants under the brand names Kylin Premier, Kylin Experience, Kylin Skybar, Go Kylin and Kylin Express.

Then, it has numerous real estate companies in its fold. Some of them are: Adhbhut Infrastructure Ltd, Lotus Infraestates Pvt. Ltd, Hazel Real Estate, Forbes Builders Pvt. Ltd, Ashoka Developers & Builders Ltd, Chandni Realtors Pvt. Ltd, Dhanpat Properties Pvt. Ltd, Dilkhush Buildtech Pvt. Ltd, Ghanshyam Realtors Pvt. Ltd, Kusham Real Estate Pvt. Ltd, Rista Developers Pvt. Ltd and Radhika Buildprop Pvt. Ltd.

Yes, there are other businesses too—OCL Iron and Steel Ltd, Amtek Travels Pvt. Ltd, Amtek Lifestyle Tour Pvt. Ltd, SPT Infotech Pvt. Ltd and Kamakshi Silk Mills Pvt. Ltd. The list could be even longer.

For the lenders, Amtek Auto had been a time bomb ticking away. It failed to repay its institutional holders nearly Rs 8 billion in bonds that were due for redemption on 20 September. Before that, in August, JPMorgan Mutual Fund restricted withdrawals from two of its funds—JP Morgan India Treasury Fund and JPMorgan India Short-Term Income Fund—which have a collective exposure of about Rs 2 billion in Amtek Auto.

The bonds were issued in 2010. Axis Bank Ltd was the lead arranger for the bond issue. Amtek Auto has defaulted on Rs 8 billion of non-convertible debentures (NCDs), including to lenders such as JP Morgan Mutual Fund, IDBI Bank and Axis Bank. Non-convertible debentures are unsecured bonds that cannot be converted to company equity or stock. Media reports indicate that Amtek Auto has selectively repaid high-net-worth individuals holding these bonds, including Bollywood star Aishwarya Rai Bachchan, moviemaker David Dhawan and a few others. Amtek's promoters denied this to the bankers.

BANKS AND THE BLOATED DEBT OF AMTEK AUTO

(Part II)

14 December 2015

On 9 October, Brickwork Ratings India Pvt. Ltd downgraded non-convertible debentures worth Rs 4.84 billion issued by Amtek Auto to a D rating because of delays in servicing debt. Instruments with this rating are in default or are expected to be in default. The revision was on account of delays in the servicing of coupon to debenture holders due on 1 October. There had been a rapid deterioration in the rating. Brickwork's July 2015 rating of Amtek was A+, dropping to C in August and finally D in October.

Care Ratings suspended its ratings in August following the company's failure to furnish information required for monitoring the rating. Till April, Amtek enjoyed an AA rating for its bonds as well as long-term bank debt and A1+ rating for short-term bank debt from Care. In May, the bonds and long-term bank debt ratings were brought down a notch, but the short-term loan continued to enjoy an A1+ rating. A Care note, dated 27 May, said, 'The ratings . . . continued to deliver strength from the experience and the resourcefulness of the promoters.'

In medical parlance, it was like detecting stage 4 cancer in a patient all of a sudden. The only difference is—a patient needs to go to a doctor, but rating agencies are expected to monitor the companies on their own. It seems that they did not smell the rat.

Incidentally, Crisil Ltd, a Standard & Poor's company, too gave the highest rating to the JP Morgan fund that had Amtek paper in its portfolio. It had assigned the AAAmfs rating to the JP Morgan India treasury scheme in May, signifying the highest portfolio credit quality. Such a rating is normally arrived at after examining the ratings of the outstanding portfolio of a mutual fund. The methodology of assigning ratings to a mutual fund scheme is typically based on shadow ratings of the papers of the companies in which the fund has invested and the ratings of which may not be available in the public domain.

In August, after the public ratings of the automotive components firm were either suspended or downgraded by other raters, Crisil revised the scheme rating in three stages over two months: first, on 1 September, it downgraded it from AAAmfs to A+mfs and then, on 29 September, to BBBmfs (overall, an eight-notch downgrade in one month), and then on 15 October, it placed the scheme on the so-called 'notice of withdrawal'.

What Has Amtek Been Doing to Get Out of the Mess?

First, in September, $80 million worth of foreign currency convertible bonds (FCCBs), floated by Castex Technologies Ltd, got converted into equity, giving breathing space to the group. Or, so it thought.

The FCCB holders have written to India's capital markets regulator Securities and Exchange Board of India (SEBI) and the bourses, saying the prices of Castex Technologies shares were artificially pushed up for a certain period of time, triggering a clause in the agreement that permits the company to enforce the conversion of FCCBs into equity. A foreign currency convertible bond is a type of convertible bond issued in a currency different from the issuer's domestic currency.

In other words, the money being raised by the issuing company is in the form of a foreign currency. A convertible bond is a mix between a debt and equity instrument. The clause states that if the Castex share trades at a price higher than approximately Rs 160 for a period of one month, the company can enforce conversions. Castex shares rose from a low of Rs 40 in March to consistently trade above Rs 160 a share between June and August, reaching a peak of Rs 360 in July, inducing the conversion of the FCCBs. However, after August, the price is back to Rs 40 per share.

Although a SEBI investigation is under way, recent media reports indicate that the ongoing investigation has not yet found any evidence of market manipulation.

Bank Exposure to the Group

As of 31 May, a group of nineteen banks and financial institutions had major exposure to the group in the form of term loans, besides many other banks that had given working capital loans and foreign currency loans, and subscribed to its bonds. The consortium had sanctioned Rs 37.95 billion worth of term loans and disbursed Rs 33.2926 billion. IDBI Bank Ltd and State Bank of India are the leaders of the consortium. IDBI Bank sanctioned Rs 4.5 billion and disbursed Rs 2.62 billion. SBI sanctioned and disbursed Rs 3.5 billion. Others include State Bank of Bikaner and Jaipur (Rs 2.2 billion sanctioned and Rs 1.5 billion disbursed, respectively), Canara Bank (Rs 3 billion, fully disbursed), IFCI Ltd (Rs 3.5 billion), Life Insurance Corp. of India (Rs 3 billion), State Bank of Mysore, State Bank of Patiala and Bank of Baroda (Rs 2 billion each), Oriental Bank of Commerce, Allahabad Bank and ICICI Bank Ltd (Rs 1.5 billion each).

Additionally, Amtek had sold bonds worth Rs 19.30 billion. The Rs 8-billion default is part of this.

IDBI Bank, Canara Bank, Punjab National Bank, Bank of Baroda and a few others have exposure to Amtek to the tune of $350 million worth of foreign currency loans, with IDBI Bank having the maximum exposure, $185 million.

IDBI Bank has also given the Amtek group working capital loans, albeit in a small quantity—Rs 47.50 billion out of Rs 15.97 billion. Corporation Bank, Andhra Bank and Indian Overseas Bank together account for the rest.

Then, there is a group of unsecured creditors too, mostly foreign banks such as Deutsche Bank AG, Crédit Agricole SA, Citibank NV, Standard Chartered Bank PLC, Bank of Nova Scotia, among others. The total exposure here is a little over $163 million. Two Indian entities on this list are Kotak Mahindra Bank Ltd and Yes Bank Ltd.

None of the banks have classified its exposure to Amtek as a bad loan and hence have not provided for it. Amtek has managed to keep its outstanding dues to within ninety days—and continues to do so.

Which is why almost all the lenders have classified Amtek as SMA-2, or special mention account.

As written earlier, the SMA-2 category refers to those accounts where the principal or interest payment is overdue for sixty-one to ninety days. This is the third stage in an account's progress to becoming a non-performing asset after SMA-0 (where the principal or interest payment is not overdue for more than thirty days, but the account shows signs of incipient stress) and SMA-1 (where the principal or interest payment is overdue for thirty-one to sixty days). Once a borrower is not able to service the account for ninety days, it becomes an NPA and the lenders need to set aside money for such an account.

Once a loan account worth Rs 50 million or more is classified as an SMA, banks are expected to report all relevant data to the Central Repository of Information on Large Credits, set up by the Reserve Bank of India. In accordance with the RBI norms, when a loan account starts showing signs of stress, bankers are required to create a Joint Lenders' Forum (JLF) to chalk out an action plan. The creation of a JLF is mandatory when a relatively large account—with an exposure of at least Rs 1 billion—is categorized as SMA-2, even as the lenders always have the option of setting up the forum for smaller accounts.

If the existing promoters are not in a position to bring in additional money or take any measures to regularize the account, the JLF can explore the possibility of getting new investors in the company in consultation with the borrower. The account can be restructured if it is prima facie viable and the borrower is not a wilful defaulter who has resorted to fund diversion. If these two options are not feasible, the JLF can initiate a recovery process. All decisions of the JLF need to be endorsed by a minimum of 75 per cent of lenders by value and 60 per cent by number.

The Amtek management has indicated to the banks that the majority of lenders have agreed to the proposal under the JLF and received internal approvals for rollovers, interest financing, etc. It is urging others to give their approval to get it going. According to Amtek, the delay in completion of the financing is because the group has had to deal with multiple banks on a one-on-one basis and that has taken time, although the recent RBI guidelines in this regard are helpful and will speed up the process.

Three group firms are involved in debt restructuring: Amtek Auto, Ahmednagar Forging and Castex Technologies. IDBI Bank is leading the discussion on Amtek Auto, while SBI is leading on Ahmednagar Forging and Castex Technologies. Discussions have been veering around the restructuring of the group debt into two parts—the infusion of funds by its promoter and the banks to take care of immediate working capital needs and the recasting of existing debt by extending maturity to ten years, including a two-year payment holiday. This is to take care of the firm's tight liquidity situation.

As a precondition for pumping in Rs 12.50 billion of fresh loans, the banks are asking the promoters to infuse Rs 2.20 billion. So far, the promoters have infused Rs 750 million as part of their contribution. For additional cash infusion, the promoters may need to rely on the sale of their interests in other businesses, including food, hospitality and real estate.

Given that the domestic business performance has not yet shown signs of revival, the company has very little option but to rely on divestitures to pare its debt. It has appointed Morgan Stanley to evaluate sale options for international assets as well as for a significant minority position (up to 40 per cent) in its international business holding company. Media reports suggest that Amtek Auto might end up selling Tekfor, the German forging company it had acquired in 2013, for Rs 60 billion.

The Lesson for the Bankers

What are the lessons for the bankers from the Amtek story? Nothing can substitute close monitoring of the businesses of a borrower. In this case, they did not do that. How could a company keep on building capacity when there was no demand and when it has been on a buying spree overseas supported by debt from domestic banks? A loan restructuring may give them temporary relief and postpone the inevitable, unless promoter Arvind Dham is serious about going to the Himalayas and selling off all non-core businesses and some of the overseas assets to clean up the balance sheet.

Even if a bankruptcy law comes into force and banks are empowered to take over a company, they do not have the expertise to run it. And if they make use of the current strategic debt restructuring programme, which gives them the right to change the management of a stressed company, who will run such units?

Bhushan Steel Ltd is a case in point. Banks have a collective exposure of Rs 350 billion to the steel company and it is now an albatross hanging around their necks. Along with project appraisal, risk management and strict monitoring, Indian banks also need to develop the outsourcing skills to run companies if they need to clean up their balance sheets of bad loans.

6

Corruption: The Soft Underbelly of Indian Banking

It doesn't happen often, but there have been instances when a bank chief's tenure has been cut short by the government for alleged irregularities. There have been arrests too for taking bribes and approving loans without discretion.

The columns in this chapter discuss in detail the modus operandi of such deals, the banker–broker nexus, the gift culture and the phenomenon of 'suitcase' banking. Each column was provoked by a specific event—such as the arrest of a CEO of a bank or his removal from office—and delved deep into the problem of corruption in public-sector banks.

Are most bankers corrupt? Do the low pay structure and lack of financial incentives lead to corruption? The answer to both these questions is an emphatic 'no'. There are public-sector bankers who take enormous pride in what they do despite the abysmally wretched pay they get compared to their private peers. They may be efficient or not so efficient, but no temptation can taint them. But there are a few—as in all other professions—who spoil the pack. Also, not all private-sector bankers have impeccable integrity, but since they are not subjected to the scrutiny by the investigative agencies, we do not hear much about corruption among them.

As bankers deal with money and as banking is all about trust, the tolerance for a corrupt banker is extremely low. A banker taking bribe is as bad as a murder or a rape in police custody.

The pieces in this chapter detail the 'whys' and 'hows' of corruption—something to which this author has had a ringside view. They are all real-life stories; only the characters are not named.

THE BANKER–BROKER NEXUS

20 December 2010

If a non-banking financial company official receives a text message from a banker saying 'all is well', what does the banker actually mean? Is he making a vanilla statement saying everything is fine at his end? The company secretary of a large corporation tells me this means the loan for which the NBFC is lobbying with the bank as a broker is through. 'All is well' indicates the banker's confirmation of a deal.

At the next stage, more text messages follow. They could be saying 'Chinese cuisine', 'Punjabi food' or 'Gujarati thali'. What do these mean? While the first message refers to the scale (a buzzword in China, this means the quantum of the bribe that the banker needs to close the deal is hefty), the other two messages explain the mode of transaction. So, when an NBFC official sees his mobile phone screen flashing two words—'Punjabi food'—he knows the banker's objects of desire are consumer durables, expensive watches or gold ornaments, while 'Gujarati thali' refers to crisp currency notes.

The banking and broking circle in Mumbai have been talking about these text messages between greedy bankers (not too many of them are around, but as you know, one rotten apple spoils the sack) and a few smart officials of the so-called boutique NBFCs who bribe the bankers to get loans for their corporate clients (here again, not all of them fall in this category).

The provocation for this article is the Central Bureau of Investigation busting a loan racket and arresting quite a few officials of banks and housing finance firms for giving loans to private builders after taking bribes from NBFCs who brokered such deals. In the eye of the storm is Money Matters Financial Services Ltd that recently raised Rs 4.45 billion from institutional investors, and has a phenomenal track record of raising debt for corporations.

My company secretary friend, who does not want to be identified (his firm has not raised any money using Money Matters as a broker) and a few bankers have told me that the practice of giving bribes to get a loan sanctioned is rampant in the Indian financial sector, particularly among public-sector banks.

While the bankers say small loans of up to Rs 50 million that get sanctioned by relatively lower-level officers are susceptible to such a practice, the company secretary says bribes are given even for large loans, particularly those given to builders. I am not privy to any specific case, but after talking to many in the industry, have got a sense of how such deals are struck.

There are many boutique NBFCs that provide debt advisory and syndication services, and bright young B-school graduates work for them. They are creative in their approach to work. They call themselves investment bankers, arrangers, loan syndicators, financial intermediaries, and hate to be dubbed as brokers. In most cases, they handhold corporations during the first stage of arrangement of a loan; however, there are instances when they step in at the last moment on the insistence of bankers to rescue a deal.

Typically, the lenders are public-sector banks. Since they are listed entities, business growth, valuations and price-earnings multiples are critical for them. They make conference calls with investors every quarter after announcing their earnings, and the pressure is always there to grow the asset book.

When a loan proposal comes from a firm, banks generally take their own time to discuss it. An impatient firm, with a broker in tow, follows up with a junior officer who introduces him to his proximate boss. At this stage, the senior officer explains to his colleague how such loans can be sanctioned without violating any credit appraisal norms and asks for elementary stuff such as outstanding bank loan rating, promoter holding, names of existing bankers, etc.

At the next stage, the firm returns with all relevant data to the senior officer's cabin (as contact is already established). The loan proposal is now ready to travel to the meeting of the credit committee, but the senior officer suddenly digs holes in the proposal and only the financial intermediary can fill in those holes. The banker sends the text messages to the intermediary ('all is well', and so on) who charges fee for bailing out the firm and spends part of the fee to arrange for the

'Punjabi food' or 'Gujarati thali' for the banker. The top management often does not take a critical look as it is chasing growth in assets.

The professional charges towards arrangement and structuring fees usually range from 0.5 per cent to 3 per cent of the money raised, or even more, depending on the financial health of the firm. This makes the cost of money more expensive for firms, but those who do not have the bandwidth to negotiate with lenders have no other choice. They treat this as part of the financing cost and amortize it over the loan tenure. Theoretically, all loans are required to be rated by credit rating agencies, but banks' internal rating mechanism is also important while sanctioning a loan and fixing the price.

Besides, the credit rating business itself is number-driven, and the rating agencies, in their aggressiveness to grow market share and retain existing clients, are not always particularly careful about their job. I am told this practice is rampant in public-sector banks while private-sector banks are more sophisticated and clinical in their approach while appraising a loan.

My take is that bribes can swing small loans for firms, but it's extremely difficult to 'manage' big loans as too many committees are involved in sanctioning such loans, and you can't bribe all senior executives who are members of such committees. But 'speed money' can sometimes change hands for faster appraisal of loan applications and sanctions. Also, when such exposures are taken through other debt instruments in the form of investments, decisions can be influenced. Finally, a bigger area of concern for an investigating agency could be settlement of bad loans.

Often such loans are settled at hefty discounts and the beneficiaries (corporations) wouldn't mind bribing bankers to get it done. The housing finance scam is unlikely to have any systemic impact as a minuscule portion of banking assets is involved. Besides, bribes may have influenced the loan appraisal and sanction process, but that doesn't necessarily mean that the quality of these assets is suspect. However, this may slow down the decision-making process in public-sector banks that are anyway not known for speedy appraisals and loan disbursals. This is bad news for consumers.

THE MURKY WORLD OF 'SUITCASE BANKING'

25 August 2014

Investors rushed to buy public-sector bank stocks last week after the finance ministry made it clear that the government would look into corporate governance issues and strengthen risk management in these banks in the aftermath of the bribe-for-loan scandal that hit Syndicate Bank and employees of two other state-run banks who were found to have gobbled up depositors' money.

Both the banking regulator and the government, the majority owner of such banks, now seem to be determined to clean up the system. It's not an easy job as the major risk, in some cases, is the senior management itself. But that's one leg of the problem. Who will look into the other leg—the investment banks, non-banking financial companies and advisory services firms that entice bankers to indulge in what the industry calls 'suitcase banking'? Investment banks are regulated by the Securities and Exchange Board of India while the Reserve Bank of India oversees NBFCs. Will they take a close look at the murky world of suitcase banking?

Early this month, when a broker was arrested by the Central Bureau of Investigation in Delhi for his alleged involvement in paying the Syndicate Bank chairman Rs 5 million for approving a loan to a steel company, another broker in downtown Mumbai celebrated the arrest. According to some of his friends, he apparently claimed to have played a part in the arrest by tipping off the investigating agency. Back in November 2010, when this Mumbai broker had been arrested by CBI for his alleged involvement in a similar scam, the other broker—who is currently in judicial custody—had uncorked a bottle of champagne.

For two years, in 2008 and 2009, they had worked together before falling out over differences on profit-sharing. Indeed, profits were huge. Presentations and annual reports of the Mumbai broker's company firm show that he was instrumental in syndicating Rs 500 billion across sectors between 2008 and 2011. He had a virtual monopoly over a government-owned insurer and many public-sector banks. He also tries to use the media to plant stories against his former colleague-turned-foe.

I am not naming either as I could not reach out to them, but I have spoken to many of their employees, friends and 'admirers', former directors of the boards of group companies, regulators, bank officials and peers to get a sense of their world of operations.

Both are chartered accountants. One now runs a publicly traded NBFC with at least Rs 9-billion capital and is planning to delist it. After being charge-sheeted in the 2010 bribes-for-loan scam, he had transferred a bulk of his holdings in his father's name, but he actively runs the company, which has stopped debt syndication and runs a real estate and small and medium enterprise lending business. The debt syndication business is now managed by a different company controlled by the broker and run by his man Friday, a former employee of the NBFC.

The core strategy is to do real estate financing by the listed NBFC, and apart from earning interest, enjoy other benefits in the form of sharing developed space in commercial buildings and residential flats being bought at hefty discounts by companies controlled by the broker and his associates. These deals are under the scrutiny of the regulator and rating agencies.

Pseudo Partnership

The company has been rechristened thrice in the past few years. Originally, he bought one listed NBFC with whom his debt syndication business was merged. After the 2010 bribes-for-loans scam, when his NBFC found it difficult to do business, he forged an alliance with a US-based fund house that agreed to lend one of its group's shell asset management company's name to the broker firm. There was no equity infusion, but the company's name was changed to reflect the relationship with the US outfit.

It is a pseudo partnership which in reality is a trademark and licence agreement without any investment or equity infusion sealed by paying close to $1million to the US fund house for the brand licence. He had raised $100 million in October 2010 through a qualified institutional placement from leading private equity funds.

The broker was arrested in November 2010 in the bribe-for-loan scam. His NBFC does not take public deposits. The bank lines were dried up after he was arrested by the CBI. Currently out on bail, he has been able to revive at least two bank lines of credit (both are based in Maharashtra)—for Rs 500 million each—because of his relationship with bank bosses. He boasts in banking circles that many more are in the pipeline.

He also knows well an asset reconstruction company and often buys at a special rate flats and other properties sold by the company to recover dues. The first information reports in five cases where he was involved allege that this broker, in cahoots with a few others of his company, offered 'illegal gratification' to public servants of banks and institutions for 'arranging suitable investments'. While the CBI cases are on, the Enforcement Directorate (ED) has also apparently stepped in to probe allegations of 'disproportionate wealth'.

The second broker cut his teeth in banking with a Delhi-based financial institution. Later, he worked with new private and foreign banks. A wizard in corporate bond markets, he is soft-spoken and knows well how to cultivate bankers in the right places to get his job done. He is the head of a boutique financial advisory firm and a director on the board of at least five other group companies. Both the gentlemen offer credit solutions, debt capital market and investment banking—a euphemism for bribing bankers to get loans. The second broker apparently has more professional knowledge and capability, and was perceived to be more credible than the first one till he was caught early this month.

Favourite 'Pickup' Line

'Chai' is the favourite beverage of the first broker, as that gives him reason to catch up with high-ranking officials. *'Sir, chai peene aata hun chaar baje aapke paas'* (Sir, I'll be coming to you for a cup of tea at 4 p.m.) would be the favourite 'pickup' line. He has a liking for expensive cufflinks, watches and pens. He would have the latest models of iPhone, iPad, Blackberry, and would be seen juggling between these gadgets while having a conversation with bankers.

Till sometime back, BlackBerry Messenger (BBM) was his preferred mode of communication as it could not be tracked by the government, but now WhatsApp is catching up. Apart from these high-end gadgets, he would always have a few low-end Nokia phones in his car, with SIM cards taken in the names of loyal and long-serving 'office boys'. These phones carry out the 'transactions'. At times, a wireless landline phone would also be seen in the car. Typically, he drives an Audi A6 in Mumbai and a BMW 7 Series while in Delhi. He changes his cars regularly to be in sync with the trend.

The display of expensive cufflinks, watches, pens and phones helps him lure in 'poor' bank officials. A middle-level bank official whose monthly salary would be less than the value of his Swarovski crystal cufflinks or Montblanc pen or BlackBerry Porsche or an iPhone 5, may compliment him on his prized possession. And lo, before his next visit, he would ensure that it reaches the banker's table.

Recently, he bought a watch worth Rs 150,000 to wear to a meeting with one of India's wealthiest men at a wedding in the family of the Gujarat-based businessman. He is a non-smoker and a teetotaller, but knows that popular brands of liquor—Glenfiddich, Talisker, Laphroaig—are all acceptable gifts to senior bankers. 'Sir, I picked it up from duty-free. . . You know I don't drink and I know you're a single-malt connoisseur,' he would say while handing over the bottle sheepishly. Both his office and home are stocked with bottles of single-malt whisky to cater to the corrupt connoisseur.

For bank officials who are not that corrupt, god comes to the broker's rescue. A silver Ganapati idol for Maharashtrians, a silver Balaji wall piece for South Indians, and an expensive Radha–Krishna for North Indians come in handy. He would say, *'Sir, Bhagwan khud dwarpe aye hain, vaapas bhejna theek nah hai'* (God himself has appeared at your doorstep; it's inappropriate to send him back), and a typical God-fearing banker would oblige him.

A fortnight ahead of Diwali, his entire office gets involved in the gifting process. Everybody has to submit their requisition, based on the might of the official concerned and his prospect of becoming an executive director or the chairman of a bank, and the gent would personally oversee the entire process. Vouchers of a retail chain worth Rs 5000 to Rs 50,000 would accompany gold coins for bank officials who don't have the courage to ask for cash.

Round the year, one of his trusted lieutenants runs a 'travel desk' for the corrupt officials. She would book flights, hotels, trips to hill resorts, first-show tickets of movies—whatever the officials want. Standing instructions are issued by him to oblige all requests.

Net Cast Far and Wide

Incidentally, these brokers do not target the banking community alone—insurers, mutual fund managers and even private equity funds also get trapped in their net, cast far and wide. One of the fund managers of an asset management company, owned by a large insurance outfit, used to frequently travel overseas at the expense of the Mumbai-based broker who believes he can buy anybody with wine, women and wealth—not necessarily in this order, though. He has flats in Mumbai to entertain the bankers; at times, even hotel rooms are booked by his company for this purpose. The fund manager was given two high-end cars—a Ford Endeavour and Porsche—registered in the name of the broker's NBFC and he used to stay in a flat provided by the broker.

In 2010, when SEBI mandated that liquid funds also needed to be valued at their market price following the mark-to-market accounting procedure, the asset management company owned by an insurance firm had to take a hit of more than Rs 1 billion as this fund manager had bought all sorts of short-term debt papers under the influence of the broker at a price higher than what was prevailing in the market. The entire money market was aware about his dealings, but because of his clout and blessings from senior officials from the parent company, nobody dared to touch him.

In fact, he was featured as one of India's best fund managers by a financial magazine in 2010. After he was exposed following the arrest of the broker by the CBI, the fund manager was shunted from Mumbai to Delhi and then to Guwahati. A Japanese company later picked up a stake in the asset management firm and the entire loss was absorbed by the insurance company owned by the government.

This broker, who originally hails from Rajasthan, would invest in 'relationships' with high-ranking officials who may not be in a direct position to take decisions, but would pass on information on policy changes and other investment criterion, which he uses deftly.

For instance, the investment committee of a state-run insurance company once decided to pick up double-A rated papers too, besides triple-A rated papers. This piece of information, passed on time, was too precious for the broker. He used it to claim a hefty fee from double-A rated companies (who were not aware of the internal decision) to place their papers with the investment company. In addition to cash benefits, the officials who pass on such information are also promised directorship and advisory roles in his companies, post-retirement. Some of them are now on the board of the broker's NBFC.

This broker prefers to work on 'all-inclusive' mandates. Such mandates do not talk about fee explicitly, but if he manages to get the deal done at an interest rate that is lower than what he had committed, he would pocket the difference. This means that if he commits a 14 per cent rate of interest to a client and 'manages' to get it at 12.5 per cent, he would charge 1.5 per cent as his fee. Such all-inclusive mandates illustrate his confidence in striking deals at a cheaper cost because of the nexus between him and the senior bank officials.

He also claims to play a role in the appointment of chairmen of public-sector banks and even regulators. For him, everything can be done at a price and everybody can be bought. His favourite line is: '*Kitneka aadmi hai?*' (What's the price of this man?). It's time the regulators took a close look at such intermediaries to make the financial system safe.

HOW TO DEAL WITH CORRUPT BOSSES OF STATE-OWNED BANKS

(Part I)

4 August 2014

Now you know why the pile of bad loans in India's state-owned banks has been rising and why both the banking regulator as well as the finance ministry are upset with many bank chiefs.

The official reason behind the growth in bad loans is a faltering economy but everyone knows there is more to it.

Yes, there are bank chiefs who are dishonest. They give loans to those who don't deserve them and make money cutting such deals. They make money, but their banks pay the price. The Reserve Bank of India is well aware of this practice. So is the finance ministry. But they don't openly talk about it as that may shatter public confidence in our banking system, some 70 per cent of which is accounted for by state-owned banks.

On Saturday, the Central Bureau of Investigation arrested Sudhir Kumar Jain, chairman and managing director of Syndicate Bank, for allegedly taking a Rs 5-million bribe. His brothers-in-laws are allegedly involved in the mechanics of the payoff.[1]

Jain, who took charge as chief of Syndicate Bank in July 2013, was allegedly offered the bribe for increasing the credit limit of a few companies, thereby throwing banking norms to the wind. A commerce graduate and a chartered accountant, Jain started his banking career in June 1987 in Dena Bank.

There aren't too many instances of public-sector bank CEOs being arrested by the CBI, but CEOs stepping down before the end

---

[1] 'ÇBI Arrests Syndicate Bank CMD in Rs 50 Lakh Bribery Case', *Times of India*, 3 August 2014, http://timesofindia.indiatimes.com/india/CBI-arrests-Syndicate-Bank-CMD-in-Rs-50-lakh-bribery-case/articleshow/39516363.cms.

of the tenure or being sacked are no novelty. More on them later, but let's first try to understand the modus operandi.

One way of making money is to give loans to a creditor who does not deserve it. The second popular way is giving loans at a price which is lower than what it should have been.

In both cases, the dealmaker pockets a certain portion of the load value (could be a few basis points for big-ticket loans or even a few percentage points for small loans). The third way of money-making is restructuring a weak loan account and giving breathing time to a rogue borrower. I am aware of a former chief of a large public-sector bank whose wife used to cut such deals.

In banking lexicon, such deals are called 'an accommodation', but all such transactions do not necessarily need to involve money. Often a bank chief indulges in such a deal under the influence of politicians in power to ensure a smooth future. And many public-sector bankers entertain politicians from their days as general manager, because this helps them climb the greasy pole and become chairman of the bank.

Many appointments of public-sector bank chiefs are such quid-pro-quo deals. The favour is returned in the form of loan sanctions and other accommodations.

Last year, the CBI arrested Shyamal Acharya, a deputy managing director of State Bank of India, for allegedly taking a bribe in kind—an Omega and a Rolex watch worth Rs 775,000 each. Both the watches were seized from Acharya's cabin by the CBI.[2]

Allegedly, Acharya violated norms for a loan approval. The CBI had filed a case against Acharya, K.K. Kumra, who was an adviser at Worlds Window Group (WWG), and Piyoosh Goyal, founder, WWG. Apparently, Goyal had sought a Rs 4-billion loan from the bank, and Kumra, a former bank official, in turn, got in touch with

---

[2] Virendrasingh Ghunawat, 'CBI Arrests SBI's Ex-official, Interrogates Deputy MD for Taking Bribes', *India Today*, 25 November, 2013, http://indiatoday.intoday.in/story/cbi-arrests-sbis-ex-official-interrogate-deputy-md-for-taking-bribes/1/326495.html.

Acharya, who allegedly influenced his juniors and got Rs 750 million sanctioned, to begin with.

The CBI conducted simultaneous raids at various locations, including offices and residences of Acharya, Kumra and Goyal, and Rs 700,000 in cash was found in Acharya's residence.

The State Bank of India instituted a two-member internal panel to look into the allegation, but could not find any procedural lapses in the Rs 750-million loan sanctioned to the Delhi-based WWG. Acharya's colleagues in the bank say he was 'framed' and that he could never compromise his integrity but the damage has been done to his reputation and he is avoiding public life.

In 2013, the finance ministry sought an explanation from Corporation Bank chairman and managing director Ramnath Pradeep on charges against him by the Central Vigilance Commission over alleged violation of norms.[3] Pradeep faced eight key charges that include sanctioning loans to a few companies in contravention of regulations, extending a big-ticket loan to a tower construction company that had already defaulted on payments to another state-controlled bank, and changing the rules in a bid to appoint a consultant at the bank.

I am not aware of the latest development on this case.

The CBI, in late 2011, had arrested eight senior officials belonging to nationalized banks and financial institutions for allegedly accepting inducements to issue loans to vested parties or leak vital information from their top committees in the so-called loans-to-bribe scam. They were later released on bail.

Tenure Cut Short

There have been many instances when a bank chief's tenure has been cut short by the government for alleged irregularities. For

---

[3] 'Corporation Bank CMD Indicted by CVC on Charges of Corruption and Misuse of Authority', *Moneylife*, 19 August 2011, http://www.moneylife.in/article/corporation-bank-cmd-indicted-by-cvc-on-charges-of-corruption-and-misuse-of-authority/19070.html.

instance, S.C. Basu of Bank of Maharashtra Ltd could not complete his full term in 2006. Ditto N.S. Gujral of Punjab and Sind Bank in Delhi. Chairperson and managing director of United Bank of India, Archana Bhargava, too has recently settled for a shorter tenure, citing health reasons. Other bankers say there was something more to it, but nobody has spoken about corruption.

When it comes to being discredited, none can beat the record of former Indian Bank chairman and managing director M. Gopalakrishnan. He was sentenced to one year's rigorous imprisonment by a CBI court for allegedly causing a loss of Rs 317.5 million by granting loans without proper security between 1992 and 1996.[4] He was found guilty by the court of conspiracy, criminal breach of trust, misconduct and cheating under various provisions of the Indian Penal Code and Prevention of Corruption Act.

Is there any way to make all bankers, who are custodian of public money, honest and incorruptible? And how to punish a corrupt one?

One way could be offering them a respectable salary. Currently, they earn a pathetic pay packet. Take a look at the chief of State Bank of India who handles a balance sheet of Rs 22 trillion. (I am in no way suggesting that the State Bank chief is corrupt.) And compare it with the chief of any private-sector bank who oversees a balance sheet which is one-fifth of the size of State Bank or even smaller. Yes, the State Bank chief lives in a big bungalow in Mumbai's posh Malabar Hills, but that doesn't add to the salary.

To start with, if the government decides to monetize all benefits that a public-sector bank chief earns, their salary will be many times more. Open up the sector, pick up competent people from the market, give the CEOs more money, keep them happy, and put them under 24/7 surveillance. If they are caught taking money, punish them. They are playing with the public's trust, and deserve exemplary punishment.

---

4 'Ex-CMD of Indian Bank, 14 Others Get 1-yr Jail', *Business Standard*, http://www.business-standard.com/article/pti-stories/ex-cmd-of-indian-bank-14-others-get-1-yr-jail-113090700046_1.html.

HOW TO DEAL WITH CORRUPT BOSSES OF STATE-OWNED BANKS

(Part II)

14 August 2014

The 2013 appointment of S.K. Jain, the suspended chairman and managing director of Syndicate Bank, 'lacked transparency and smacks of unfair practices', the *Indian Express* reported on 11 August.

The cat is finally out of the bag.

The biggest bane of public-sector banks in India is the opaque appointment process of the top bosses. There is hardly any norm there; most appointments are based on the discretion of the bureaucrats involved in the process, with the Reserve Bank of India deciding to look the other way.

Should an executive be first made the CMD of a relatively small bank and then move on to head a bigger bank? Or, should the person be straightaway made the boss of a large bank?

Can a banker who has spent close to three decades in a small bank be suddenly catapulted to the corner room of a very large bank?

Or, should he be chosen to head a small bank first because of his background?

Nobody knows the answers to these questions. Rules are made and broken on the whims and fancies of a few in the North Block that houses the finance ministry which appoints top bankers. Often, a shortlist of successful candidates is made up to a year ahead of the vacancies. This leads to intense lobbying where individuals and industrial houses are involved.

Nothing comes for free. So, the industrial house which lobbies hard to get its candidate the plum post demands its pound of flesh in the form of loans, and the banker has no option but to oblige. An executive director of a large bank based in South India told me that he received a call from somebody he did not know promising to 'fix' his appointment a few days before he was to appear for an interview for a CMD slot. 'To be fair to him, he didn't demand anything, but I didn't want it this way,' this person said. He faced the interview board, but did not make it.

Many appointments of CMDs and executive directors are a result of lobbying. That's one aspect. The other is that the process itself is rotten. There have been instances where an executive director becomes the chief after spending only a few months at a bank. There is no clarity even on how many years of residual service is required to become the boss of a bank. The norm is two years, but there have been instances where CMDs have been appointed for one and a half years.

A senior banker, who headed two banks, says the entire system is rotten.

It starts innocuously.

A farmer who has been sanctioned a loan gives a junior agriculture officer a watermelon.

As the officer progresses in his career, the offerings become costlier.

A chief manager gets a 2 gm gold coin on Diwali while a general manager gets a 50 gm gold coin.

There is a very thin line between a bribe and a gift. A box of Alphonso mango in April (when Alphonsos are sold at Rs 1600 a dozen), a gold coin or dry fruits in silver bowls on Diwali, an expensive saree or a diamond earring for the banker's wife on New Year—are these gifts or bribes? It's difficult to classify them, but I understand that officers' manuals in some banks prescribe what a banker can accept and what he cannot.

Globally, different entities adopt different approaches towards gifts. For instance, an executive of the US Federal Reserve will never accept an invitation for dinner while a Financial Services Authority (FSA) executive in the UK will attend the dinner and send a 'thank you' note the following day. Bankers would do well to deal transparently and put all such items that they accept on record the way FSA executives do.

Transparency is the key. Apart from lack of expertise in skill, risk management and credit monitoring, public-sector banks are non-transparent in dealing with loan accounts, and there are no set norms for who can get loans and who cannot, the pricing of loans, even the nature and quantum of the collaterals.

The deputy general manager of a bank, based in Kolkata, told me that his bank doesn't appraise a loan proposal but assess how much money should be given to the borrower. 'We do the reverse. We first assess and decide how much money we should give and then do a mock appraisal,' he says.

Norms for collateral are typically there for small loans. 'How authentic are the stocks and receivables audits? And often we give loans against fake book debts,' he adds.

Riding a Tiger

There are many occasions when a fresh loan is given to enable a borrower to service the interest cost of a loan already given. The cycle goes on till the borrower crumbles under the burden of debt and fails to service it. In that sense, the banks are riding a tiger for many accounts.

The investigative agencies are selective on whom they go after. Jain was caught taking bribe for extending fresh loans to Bhushan Steel Ltd, but the company already has an exposure of Rs 400 billion to various banks and is on the verge of default. What about other banks that have loaned money to Bhushan Steel?

Similarly, IDBI Bank Ltd is under the scanner of the CBI for giving loans to Vijay Mallya's grounded airline, Kingfisher Airlines Ltd. Many other banks too had given loans to Kingfisher, and a consortium of banks, led by the State Bank of India, even restructured loans by converting part of debt into equity at an unbelievably high price.

Have any of them been taken to task?

In November 2010, banks in the consortium converted Rs 13.55 billion of debt into equity, at a 61.6 per cent premium to the market price of Kingfisher Airlines' stock. Apart from this, the bankers also stretched the period of repayment of loans to nine years with a two-year moratorium, cut the interest rates, and sanctioned a fresh loan.

The brokers also play a big role in this game of bribing bankers to facilitate loans for their corporate clients. One such broker syndicated Rs 500 billion worth of loans between 2008 and 2011 across sectors till it was caught while bribing bankers. Typically, broker fees are 2 per cent of the loan amount sanctioned, but this could vary depending on the sector. For instance, a real estate company may have to pay as much as 5 per cent to get a loan sanctioned, as banks are not willing to take exposure to this sector.

On top of that, if the price of the loan is lower than what a borrower expects, the broker gets a cut. And they share their booty with the bankers. Such brokers literally carry money in suitcases to distribute. One individual broker owns seven flats in Mumbai and its suburbs where senior bankers are regularly entertained, and another uses a helicopter for meeting bankers in different cities and closing deals.

There are other ways of pleasing bankers. One media company was looking for a Rs 8-billion loan from a bank whose CMD was on the verge of retirement. It simply bought a flat in UK where the banker's son is based, spending £800,000, or about Rs 80 million. It was a win-win deal for both the sides, as otherwise the media company would have needed to spend at least 2 per cent, or Rs 160 million, to get the deal done through a broker.

There are retired public-sector bank chiefs who live in large flats in posh areas in Mumbai. Does their income justify ownership of such properties, or is there a builder–banker nexus? I don't know the answer. Offering apartments at highly discounted rates could be a builder's way of influencing a commercial banker.

Similarly, there are financial intermediaries who influence even central bankers by offering lucrative jobs to their children. Here too, it is difficult to prove any mala fide intention. One way of tackling this could be making disclosures mandatory. Regulators overseas do this.

How do we deal with corrupt bankers? To start with, split the top position in public-sector banks between chairman and managing director. Right now, too much power is confined to one person and not everyone knows how to handle absolute power. The chairman can keep a check on the misuse of power. Also, the MD should start with a two- or three-year stint that can be renewed. The corrupt ones should not get their term renewed and must face the risk of termination even before the expiry of the first term.

At the risk of sounding repetitive, let me make a pitch for raising the salaries of public-sector bank chiefs manifold, but don't offer them the entire package in hand. There should be a clawback clause and a portion of the salary should be given two years after the chief's retirement—once it is clear that bad assets haven't swelled after the person's departure because of indiscriminate lendings.

Finally, the boards must be restructured. Currently, instead of giving vision and strategic inputs, some board members are facilitators for unworthy borrowers—they play the role of brokers. This practice must be stopped.

HOW CORRUPT ARE OUR BANKERS?

26 September 2016

On 15 September, the Central Bureau of Investigation registered a case of corruption against Archana Bhargava, a former chairperson and managing director of United Bank of India (UBI), after the agency carried out raids at multiple cities and recovered cash, jewellery and investment of over Rs 135 million.[5] Allegedly, Bhargava had abused her official position, first as an executive director of Canara Bank and later as the boss of UBI, to make money for herself and/or for a company in New Delhi, owned by her husband and son.

The agency also found a fat sum kept in the bank accounts of Bhargava and her family members, and properties in Delhi and Mumbai which the sixty-one-year-old retired banker, a postgraduate gold medallist in biochemistry from Delhi's Miranda House and a National Science Talent Scholarship holder, may find difficult to explain.

A month before that, on 14 August, an assistant general manager of a south-based bank committed suicide by jumping in front of a running train, as the loans he sanctioned turned bad. Apparently, he was suffering from depression, being persistently questioned by senior officials of the bank and an investigative agency. His suicide note talks about certain loans sanctioned in Kolkata which turned bad. It is not clear whether he had sanctioned such loans on his own or at the insistence of his seniors in the bank.

These two incidents point to one malaise that has been plaguing the Indian banking system, particularly the public-sector banks: corruption. Referring to corruption among government officials,

5 'CBI Registers Corruption Case against Archana Bhargava, Former CMD of UBI', *Economic Times*, 15 September 2016, http://economictimes.indiatimes.com/news/politics-and-nation/cbi-registers-corruption-case-against-archana-bhargava-former-cmd-of-ubi/articleshow/54348329.cms.

Chanakya, an Indian economist of the fourth century, in his political treatise the *Arthashastra*, had said that detecting corruption among revenue officials is as impossible as knowing when a fish is drinking water. The same holds true for the bankers. They are in an industry where money is the raw material and it is not easy to find out how they use their official position to make money for themselves.

Bhargava had started her banking career with Punjab National Bank as a management trainee in 1977. In February 2014, she sought voluntary retirement, citing health reasons, ten months after she took charge of the Kolkata-based bank. Her tenure would have ended a year later. Citing two unidentified bank officials, a newspaper report then referred to a Rs 1-billion loan to a real estate developer despite opposition from directors of the bank's board, as the reason behind her quitting in a huff.

She had mostly been on leave ever since the bank's board met on 7 February 2014 to take into account the December (2013) quarter earnings in which it reported a Rs 12.38-billion loss after it set aside money to provide for its rising bad assets.

In UBI, she allegedly cleared loans overriding the board's dissent and restructured troubled accounts without assessing the viability of the projects. Incidentally, her stint as an ED in Canara Bank was quite turbulent. S. Raman, then CMD of Canara Bank and now a director at the capital market watchdog Securities and Exchange Board of India, had found her interfering with the auditors of the bank and wrote to the finance ministry to get rid of her.

This is not the first instance of CBI looking into corruption in this sector. In August 2014, the agency arrested Sudhir Kumar Jain, then CMD of Syndicate Bank, for allegedly taking a Rs 5-million bribe. His brothers-in-law were allegedly involved in the mechanics of the payoff.

Typically, a corrupt boss uses senior executives such as general managers and deputy general managers for sanctioning loans to undeserving borrowers and pockets a small portion of the loan amount. It could vary from 0.5 per cent to 2–3 per cent, depending on the profile of the borrowing company. This means for a Rs 1-billion loan sanction, the 'earnings' could be Rs 500,000 to Rs 30 million. The money could be paid in cash or in an overseas bank account (one banker is known to keep this money in his own bank overseas, through the so-called hawala route).

In most such cases, the pressure on giving loans without proper risk assessment mounts on senior executives just ahead of their interviews for promotion. If they don't oblige, the risk of missing promotion is high. The senior executives also run the risk of being transferred to places not to their liking if they reject a loan proposal recommended by the boss.

The current boss of a government-owned bank has recently told his executives to sanction loan proposals that he recommends (of course, verbally) and not bother about whether they will turn bad. His philosophy is: as long as the loan book is growing, none should bother about non-performing assets as bad loans as a percentage of overall loans can be contained through aggressive loan growth.

It's another story that the corrupt bank bosses do not use their subordinates only for clearing loan proposals that should not be cleared. Once, a senior executive of a bank had to spend almost an entire day searching for a particular brand of dog biscuit in Bengaluru markets for the dear pet of the bank chief.

Different Shades of Grey

There are many ways of making money. For instance, there could be 'consideration' behind the alliances for selling non-banking products such as insurance and mutual funds. Also, many brokers and consultants involved in sourcing loans for banks (not all banks entertain such intermediaries) are known to offer a cut to the senior bankers who sanction the loans. One such broker has confided in me that these days, many prefer 'skin' (women) to cash for fear of being caught by investigative agencies.

I am also aware of at least one senior banker who has employed a 'portfolio manager' to manage his money. The manager collects money on the banker's behalf from borrowers and even helps distressed borrowers by offering short-term loans from the 'fund' he manages to keep the loan as a 'performing' asset. Such loans can continuously be milked as only a performing asset or loan can get fresh disbursements of money from the bank and such disbursements keep the money flowing for the portfolio he handles. When a loan turns bad, the bank cannot give more money to the defaulting borrower.

If one thinks that such 'transactions' are restricted only to the higher level, one is mistaken. Junior officers too are involved in 'deals'. Such practices are particularly prevalent in small, unsecured loans. Even junior officers enjoy reasonable freedom to choose the borrowers who do not need to offer any collateral to get such loans and often default.

Gifts Galore

While corruption remains a hot topic, it may not be a bad idea to look at the gift culture prevalent among most banks. During Diwali, relatively junior officers of banks are seen hailing cabs to home in distant suburbs in Mumbai as they cannot carry the dinner set, thermos and other such items in crowded local trains.

The nature of the gifts changes in accordance with the profile of the bankers. While the junior-most employee in a branch may have to be happy with a Prestige pressure cooker or a Titan watch, gift vouchers, Montblanc pens, fancy mobile phones, iPads and Kindles, Nalli sarees, silver utensils, gold coins and jewellery make their way to the cosy cabins of senior officers in branches and to other office managers.

Instances of borrowers taking care of the overseas educational needs of a senior banker's child or picking up the tab for the wedding reception of his daughter and even a Bali honeymoon are not rare.

There are a few banks which do not allow the entry of any gift in their corporate offices, but I am not sure whether there is any code of conduct for acceptance of gifts which has been framed either by individual banks or the industry lobby, the Indian Banks' Association. Of course, the service regulations spell out the dos and don'ts, but not everybody cares for them.

Also, the prevention of entry of gifts into the corporate office does not necessarily mean that the bankers are not accepting gifts. Once, the CMD of a south-based bank got upset seeing many gifts in the boot of the official vehicle while leaving for the airport from a meeting with borrowers in an eastern city; in the presence of all, the bank's manager of the zone was asked to remove them. Later, the same zonal manager was entrusted with the task of delivering them to the CMD's house!

This culture is not confined to the bankers alone. Many government nominees on the boards of the banks too are afflicted with greed for gifts. One such nominee on the board of a large public-sector bank once wished to buy a pullover during a meeting in Mumbai as Delhi winter was cruel that year. Since he did not have the time to visit a shop, the bank arranged to show him four fancy pullovers fetched from a departmental store, giving him choices. The director liked all four and asked the CMD's secretariat to pack them for him!

Similarly, a real estate firm may not mind selling a flat to senior bankers at a hugely discounted price to ensure speedy appraisal of the loan process. There are also borrowers who offer 'annuity' to bank chiefs after their retirement to express their gratitude for the support extended to them in the appraisal of loan proposals and disbursement of loans.

The annuity comes in the form of annual holidays, chauffeur-driven cars and guest house or hotel accommodation at certain cities. This 'give and take' culture between a few bank chiefs and corporate borrowers start with the appointment of the person as the managing director or executive director. Till recently, the appointment process was opaque and many in the industry say that top seats could be bought. Typically, borrowers pay the money involved in such deals and the banker returns the favour after assuming the office.

How to Change the Culture

Why do some bankers entertain such things? Will they change if the government raise their salary and perks manifold? The little-known fact is that while senior public-sector bankers get far lower salary than their counterparts in the private sector, at the lower level, employees of public-sector banks earn higher than the private bankers besides enjoying the job security. Allowing the senior bankers to monetize their perks and stock options could be good incentives. In most cases, the senior bankers become a victim of greed out of insecurity post-retirement when their lifestyle takes a big hit.

However, there is no uniform culture among all public-sector banks. Some banks are known for transparency and free flow of information and some are not.

There has been no survey on the level of corruption, but I would imagine a few senior bankers love wealth and they will not change even after their salary is raised manifold, as corruption is in their DNA. Some of them, who do not suffer from any ethical dilemma in accepting favour in the form of someone taking care of their children's education and wedding expenses, as well as hefty discounts for buying costly flats, will stop the practice when higher salary and perks give them security. The rest believe in living within their means and are committed to a high ethical standard.

7

The Conflict between the RBI and the Finance Ministry

Financial sector commentators love to describe it as a 'spat' between the Reserve Bank of India and the finance ministry which we come across often irrespective of who the finance minister is and who the RBI governor. This happens because growth is always the government's worry and inflation the RBI's.

The columns in this chapter focus on the recurring theme of the Indian financial sector—the autonomy of the RBI or the lack of it and an overbearing finance ministry who loves to play the role of a super regulator. The tension has always been there beneath the surface, but on occasions it takes an ugly turn in full public glare. Like what happened in June 2010 when an ordinance was passed empowering the finance ministry to resolve all disputes between the regulators. The original idea behind the ordinance was to end the turf war between the Securities and Exchange Board of India and the Insurance Regulatory and Development Authority (IRDA) on unit-linked insurance plans, but the regulators were not consulted and it turned out to be an attempt by the finance ministry to officially be the super regulator which the RBI could not stomach.

Governor D. Subbarao wrote to the finance ministry: 'The ordinance has seeming implications for regulatory autonomy and sows seeds of doubt where none exist. My earnest request to you is to allow the ordinance to lapse.'

It ends with the finance ministry's attack on the newest institution—the monetary policy committee which now decides on interest rates in India in the new regime of flexible inflation targeting.

Former RBI governor Y.V. Reddy calls it 'creative tension'. That's a graceful descriptor of non-stop skirmishes that both the sides engage in, mostly on the issue of rate cut, the collective obsession of the nation.

THE RESERVE BANK OF INDIA NEEDS NEW CLOTHES

19 July 2009

Every year, a few days after presenting the Union Budget, India's finance minister meets the country's chief money man, the governor of the central bank and its central board. Pranab Mukherjee addressed the Reserve Bank of India board for the first time in 1982 as finance minister in the Cabinet of the then prime minister Indira Gandhi. This time around, in his interaction with fifteen directors (the RBI's central board has nineteen members, but four of them, including Kumar Mangalam Birla, chairman of the Aditya Birla Group of companies, were not present at the 11 July meeting), Mukherjee treated the annual ritual differently and flagged off quite a few critical issues involving the RBI.

The finance minister made it clear that he is not a believer in the UK's Financial Services Authority model of supervision, but called for better coordination among all regulators in the Indian financial sector. He also spoke about bringing all financial market regulations under the capital market watchdog, the Securities and Exchange Board of India and setting up a separate public debt office, relieving the RBI of its role as the investment banker for the government. Finally, he pointed to a few grey areas in financial sector supervision. For instance, there is no regulation to supervise non-banking finance companies in India and the RBI manages them through 'directions'.

Similarly, the Reserve Bank of India Act, 1935, that governs the seventy-four-year-old Indian central bank, is silent on the critical aspect of 'financial stability'..

Mukherjee's observations have created quite a flutter in the staid RBI bureaucracy and even some outsiders are seeing in them a conspiracy to demolish a great institution with impeccable integrity.

I am sure no one can find fault with Mukherjee's suggestion for better coordination among the regulators. Including the ministry of finance, which informally plays the role of a super regulator in India, there are some ten regulators in the financial sector. The RBI oversees commercial banks and a few other financial firms; SEBI regulates capital markets and supervises stock exchanges, asset management firms, brokerages, and so on; the Forward Markets Commission supervises the commodities markets; the Insurance Regulatory and Development Authority is the watchdog of the insurance business; the Pension Fund Regulatory and Development Authority oversees the pension business; the National Bank for Agriculture and Rural Development supervises regional rural banks; the National Housing Bank (NHB) regulates home finance firms; the registrar of cooperatives is a joint regulator for cooperative banks; and the government's department of company affairs regulates the deposit-taking activities of non-financial companies.

If not for anything else, only to prevent regulatory arbitrages by smart players, these bodies should talk to each other regularly and not waste time in turf wars.

The debate on the RBI's role as the government's debt manager is intensifying with the widening of the fiscal deficit. To bridge the fiscal deficit, estimated at 6.8 per cent of gross domestic product, the government needs to borrow Rs 4.51 trillion from the market in fiscal 2010 and many believe that an independent debt office should manage the borrowing. But there are others who strongly feel that the RBI should remain the government's debt manager when the borrowing is high because the government, being the majority owner of three-fourth of the banking industry, will end up arm-twisting public-sector banks to buy bonds if it runs an independent debt office, leading to a greater conflict of interest.

If the debt management function is actually taken away from the RBI, it will not be a big loser as now it manages some twenty-five functions and each can be independently run by an institution.

In the past, at least five institutions had been carved out of the RBI—NHB, NABARD, Exim Bank, Industrial Development Bank of India (the earlier avatar of IDBI Bank Ltd) and Unit Trust of India. The debt office will be yet another such body. The RBI should not bother much about losing its debt management function, and instead focus on changing the organization to be in sync with the new global order.

The US-based economic think tank National Bureau of Economic Research (NBER) finds the RBI the least transparent of central banks in South Asia. While the transparency level in other countries, including those in South Asia, increased over the years, that of the RBI remained the same through 1998–2006, says the latest NBER study.

The findings echo those in the Country Report on India published in February 2008 by the International Monetary Fund, which criticized the RBI's lack of transparency. The RBI also does not practise what it preaches to commercial banks. For instance, it forced banks to adopt core banking solutions to integrate all their branches on a common technology platform many years ago for customer convenience and better business management, but its own twenty-two regional offices work as islands with no technology integration!

Similarly, not too many insiders talk glowingly about its human resource policies. It has lowered its employee strength from 37,000 to 20,000 in the past twenty-five years, but only one-fourth of these employees are involved in central banking.

Progressive central banking is impossible with this skewed structure and a look at its transfer policy (or the lack of it) makes one convinced that it does not believe in creating skill and specializations. When did we last see any seminal work done by any of its research wings?

Finally, governors come and go, but a few of its central board members remain there for decades. How can it talk about corporate governance in regulated entities? The RBI needs new clothes.

SHOULD FINMIN BE THE SUPER REGULATOR?

13 July 2010

India's seventy-five-year-old central bank runs the risk of losing its autonomy. The bank, which many believe did a splendid job ring-fencing the Indian financial system from the global financial meltdown, will lose its teeth following the 18 June ordinance that has empowered the finance ministry to resolve all disputes between regulators.

The original idea behind the promulgation of the ordinance was to end the turf war between the Securities and Exchange Board of India and the Insurance Regulatory and Development Authority on unit-linked insurance plans (ULIPs), but it speaks of a statutory joint committee, headed by the Union finance minister, being set up to resolve any such disputes among any of the financial-sector regulators in future.

This is the first ordinance in independent India to quash a regulator's directive to the market players (SEBI had asked insurance firms to seek its approval before launching fresh ULIPs as these plans have substantial investments in equities which is the capital market regulator's domain) and neither SEBI nor the RBI was consulted before the ordinance was promulgated.

Now the Reserve Bank of India wants the government to take a relook at the proposal of setting up the panel—the joint committee which is statutory in nature. Unlike the existing high-level coordination committee on financial markets (HLCCFM) which is an informal forum, the decisions of a statutory panel are binding. To that extent, the finance ministry becomes the super regulator—which neither the HLCCFM nor the proposed Financial Stability and Development Council (FSDC) is—and erodes the RBI's autonomy.

To be sure, RBI is not an autonomous institution. It is answerable to Parliament and each of its policy decisions on interest rates needs to be ratified by the government (no one will officially admit this, though). But as the RBI governor

D. Subbarao's recent letter to Finance Minister Pranab Mukherjee points out, 'The appearance of autonomy is as important as the actual autonomy itself' and 'the very existence of a joint committee will sow seeds of doubt in public mind about the independence of regulators'.

Apart from setting up the joint committee, the ordinance also amends a chapter in the RBI Act by proposing a mechanism to resolve differences of opinion on the regulatory jurisdiction of certain financial instruments that are currently regulated by the RBI. These instruments are interest rate futures, credit default swaps, and currency futures. They are exchange-traded and a 2006 amendment to the RBI Act has 'clearly demarcated the responsibilities of RBI and SEBI on exchange traded products'.

'Experience shows that this system has been working well without any ambiguities, doubts or disputes. In such a situation, the need for the amendment to the RBI Act contained in the ordinance becomes questionable,' Subbarao's letter said.

Business Standard wrote last week that the Indian central bank has urged the finance minister to allow the ordinance to lapse. If the government does not bring a bill to this effect within three months, it will lapse automatically.

Let me extensively quote from the letter to understand the RBI's point of view:

> It is possible to argue that a mere enabling provision for resolution of disputes as contemplated in the ordinance should not, by itself, be a matter of concern. However, an ordinance makes what is now a clearly demarcated regulatory jurisdiction . . . It will sow the seeds of ambiguity where none now exist, impact the credibility of regulatory actions and constrain the effectiveness of prudential framework . . .
>
> The establishment of a statutory joint committee is itself problematic and raises issues about its potential misuse in ways that impair the autonomy of the regulators. We are all aware that

> both the Prime Minister and you have strong and impeccable commitment to regulatory autonomy. But we must evaluate the arrangement . . . in a long-term perspective when personalities change; the misuse of the ordinance is not beyond the realm of possibility for several reasons.
>
> First, the jurisdiction of the joint committee could 'spillover' to issues strictly beyond issues of difference of opinion on specific products to issues of policy. Second, the joint committee mechanism could be invoked to decide on issues involving mere differences in judgement . . . Third, it could provide a perverse incentive for regulatory arbitrage if the market has issues with the existing regulatory framework . . .
>
> Is the joint committee mechanism the optimal way out (to settle jurisdictional disputes over regulation)? . . . The government can act through its nominees on the boards of the regulatory agencies. The specific Acts relating to the various financial sector regulators vest the government with powers to issue directions on policy issues, and these powers can be effectively used. . . .
>
> Finally, there already exists a high-level coordination committee on financial markets (HLCCFM), which is the nodal forum to discuss regulatory coordination issues. Though the HLCCFM is constrained by its non-statutory nature, the government can very well direct the HLCCFM to make a specific recommendation on any issue having inter-regulatory implications.
>
> . . . The ordinance has seeming implications for regulatory autonomy and sows seeds of doubt where none exist. My earnest request to you is to allow the ordinance to lapse. If that option is not acceptable, the portion of the ordinance relating to the RBI Act may be deleted . . .

Irrespective of how this plays out, it's time the RBI too took a close look at itself at a time when global financial sector regulators are redefining their roles. For instance, financial inclusion, financial literacy and consumer protection functions of the RBI can be handled by the FSDC; and the micro regulations part of the central bank's job can be taken away. The RBI can concentrate on monetary policy, exchange rate management, payments and settlements, and the macro regulations for the financial system as a whole. It should also get out of its role as the government's debt manager when India's fiscal deficit comes down and the banks won't need to buy the government bonds heavily to see through the annual borrowing programme. It also needs to disclose more in its balance sheet.

Overall, the regulator needs to reinvent itself. This could happen sooner than expected.

THE UNTOLD STORY BEHIND THE QUICK-FIX ORDINANCE

18 July 2010

This is yet another piece on the 18 June quick-fix dispute resolution ordinance. Why am I writing this? Simply because I haven't been able to unravel the mystery behind it. The objective is to raise some questions and flag certain issues.

Before doing that, let me look at the context. The ordinance was the government's answer to the spat between two regulators—the Securities and Exchange Board of India, and the Insurance Regulatory and Development Authority—on which will regulate unit-linked insurance plans. A ULIP is a hybrid product with two components—insurance and investment. Since a substantial portion of the money is invested in equities, the capital market watchdog argued that it had every right to regulate such products, at least partly, but IRDA did not agree.

According to the insurance regulator, it's an insurance product and SEBI has no business to interfere in its oversight. The turf war continued for years as both regulators refused to budge. Even the high-level coordination committee on financial markets, chaired by the Reserve Bank of India governor, could not sort out the differences. The HLCCFM is a nodal forum to discuss regulatory coordination issues. In January, the turf war intensified, with SEBI issuing show-cause notices to some insurance firms on ULIPs.

While the firms kept quiet, IRDA responded quickly in their defence. At this stage, the government stepped in and meetings were held with both regulators to find a way out, but no solution was reached. At the end of March, SEBI informed the finance ministry about its intention to write to insurance firms directing them to seek the capital market regulator's approval before launching new ULIPs. The ministry kept silent and SEBI went ahead with its plan in early April. This time too the insurers stayed quiet and IRDA asked SEBI to keep its hands off ULIPs.

With the two regulators sticking to their guns, the ministry advised them to seek a legal solution that would be binding on both. With public interest litigations being filed in two high courts, in Mumbai and Allahabad, SEBI, without wasting time, moved the Supreme Court in May.

Until this time, there had been no surprise in the sequence of events, but suddenly things took a different turn. As the court was going on vacation, the matter was to come up for hearing in July. On 18 June, the President of India promulgated an ordinance settling the matter in favour of IRDA by amending the Insurance Act. The ordinance also amended the Reserve Bank of India Act and set up a statutory joint committee, headed by the finance minister, to resolve any disputes among financial sector regulators on hybrid financial instruments that combine features of bonds, equities and insurance.

Many Unanswered Questions

There's nothing wrong in the government stepping in and sorting out the issue when the regulators themselves fail to do so. But I have the following questions: why didn't the finance ministry prevent SEBI from issuing directives to the insurance firms in April that escalated the fight? After all, the capital market regulator informed the ministry about this in advance and waited for a week before issuing the directives.

Why did the government first ask SEBI and IRDA to seek a legal solution and then change its mind? Did the government feel that SEBI had a stronger case, but it didn't want the capital market regulator to win the case in a court of law? Was there pressure from insurance firms and distributors of ULIPs that the government could not overcome?

The government might have felt the court would take longer to sort out the issue and hence, decided to opt for the ordinance route. If indeed this was the case, why was it so wary of consulting the regulators? Neither SEBI nor the RBI was consulted on the ordinance.

This is surprising because the government has the power to give directions to any of these regulators on policy issues. Since the government has the absolute power to overrule any of their policy decisions, there was no necessity to take the ordinance route to resolve the ULIP controversy.

I am sure that had the finance ministry told SEBI to keep off ULIPs, it would not have questioned the ministry's decision. And precisely because of the special power that the government enjoys, there is no need to set up a statutory joint committee. Then how would one sort out regulatory spats?

Let's make it clear first that fights between regulators are rare and even when they take place, in most cases, the regulators act with patience and maturity to understand each other and sort them out. Take the case of exchange-traded currency derivatives. Both the RBI and SEBI claimed the right to regulate such products initially, but instead of fighting, they constituted a six-member joint committee to find ways to bridge the differences. The understanding was that any issue on which any of the regulators is not comfortable would not be pushed. That arrangement is working fine.

Whenever there is a conflict between two regulators, at the first stage, both of them should try to resolve it between themselves. SEBI and the RBI could do that on exchanged-traded currency derivatives, but IRDA and SEBI couldn't on ULIPs.

At the second stage, it can be discussed at the institutional forum, the HLCCFM. This committee could not sort out the ULIP issue, but that does not mean we need a statutory panel, headed by the country's finance minister, particularly when the government has the absolute power to intervene on policy issues.

The lessons of the 2008 global financial crisis are obvious: a central bank, despite being the lender of last resort, cannot have the last word any more as the buck stops with the government, which needs to open its coffers and offer taxpayers' money to bail out troubled institutions. But that doesn't justify the constitution of a statutory panel, headed by the finance minister, to interfere with the regulators' autonomy. Such a committee could be the proverbial thin end of the wedge.

It may start as an arbitrator for hybrid products, but later may start dictating terms on issues such as which industrial house should get a banking licence or on whom should the capital market regulator go soft in dealing with insider trading charges. That's the real danger.

EMPEROR, LOOK AT YOUR OWN CLOTHES

3 September 2012

The State Bank of India chairman Pratip Chaudhuri and the Reserve Bank of India deputy governor K.C. Chakrabarty have been exchanging ideas on the central bank policy of impounding banks' cash—technically known as cash reserve ratio—through media. Chaudhuri wants the banking regulator to abolish CRR, the portion of deposits that banks need to keep with the RBI, as banks do not earn any interest on it. If this is done away with now, at least Rs 2.6 trillion will be released into the system (CRR is now 4.75 per cent of deposits). This will help banks meet the borrowers' need and fuel economic growth. (Plenty of money in the banking system will also stoke inflation and this is why the RBI is not paring it.) Besides, banks' income will also go up as they will earn interest deploying the money through loans or investments.

Chaudhuri's argument is: why should banks be subjected to CRR and why not insurers and mutual funds who also deal with public money?

Chakrabarty doesn't find any merit in the argument and has apparently said the SBI boss will have to work within the existing regulatory framework and if he cannot do so, he has to find some other place. The central banker possibly meant Chaudhuri can run an insurance company or a mutual fund where there is no CRR.

Chaudhuri's retort is equally interesting—Chakrabarty himself had made such a demand when he was a banker. (Chakrabarty headed Indian Bank and Punjab National Bank before moving to the Mint Road headquarters of the RBI.)

The demand for CRR abolition and/or interest payment on CRR in India has been as old as CRR itself and there is nothing new about Chaudhuri's argument. Comparing banks to insurance companies and mutual funds is not fair though, as unlike the RBI, their regulators do not create money and hence, the question of impounding money does not arise.

What does the RBI do with its money? This year, the Indian central bank transferred Rs 160.1 billion to the government, its surplus profit for the year, more than what it had transferred the previous year, which was Rs 150.09 billion. The RBI follows a July–June financial year.

Its gross income for the year was up at least by 43 per cent to Rs 531.76 billion, primarily from its domestic operations where the earnings rose by 110 per cent. Its income from foreign currency assets dropped by more than 6 per cent because of low interest rates in international market. The higher domestic earning of the central bank is not good news, as this means commercial banks are borrowing from it heavily and there is not enough money in the system. The RBI earns interest when it lends to banks.

Since there is no cost of money for the central bank—the RBI itself creates money—how much it earns entirely depends on the liquidity in the system (for its domestic income) and interest rate overseas (for earnings on foreign currency assets). It can show its efficiency in expense management. In 2011–12 (July–June), the RBI's establishment expenditure rose by 30 per cent as it had to set aside money for employees' gratuity and superannuation funds.

That's fine, but what is frustrating is that the RBI balance sheet does not clarify many things. In fact, the Central Bank of Sri Lanka balance sheets says more than what the RBI balance sheet tells us. For instance, its gross income last year was Rs 531.76 billion and net income Rs 261.51 billion after Rs 270.25-billion provisions, but it does not give the details of such provisions. The RBI does not pay any income tax.

Similarly, its foreign currency assets consist of deposits kept with the Bank for International Settlements, other central banks and commercial banks, and securities but it does not give any break-up of such assets. One can appreciate its reservations about revealing the currency profile of foreign assets, but why can't it classify such assets? The balance sheet also does not have the cash flow statement.

The balance sheet of the Sri Lankan central bank gives the cash flow statement, classifies its foreign currency assets, including derivatives, and says how much of these assets it is holding till they mature and how much it can trade. It also gives a clear picture of the credit risk by explaining the bank's exposure to different locations such as the US, Japan, the UK, Europe, etc. It also gives a detailed presentation on how many pension, gratuity and other employee welfare schemes it runs.

The RBI was set up as a private shareholders' bank in 1935 with an initial paid-up capital of Rs 500,000. It was nationalized in 1949 and there has been no change in its balance sheet structure since then. It continues to carry two balance sheets—one relates to currency management and the other to all other functions as a monetary authority.

It is high time it changed its balance sheet structure and opted for more clarity and transparency. The RBI's board—with eminent people as directors—does not have any regulatory function. It meets at least six times a year and there is enormous curiosity about such meetings. How about putting up the minutes of the board meetings on the RBI website?

Also, why shouldn't the RBI be subjected to Comptroller and Auditor General of India's audit? I am in no way suggesting the central bank is doing things that it should not do. In fact, as an institution it is known for its integrity and intellectual honesty even as it continuously fights with the finance ministry for its independence, but there is no harm in being scrutinized by CAG and the Public Accounts Committee (PAC).

With the changing times, the emperor should look at his own clothes. Otherwise, it loses the right to point fingers at its naked subjects.

FINANCE MINISTRY, RESERVE BANK AND AUTONOMY

16 January 2017

A finance ministry statement on Saturday said that 'the government fully respects the independence and autonomy of the Reserve Bank of India'.

It's very reassuring to hear this.

There have been talks on the Indian central bank's autonomy being compromised in various circles against the backdrop of the demonetization move—how the decision to replace 86 per cent of the currency in circulation was taken in Asia's third-largest economy and the way it has been implemented. Apart from many others, two former Reserve Bank of India governors—Y.V. Reddy (governor from 6 September 2003 to 5 September 2008) and Bimal Jalan (22 November 1997 to 6 September 2003)—have recently joined the debate. Reddy has gone to the extent of saying that he would have resigned had he not been able to convince the government against this exercise.

However, the finance ministry chose not to react to them. It did so after four RBI employee unions wrote to the central bank governor Urjit Patel objecting to the ministry's move to send a joint secretary to coordinate cash operations at the RBI. The unions have found this 'unfortunate' and something which 'impinged on RBI's autonomy'.

Probably it doesn't really matter to the government how the experts and the intelligentsia react to demonetization, but employees' unions do matter as they represent the masses. Besides, they are also part of the RBI and hence they must know the truth (that is, the RBI is independent).

I heard P.N. Vijay, an expert in investment banking and wealth management services who also assists the ruling Bharatiya Janata Party on economic and financial matters, speaking from his heart on a television channel. He would not like to give much importance to the governors of Reddy's ilk. They are the 'Lalu Prasad Yadavs' of the central bank—bureaucrats sent from Delhi to the RBI who do not have much understanding of how the system works. Or something on this line.

To be fair to him, he did not say that Yadav would have been a better RBI governor than Reddy the way Haryana health minister Anil Vij said Prime Minister Narendra Modi is a better brand than Mahatma Gandhi for the Khadi and Village Industries Commission's calendar and diary. (Later, he retracted the statement.)

An Old Debate

The debate on RBI's autonomy is as old as the central bank itself. What exactly has happened this time? Why is there so much noise? The government advised the RBI to take the call on demonetization and the RBI board obliged the government without losing time. Is this something unprecedented? Does this violate the norms laid down by the RBI Act?

Two sections of the Act deal with this.

Section 26(2) of the Reserve Bank of India Act, 1934, says that on the recommendation of the RBI's central board, the government may, by notification in the *Gazette of India*, declare that with effect from a date specified in the notification, any series of bank notes of any denomination shall cease to be legal tender. So, there is nothing illegal about the RBI board recommending the withdrawal of Rs 1000 and Rs 500 notes from the system.

And Section 7 of the Act says 'the central government may from time to time give such directions to the Bank as it may, after consultation with the Governor of the Bank, consider necessary in the public interest'. So, the government's advice to the RBI on demonetization is in sync with the Act even though I am not sure whether it was done under Section 7 of the Act or not. I presume that the governor was consulted on this.

In Public Interest?

The moot question is: was demonetization 'necessary in the public interest'? Many feel that it was not and the intense debate stems from there. If it was not, the RBI should have put up at least a semblance of a fight, they feel. Since the RBI has not done that, I think at this point both the government and the RBI are on the same page—both believe that demonetization is for the greater good of the public and the long-term gains will more than compensate for the short-term pains. Had the RBI board deliberated on this a little longer, probably people would have been convinced on this. Anyway, only time will tell whether this prognosis is correct or not.

Five Indian states are going for polls, beginning 11 February. Will these polls be a referendum on demonetization? May or may not be. The narrative of the demonetization story is a fight between good and evil, poor and rich, the oppressed and the oppressor. Told nicely, the story can touch the heart of the masses and despite sufferings, they can continue to give a thumbs-up to demonetization.

Had the RBI not been convinced about the efficacy of the move, could it have stopped it? Probably not, as under Section 7 of the Act, the government can 'direct' the central bank. However, it could have fought against it—in private as well as in public—as the appearance of autonomy is as important as actual autonomy itself.

Incidentally, on earlier two occasions—in 1946 and 1978—the government demonetized high-value currency notes in circulations through an ordinance even though the respective RBI governors were not in favour of the move.

The history of central banking in India is replete with many fights. The title of the book of former governor D. Subbarao (whose tenure ran from 5 September 2008 to 4 September 2013), *Who Moved My Interest Rate?*, itself is a testimony to this. His predecessor Reddy too was involved in similar fights—which were more severe than an India–China war, a colleague of Reddy says in jest—but the details are not in the public domain. Reddy's run-ins with the finance ministry were more on specific issues while Subbarao fought on broader policy issues.

Creative Tension

Reddy always downplayed the fights, terming them 'creative tension', but those who had seen the period from close quarters vouch that there was nothing creative about it and the tension was at times unbearable. Reddy fought hard against the government's plan to create sovereign wealth funds and the use of foreign exchange reserves for infrastructure development. The finance ministry went to the extent of reaching out to the board of the central bank, seeking help to convince Reddy, but he did not budge an inch from his stance.

He also made the finance ministry accept that the RBI should have the last word on foreign investment in a holding company of a large private bank (ICICI Bank Ltd). The bank had planned to float an intermediate holding company for its insurance and mutual fund businesses, and even sold a substantial stake in the proposed holding company to a few foreign investors. The government approved the plan and even the Foreign Investment Promotion Board (FIPB) that deals with overseas investments in local firms cleared the proposed investment by foreign funds in this venture.

The RBI refused to clear it and, with extreme reluctance, the finance ministry accepted the central bank's proposal to form a working group to look into the proposal. The working group took its own time to frustrate the bank and prospective foreign investors in the venture before saying it was not 'desirable'!

When former finance minister P. Chidambaram called the then deputy governor Rakesh Mohan for an 'interview', which the ministry was conducting through a committee to identify Reddy's successor, Reddy was not kept in the loop. That was the finance ministry's way of insulting Reddy. The ministry did the same thing to Subbarao—by not accepting his recommendation for giving another term to his deputies, first Usha Thorat and then Subir Gokarn. In Subbarao's own words, this is the price he paid for asserting autonomy.

His first brush with the ministry came in June 2010 when an ordinance was promulgated empowering the finance ministry to resolve all disputes between the regulators. This was when the Financial Stability and Development Council was being constituted. Subbarao immediately wrote to the then finance minister Pranab Mukherjee, saying, 'The very existence of a joint committee (the council) will sow seeds of doubt in public mind about the independence of regulators'.

'The ordinance has seeming implications for regulatory autonomy and sows seeds of doubts where none exist. My earnest request to you is to allow the ordinance to lapse. If that option is not acceptable, the portion of the ordinance relating to the RBI Act may be deleted.'

Mukherjee did not pay heed.

Subbarao was also not comfortable with the idea of divesting the RBI of its debt management function and had strong reservations on the report of the Financial Sector Legislative Reforms Commission, which has proposed taking away many of RBI's functions.

A Governor, Annoyed and Upset

The RBI employees unions' objection to a joint secretary coordinating cash operations at the RBI reminds me of Subbarao's reaction when in October 2008, in the aftermath of the collapse of Lehman Brothers and the acute liquidity crisis, the then finance minister Chidambaram appointed the then finance secretary Arun Ramanathan as the chairman of a panel on liquidity management, without consulting the RBI. Subbarao was 'annoyed and upset' and called up the finance minister, saying the regulator would not participate in the committee.

The governor's frequent fights with both the finance ministers Mukherjee and Chidambaram on interest rates too are well known.

Subbarao's successor Raghuram Rajan (whose tenure was from 4 September 2013 to 4 September 2016), who received a lot of flak from some quarters for talking beyond central banking in public fora (on intolerance, 'make for India' instead of 'make in India', among others), also had his quota of fights with the ministry on issues such as funding the Punjab government's food purchases (there was a massive gap between the worth of the food stock and the money borrowed from banks) and the trillions of rupees of debt restructuring of power distribution companies.

Rajan also put his foot down when the finance ministry in February 2014 wanted the RBI to pay an interim dividend ahead of the end of its accounting year in an effort to bridge India's fiscal deficit and stick to the estimated deficit target.

The RBI follows a July–June accounting year and transfers the surplus in August. In 2015–16, it transferred Rs 658.76-billion surplus as dividend to the government, Rs 0.2 billion less than the previous year.

Rajan was also against the idea of using the RBI's surplus fund to take stakes in banks or create a state-owned bad bank. The idea was first floated by Chief Economic Adviser Arvind Subramanian in the Economic Survey for 2016–17. 'RBI's capital could be used in two ways. It could be injected directly into PSBs which will give them financial room to accept losses on bad assets and continue lending. Alternatively, funds could be used to create a "bad bank" that would be used for resolving bad loans, thereby forcing PSBs to focus on their normal commercial activities,' the survey said.

Successive RBI governors have also resisted government pressure on making the central bank's staff regulations statutory in character. Currently, the staff regulations are governed by the RBI's administrative decisions, but once they become statutory, the approval of the government would be mandatory.

Is the Cause Worth Fighting For?

In short, there have been innumerable instances of the Indian central bank fighting with the government on many fronts—it has lost in many cases and won quite a few. The core of the debate is whether the cause is worth fighting for. So far, most cases where the RBI has chosen to fight—and has lost or won—have been related to certain segments of the economy and they did not have the kind of impact on a nation of 1.3 billion people, which demonetization is envisaged to have.

Many in the ruling government feel this is the biggest economic reform India has witnessed since Independence—bigger than the goods and services tax, or GST, and even the 1991 chapter when, under the pressure of the worst-ever balance of payment crisis, the Indian economy embraced liberalization. It would change India forever by stamping out the parallel economy and ushering in a cashless payments system.

Is the RBI a believer in the demonetization exercise or a reluctant supporter of the move? If it is the latter, then it should have put up a fight. Irrespective of a win or a loss, that would have made people perceive that the central bank is independent, as public perception about autonomy is as important as autonomy itself.

Former RBI governor I.G. Patel (tenure from 1 December 1977 to 15 September 1982) once said: 'Don't nitpick. Pick your battles. Once you have picked your battles, fight those battles valiantly.' This was an opportunity for a valiant fight only if the RBI was not convinced about demonetization's success. But the regulator gives the impression that it is convinced of its success. So, why believe that it has surrendered its autonomy? Wait till we see the end or question its wisdom.

Meanwhile, since this government wants to change India, it can do many other things. They may not be as seminal as demonetization, but nonetheless can change the contour of the financial sector and regulations. Two such things could be dropping Section 7 from the RBI Act and bringing down the government's stakes below 51 per cent in public-sector banks through amendments of Acts.

I am sticking to only the financial sector and not talking about making political parties disclose donations of even less than Rs 20,000 and paying income tax on all donations.

THE NEW PHASE OF THE RBI–FINANCE MINISTRY CONFLICT

19 June 2017

In media and India's financial circle, speculation is mounting on the 'deteriorating' relationship between the finance ministry and the Reserve Bank of India and the 'attack' on the central bank's autonomy.

During the demonetization exercise in November–December 2016 when high-value currency notes worth 86 per cent of the money in circulation were withdrawn all of a sudden, the Indian central bank did everything it could do to support the government move. This annoyed many, including a couple of past governors of the RBI, who found the central bank being subservient to the government.

The April policy statement in which the RBI sounded pretty hawkish (after changing the monetary policy stance from accommodative to neutral in February) led to the first outburst by the government. Arvind Subramanian, Chief Economic Adviser to the Government of India, has been vocal against the monetary policy committee (MPC) as well as the central bank for not cutting the policy rate despite considerable easing of inflation pressure.

The analysts' community largely ignored that as yet another instance of the classic conflict between growth and inflation in Asia's third-largest economy. By tradition, the government pushes for rate cuts for short-term growth, while the central bank's primary mandate is curbing inflation, and in the long run only low inflation can fuel sustainable economic growth.

The finance ministry summoning members of the MPC for a meeting is the latest provocation for the speculation on the RBI–finance ministry relationship.

What exactly happened?

A not-so-senior bureaucrat of the finance ministry wrote to the MPC members, inviting them for a meeting in Delhi just two days ahead of their meeting at the RBI headquarters in Mumbai, ostensibly to put pressure on them for a rate cut. The MPC has six members, including three from the RBI—Governor Urjit Patel, Deputy Governor Viral Acharya and Executive Director Michael Patra. The finance ministry wanted to have two separate meetings, one with the MPC members from the RBI and another with the outsiders. All the MPC members declined the request for the meeting.

Had they met the ministry officials ahead of the policy meeting, they would have ended up compromising the credibility of the MPC. Even if they had chosen to only listen to the finance ministry officials and not acted on their 'advice', it would not have been easy to communicate to the market the stance of the monetary policy. After such a meeting, had the MPC decided to cut the rate, it would have been obvious that it did so under pressure from the government; and had it not gone for a rate cut, the interpretation would have been that the MPC is extra hawkish.

The RBI Act was amended last year to provide for a statutory and institutionalized framework for the MPC whose objective is to maintain price stability, 'while keeping in mind the objective of growth'. The members of the MPC are to be appointed by the government, but it has no business to directly interfere in the functioning of the MPC.

Calling the MPC members for a meeting in Delhi ahead of the policy is an open attack on it. The MPC is not even a year old (it was constituted in September 2016) and the June meeting was its fifth since inception. Such an attack on the fledgling MPC will considerably weaken it even if certain finance ministry officials do not care about their own credibility.

If the past meetings of the MPC are anything to go by, it has started showing signs of maturity. While decisions at its first three meetings were built on consensus, in the April meeting, the RBI's Patra almost pitched for a rate hike (it's another matter that he misread the inflation trajectory) and Professor Ravindra H. Dholakia in June was strongly in favour of a rate cut.

The June monetary policy statement (the MPC deliberations are not in the public domain as yet) makes it clear that the members of the committee do appreciate that the risks to inflation are lower now than what they were in April. The mid-year and the year-end projections for retail inflation have also been pared considerably; yet most members of the committee were against a rate cut as they wanted to be sure that in the medium term, retail inflation would stay within the 4 per cent limit that the committee is targeting.

The government can always have a different view, but it could have been communicated to the RBI in a different way. Typically, ahead of every monetary policy, the RBI governor always meets the finance minister in the North Block that houses the ministry. This had been the tradition till the MPC was constituted. In fact, I always wondered why the governor would meet the finance minister carrying the policy document in a briefcase and why they could not talk on phone.

Instead of a bureaucrat writing letters to the MPC and making this public within hours of writing it, the Prime Minister's Office or the finance minister could have called the governor for an informal meeting on the state of affairs in the Indian economy ahead of the policy.

With the May retail inflation slowing to 2.17 per cent and the likely fall of June inflation to below 1.9 per cent (that's the last inflation data that the MPC will have on its table before its August meeting), it's almost a given that there will be a quarter percentage point rate cut in August. The bond market has already priced in this cut.

So, why are the finance ministry officials in such a hurry to push for a rate cut? Probably slowing economic growth since June 2016 has made them a worried lot, but the rate cut alone cannot propel growth. At the current juncture, even if the loans are given free, there is hardly any taker for the money for many other reasons. Besides, already saddled with bad loans, the banks are wary of giving loans for fear of accumulating more bad loans.

The RBI is addressing this issue on a war footing, and rightly so. Of course, a rate cut at this point will drive down the bond yield, leading to treasury profits of banks and helping them clean up their balance sheets. It will be recapitalization by stealth, but will not fuel economic growth.

Also, any attack on the MPC will not be liked by the foreign investors who are ready to pump in money into India, looking at its rock-solid macroeconomic and political stability. They are convinced that India is determined to slay inflation for good. Of course, there are many, including some foreign investors, who aren't liking the MPC delaying the rate cut, but the delay is a far better option than having an impotent MPC.

8

Demonetization: A Boon or a Bane?

The jury is still out on the impact of demonetization on the Indian economy. Everyone is convinced that the implementation was shoddy, very few believe in its long-term benefits, and many highlight the short-term pains. What started as a crusade against corruption, black money, fake currency and terrorism took a different turn midway and morphed into a movement for a cashless nation. Realizing that even that's too ambitious a mission, the terminology was later changed from 'cash less' to 'less cash'.

In the fifty days between 10 November and 30 December 2016, Rs 15.4 trillion worth of currency notes of denominations of Rs 1000 and Rs 500—some 86.9 per cent of the value of total notes in circulation—were withdrawn after a historic address to the nation by Prime Minister Narendra Modi (he also signed it off with an equally passionate address). How much of that has come back to the system? The data released by the Reserve Bank of India annual report in August 2017 show that Rs 15.28 trillion in demonetized notes had returned to the system as of 30 June 2017. This is nearly 99 per cent of the Rs 15.45 trillion in currency that had been scrapped.

At the initial stage, the quantum of unreturned currency was speculated to be around Rs 3 trillion. There had also been speculation that the Indian government could use the currency that would not be returned to solve its fiscal problems. Ironically, instead of helping the government tackle its fiscal deficit, the impact of demonetization on the RBI's balance sheet could queer the pitch in the fiscal year 2017–18. The RBI transferred Rs 306.59 billion of its surplus to the government for the fiscal year 2016–17 (July–June), less than half of the Rs 658.76 billion it had transferred in the previous year, and substantially lower than what the government had estimated in its budget document (Rs 580 billion). This is the lowest dividend paid since 2011–12, and the cost of printing new notes and stamping out excess liquidity from the system, an offshoot of demonetization, contributed to this, among a few other things.

Does this mean, the government's aim to kill black money has bitten the dust? Not entirely. Tonnes of black money may not have been unearthed, but the government has been closely following the leads given by the banks and chasing people whose official income does not justify the amount of money they had deposited in November–December 2016 to get rid of the old Rs 500 and Rs 1000 currency notes. Some people had come forward to declare unaccounted money and there is a positive impact on the mass of taxpayers; and the digitalization of financial transactions will leave a trail and ultimately help in better tax compliance and efficiency. Also, demonetization has improved transmission in the banking system and led to greater financialization of savings.

The drop in interest rates on bank deposits after demonetization and the decline in gold prices, coupled with a dull real estate market—regulations such as the Real Estate (Regulation and Development) Act, 2016, and the Benami Transactions (Prohibition) Amendment Act, 2016, have contributed to that—have been drawing savers and investors to the equity market, directly and through the mutual fund route. The assets under management by mutual funds have been rising, and the flow of money into equity schemes doubling. The premia collected by life insurance companies have also been on the rise. If the shift from physical assets such as gold and real estates to financial savings lasts for good, then the cost of capital will come down and demonetization will be a boon for the Indian economy.

The questions are: will it last? Will the government be able to block the reverse flow? Will investors permanently shift from real estate to equities? Will there be enough incentives for financialization of savings?

Only time will tell. The three pieces in this chapter have not dealt in detail with the pros and cons of demonetization; neither have they tried to pass any value judgement on the move for lack of sufficient information at this point of time. Also, you might find some discrepancies in the data. I have used the figures available while I was writing the columns and they keep changing. The story is still unfolding.

Former RBI governor Raghuram Rajan was not on the same page with the government on demonetization. Historically, the government—irrespective of its political affiliation—never listened to the RBI governor on such a move. C.D. Deshmukh (August 1943–June 1949) was against it in 1946 and I.G. Patel (December 1977–September 1982) did not support it in 1978. Patel recalled in his book, *Glimpses of Indian Economic Policy: An Insider's View*, that when Finance Minister H.M. Patel informed him about the decision to cancel high-denomination notes, he had pointed out that such an exercise seldom produces striking results, as most people who accept black money do not keep their ill-gotten earnings in the form of currency for long.

Incidentally, following the 1946 exercise, out of Rs 1439.7 million worth of high-value notes, Rs 1349 million returned to the system and a little over Rs 90 million was demonetized. While this information is culled from the RBI publications, going by a report in *The Hindu BusinessLine*, about 86 per cent of high-denomination currency returned to the banking system in the aftermath of the 1978 exercise. The result of the latest demonetization drive, purely from the point of view of how much money returned to the system, is far worse.

I am not joining the debate on the supposed political dividend it paid and the economic benefits that will accrue in future from the black swan event. I am just chronicling those fifty eventful days, the logistical nightmare, the pain that some segments of the financial system and Indian economy had undergone during that period and still suffering from it. And also, how the banking system coped with it. The last bit has been told through the diary of a branch manager.

THE WHYS AND HOWS OF DEMONETIZATION

14 November 2016

The choice before the government was to announce it out of the blue and run the risk of chaos on the streets or have a smooth transition from the old currency notes to new ones, but without getting much out of it in terms of unearthing unaccounted cash. It chose the first.

Had I been Kumbhakarna, the younger brother of Ravana in the Ramayana, and was woken up in Mumbai after a long slumber and the looked at the thousands of bank branches that dot the country's most populous city, I would have thought there's a run on the entire banking system of the country.

Why were so many people waiting with impatience outside every bank branch? Why were all ATMs closed? Why the mad rush to withdraw money? Is there a liquidity crisis? Have all the banks gone belly up?

The trigger was the banning of high-value Rs 1000 and Rs 500 notes (and replacing them with new Rs 2000 and Rs 500 notes over the next fifty days) that took effect at midnight on 8 November, hours after it was announced by Prime Minister Narendra Modi.

Is there any surprise in the move? Well, unless we were all sleeping like Kumbhakarnas, we should have anticipated it. Bringing back unaccounted money stashed in offshore accounts was a poll promise of the ruling Bharatiya Janata Party. The government had given a three-month window for compliance, but the response was not great.

The next target was black money within India. The Income Disclosure Scheme 2016 was relatively successful. It collected Rs 652.50 billion, seven times more than what a similar scheme in 1997 had mopped up. A new law to give more teeth to the authorities to curb benami transactions (or transactions done in the name of some person other than the person who has financed it) is also in place. Besides, India's Double Taxation Avoidance Agreements with Mauritius and Cyprus have been amended.

While all these aim at shrinking the size of the so-called parallel economy, which could be at least one-fifth of India's GDP, and forcing more citizens to come under the tax bracket, the Pradhan Mantri Jan-Dhan Yojana, a national mission on financial inclusion launched within months of the new government assuming power, has been trying to expand the reach of India's banking sector.

It has so far opened 254.5 million new accounts, offering access to credit and remittance facility, insurance and pension products to low-income groups.

All these, in stages, created the context for the 'surgical strike' of 8 November that attacked black money, fake currency, terrorist financing as well as people's unwillingness to say goodbye to the cash economy.

Surely, it has been a logistical nightmare for the banking system. All bank branches remained closed on Wednesday and ATMs for two days, Wednesday and Thursday, but this was too short a notice to prepare the system to meet the demand for new notes. Most ATMs were closed even after two days and bank branches do not have adequate new notes and old Rs 100 notes even now. There have been instances of a hospital refusing to release the dead body of a twenty-six-year-old man to his father as he could not arrange the cash in the denomination of acceptable currency notes; a newborn baby dying for the same reason; and a senior citizen suffering from heart attack while standing in a long queue outside a bank branch to exchange old notes.

Even on Saturday, Finance Minister Arun Jaitley said it could take as much as two to three weeks for the ATMs to start dispensing new Rs 2000 and Rs 500 notes as they are to be recalibrated to accommodate these new notes of different sizes. This means the inconvenience of the masses will continue for some more time and political parties of different hues will not end their tirade against Modi's move.

Shouldn't this have been handled better? Definitely. At least, this could have come a few days later when the Reserve Bank of India was ready with the new Rs 500 notes. Similarly, Rs 100 notes could have been pumped into the system in the run-up to it as that would have made the lives of millions a bit easy. Even if one gets Rs 2000 notes today after a long wait, it's not easy to use that in the market as the vegetable vendors, provision stores and barbers do not have enough Rs 100 notes to return.

However, could this chaos have been avoided entirely? Certainly not. Secrecy is the key to the success of such a move. There was only a three-hour window and even that was wide enough for many with unaccounted money—they bought gold and foreign currency till the wee hours of 8 November, paying as much as 50 per cent premium. Had the government and the RBI wanted a foolproof transition by stacking currency chests of all banks with new notes to ensure a smooth transition, the black money hoarders would have got wind and the very purpose of this exercise would have been defeated.

A Hobson's Choice

The choice before the government was to announce it out of the blue and run the risk of the chaos on the streets or have a smooth transition from the old currency notes to new notes but without getting much out of it in terms of unearthing unaccounted cash. It has chosen the first, and rightly so. My understanding is that the plan was to launch this a bit later, probably in January, but the image of the new Rs 2000 note making the rounds in social media last week unnerved the government and it did not want to take chances with the plan being leaked, and instead preferred to launch it immediately, even though the printing of Rs 500 currency notes had not even started at that time.

Almost everybody has been discussing how the so-called demonetization (strictly speaking, this is not demonetization—it's replacing old notes with new ones) has failed in India and globally and how it could possibly curb only the stock of the black money (that too, partially) and the flow will continue. The habitual offenders would now hoard the new Rs 500 notes, and the higher-denomination Rs 2000 notes will, in fact, make their job easier. Even now, thousands of Jan-Dhan accounts are being 'sold'—people with unaccounted money are hiring such accounts to deposit Rs 250,000, the limit up to which the tax authorities will not ask any questions on the source of money. There could be endless debates on all these and the disruption in discretionary consumption, gold and property markets, but that does not negate the enormous impact of the historic move.

As of September, the Indian economy had Rs 17.3 trillion, or $260 billion, of currency in circulation, and going by the March 2016 data, Rs 500 and Rs 1000 notes contributed to 86 per cent of the value of currency in circulation—around Rs 14 trillion, or a little over 10 per cent of India's GDP. Even if a part of this money flows into the banking system and tax is paid on that, the government stands to gain and to that extent, the country's fiscal health will improve. This will also improve India's tax to GDP ratio of 16.6 per cent, much lower than the emerging markets' average of 21 per cent.

On Saturday, Jaitley announced that around Rs 1.5–2 trillion fresh deposits flowed into the banking system and the State Bank of India alone has mopped up Rs 480 billion. In the past one year—between November 2015 and October 2016—the banking system collected Rs 8.9 trillion new deposits. At this rate, in fifty days till 30 December, the flow of new deposits would probably be higher than the yearly deposit collection. This will increase liquidity in the system and drive down the interest rates on loans and yields on bonds. The so-called monetary transmission will improve and banks' profitability too will rise as they will get more low-cost current and savings accounts, and their cost of funds will come down.

Indeed, this drive will attack the stock of black money and not the flow, and it will instil the fear of god in the tax evaders the way the new insolvency law will psych wilful defaulters. The chaos at bank branches and ATMs, and people scrambling for new currency notes will also force many to shift to plastic and other channels of payments instead of cash alone.

Anecdotally, some of the malls in Bengaluru and Mumbai saw a phenomenal rise in the use of credit and debit cards last week. There will be resistance in rural India, and low-income groups will take time to get used to debit cards, but the combination of the goods and services tax, an Aadhaar-driven financial inclusion and the latest move will change the narrative of India's formal economy.

AN UPHILL ROAD FOR MFIS

5 December 2016

Many sectors are facing enormous challenges because of the shortage of cash. Microfinance is one of them. If you have your ear to the ground, you may hear 1.2 million employees of the Indian microfinance industry singing an old song of country-and-western singer and songwriter Jim Reeves: *Where do I go from here? / What fate is drawing near?*

Around 85 per cent of the loan disbursements by the microfinance institutions and close to 95 per cent repayment or collection of loans have traditionally been in cash. The sudden disappearance of the old notes and the slow replacement by new ones hit the industry hard in the second week of November when the so-called demonetization came into effect.

Yes, the Rs 100 currency notes, the mainstay of relatively smaller MFIs when it comes to loan disbursements and repayments, have been in circulation, but people have been hoarding this as it is difficult to get change for Rs 2000, and Rs 500 currency notes continue to be in short supply even now. The industry is limping back to normalcy, but the aggressive push towards a cashless economy will force the MFIs to change their business model if they want to survive.

As I write this piece, the disbursements and collection of loan instalments have risen substantially from the week ending 12 November, but still they are far from being normal. Going by the estimate of Sa-Dhan, an industry body, in the first week of the ban on old notes, disbursements dropped by50–60 per cent. In the second week, it rose by 12–15 per cent over the first week and in the third week, it rose further by 30–35 per cent over the second week. Similarly, the collection of debt instalments dropped by 30–40 per cent in the first week, but there has been a gradual rise since then.

Some of the MFIs were planning to go cashless, and now they will speed up the process. It won't be an easy task for the industry even though there have been instances of MFIs striving to do this in different geographies. They could do so, as many of them—at least fifty for-profit MFIs—have been serving as banking correspondents of various banks.

In this avatar, in addition to their core business of giving small loans, they offer banking products to their customers for a fee earned from the banks whose products they hawk. About 70 per cent borrowers of Cashpor Micro Credit in eastern Uttar Pradesh get their loans through bank accounts. Similarly, around 200 branches of Satin Creditcare Network Ltd in western Uttar Pradesh have gone cashless.

Obviously, all MFIs will not be affected the same way. The pain for the rural ones will certainly be more than their counterparts in semi-urban and urban pockets. Similarly, those who are on their way to transform themselves into small-finance banks are better equipped to handle this phase of transition because of their relative superiority in terms of the technology platform. For most, all lendings have been so far in cash, drawn from the nearest bank branch with which the MFIs have an account. From the bank branch, the cash travels to different branches of the MFIs and from there to the community centres or the spots where the borrowers gather to collect their loans and repay at periodic intervals.

For this logistic reason, the loan disbursements are typically planned for days in advance. There are around 13,000 MFI branches across India and each branch serves many groups of women who assemble at the courtyard of the leader of such groups at a particular time on a given day.

In a similar fashion, the repayments flow back. Different MFIs follow different payment cycles. At the weekly, fortnightly or monthly meetings, the borrowers pay their loan instalments. From there, the collections flow back to the banks through the MFI branches which aggregate all loan disbursements and repayments, and keep a small amount in their custody when the repayment of loans exceed new disbursements.

What impacted the MFI borrowers who have a high repayment track record is primarily the sudden shortage of Rs 100 notes and, to a lesser extent, the slow replacement of the old Rs 500 notes. Indeed, repayments are used for fresh loan disbursals, but since all repayments cannot be absorbed in the same centre immediately, a good part of the repayment flows back into the bank account.

And once the money goes back into the bank account, it cannot come back for fresh disbursements because of current restrictions on how much cash an MFI can withdraw from banks. As a result of this, many of those that had planned big disbursements this time around cannot do so. Traditionally, a substantial part of the disbursements takes place in the so-called 'busy season' that lasts between October and March when major crops are reaped and economic activities increase across the country.

The writing on the wall is loud and clear. The MFIs must change the ways in which they have been working. They need to forge alliances with different kinds of banks—small-finance, payments and universal banks—as well as digital wallet service providers, and disburse and collect money through the banking channel which will leave a trail for audit of all such transactions. It cannot be done overnight and the RBI must give them time for the transition. For all new customers, the MFIs must create the bank linkages. Those who are not capable of doing so can convert themselves into banking correspondents, while the large MFIs can be made small-finance banks, depending on their track record. Eight of them have already been made so.

This new architecture will lead to an increase in the cost for MFI borrowers as the money cannot be disbursed at their doorsteps any more unless portable micro ATMs are used. They would need to travel to the nearest bank branch or approach the banking correspondent, and in the process they may lose half a day's wage and/or incur transport cost. For MFIs, on the other hand, the operational cost will come down as they would not need so many people for disbursements of loans and collection of repayments. It will also bring down the incidents of theft and pilferage. The new cost structure will enable them to bring down the price of loans and compensate for the additional cost that the borrowers will incur.

The small and medium enterprises, many of whom depend on the MFIs for borrowing, are also being hugely affected as they operate in cash economy. As I write this column, I hear millions are staring at the prospects of losing jobs.

The cascading effect of the move can outweigh the gains if not handled properly. Mere congratulations to 1.25 billion Indians and appeal to their patience will not work.

FIFTY DAYS IN THE LIFE OF A BANK'S BRANCH MANAGER

9 January 2017

This is from the diary of a branch manager of an Indian bank.

He lives in the Mumbai suburbs, takes a local train to work and usually heads back home by 7 p.m.

Life took a different turn after Prime Minister Narendra Modi made the historic announcement of a currency swap on 8 November 2016. Roughly 86 per cent of the Rs 15.50 trillion worth of currency in circulation was to be replaced in the world's second-most populated country where a bank branch caters to an average of 10,000 people.

For the next fifty days till the exercise ended on 30 December, the branch manager had to occasionally sleep at the branch when he missed the last train home. He had to make sure that every customer was taken care of and that the bank could use the opportunity for generating low-cost current and savings accounts. On top of that, he needed to be on his toes so that none of his colleagues were used for money laundering.

He is one of the 1,30,000-odd branch managers of banks in India—and this is a story of every branch manager in the country.

This thirty-three-year-old banker works for a private bank in Mumbai, and heads a relatively new and small branch. For privacy, I am neither naming the banker, nor his bank. Every character and incident mentioned in this diary is true.

Back from a four-day holiday in the first week of January at Matheran, a hill resort in Maharashtra, with his three-year-old daughter and wife, this man looks back at those fifty days as something surreal.

Edited Extracts from His Diary

The 7.04 a.m. Virar local at Nalasopara was late. My heart sank when I heard the late arrival announcement. Would I be able to reach office on time? How long would it take to get a taxi from Dadar station? Thank God, the train was late by just five minutes. By the time I reached the branch, there were about fifty people waiting outside, patiently. That was 10 November, two days after the demonetization announcement. The branch was closed the previous day.

The first thing that nine of us in the branch did was huddle in a corner—the way a cricket team does before taking the field. I told them that we need to serve the customers to the best of our ability and we will never compromise our integrity. This is a lifetime opportunity to prove to the world what we can do. That became a daily ritual till 30 December. We did not ask for any reinforcement of staff from the headquarters. Nine of us formed three teams—two of my colleagues were managing the queue of the customers with the help of a lone, unarmed security guard; three were handling data entry and another three were at the two cash counters. I was overseeing the work of all three groups.

Three Transactions

Many customers were making three transactions—one each for deposit of cash, withdrawal of cash and exchange of old notes. Reconciling the data was very critical as any shortfall of money was to be made good by us unless the amount was too big. In such cases, an internal inquiry could be instituted. We needed to make sure that the money deposited must tally with the amount we had in the vault. One day in the train I heard a gentleman sitting next to me, a branch manager of a large public-sector bank, telling someone higher up in his bank on phone about a Rs 18-million shortfall in his branch and begging for more staff. Thankfully, in our case we needed to make good only Rs 300 one day.

Such things can happen even if you're alert. One day, to my horror I found how ingenious people can be! A person was busy filling in the form for depositing money, but actually he was carrying no money. He probably assumed that under work pressure, my colleague at the teller would check the form and accept it, but wouldn't ask for the money! Similarly, another person wrote Rs 4500 in the form, but actually offered to deposit Rs 2000. He too thought the man at the teller was too busy to bother about this.

We needed to keep a hawk-eye on every transaction to catch such people. After every hour, we were taking a five-minute break to tally the transactions. At the first stage, we were getting all the details of the customer in terms of Aadhaar card, PAN card, address, the amount of money to be deposited, etc., and taking notes of all. Only after that, a transaction could take place. In the five-minute break after every one hour, we were checking how much money was deposited and whether the amounted tallied with the data sheet that we were creating.

On the pavement directly opposite the branch one day I saw one gentleman distributing old Rs 1000 and Rs 500 notes to at least a dozen people. After taking the money from him, those people were rushing to join the queue outside the bank branch. I called my colleague Varun out and decided to confront that man.

He claimed to be a contractor who was giving salary to his workers and immediately left the spot. We found that each of them was given Rs 4500 worth of old notes to exchange for new notes. On that day, the limit for currency exchange had been raised from Rs 4000 to Rs 4500, and the limit for drawing money from ATM had also been lifted from Rs 2000 to Rs 2500. Apparently, the man was doing this every day outside different bank branches across Mumbai. We politely told those people to leave the place.

We also put in place a system whereby I could keep a tab in real time on how much money is being withdrawn from the ATM at my branch. Before I settled down and had my first glass of water one day, I found a series of withdrawals in quick succession, with a gap of less than thirty seconds, of Rs 2400 each. There must be something wrong! I stepped out of my cabin and went into the ATM kiosk.

There were about twenty people standing in a queue outside the kiosk. I found a man inside with at least twenty-five debit cards and a piece of paper with passwords of those cards written on it. He claimed that all these cards belonged to his colleagues and he was withdrawing money on their behalf. The amount for each transaction was Rs 2400 so that he could get at least four Rs 100 notes. I had to throw him out of the kiosk.

A Car Full of Money

Another day, a man walked in with a suitcase carrying Rs 8.5 million. He was a customer of our bank, but not our branch. I decided to connect him with the Vadodara branch manager where he claimed to have his account. I don't know what they discussed over the phone, but I found him leaving my branch with his suitcase after talking to my counterpart.

Another man one day came in his Toyota Innova, full of money. He came to the bank carrying Rs 50 million worth of old notes in one bag. There were thirteen such bags inside the car, he told us. His offer was quite straightforward—50 per cent of new notes in exchange of old notes. We could not believe what he was saying, and we looked at each other for a few seconds, and then asked him to leave the branch or else we would call the police.

I also remember an occasion when a travel agent dropped by with eighty passports and other documents to complete the KYC formalities and open new accounts. We said no to him.

Since we don't have a currency chest of our own, our internal guidelines allowed us to keep Rs 1.4 million in the bank vault overnight. Every day, we needed to transfer the extra cash that was being generated through deposits of old notes to another bank which has a currency chest. It's merely 200 metres away. But under our bank's rule, we could not walk up to that bank's branch carrying money. Each day, we had to take a taxi and make several trips, as without an armed security guard we are not allowed to carry more than Rs 900,000 in one trip. Two of my colleagues needed to carry the cash each time.

On the first day, 10 November, we closed the branch at 11.45 p.m. By the time I reached Dadar station, the 12.41 a.m. Virar local had left. I came back to the branch, slept for a couple of hours sitting on my chair before taking the 4.36 a.m. train. At home, I took a bath, had breakfast and left for work at 6.30 a.m. This was not a one-off. There were many days in the past two months when I missed the last train and returned to office at midnight to catch some sleep. Many of us spent our Sundays too in the branch as on weekdays we could do nothing but handle the cash; there was no time to do other routine work such as maintenance of records and, of course, sanction and disbursement of loans.

Many a time the customers got agitated, but we could not afford to lose our cool. Most of them supported demonetization, but for some reasons they did not have much sympathy for us. They thought the move is good for the country to flush out black money, and banks had the money, but were not giving them. It was very tough to convince them that our hands were tied—there weren't enough new notes to please all. The continuous changes in the regulator's directives also complicated our job. Literally, each time I was going to the toilet, I used to ask my colleagues to keep a tab on whether there's any change in the RBI rules. And once it actually happened.

The toughest part of the entire exercise was to keep the morale of my colleagues high. Two of my women colleagues also used to stay late every day. There were occasions when they could not take it any more. One of my male colleagues cried; another wanted to quit the job. I always told them to look at this as an opportunity to learn, to excel at our job. We needed to support the country in its fight against black money.

There were days when we couldn't have a proper meal. I lost 10 kg in these two months; got a few strands of grey hair. I also quit smoking, something I had been trying to do ever since my daughter was born. In those fifty days, there was no time to step out of the bank branch for a smoke. My wife is happy. At Matheran, my daughter did not leave me alone for a moment.

PART II
The Seminal Leaders

THE PEOPLE

Who are the people that best exemplify the transformation of the Indian financial sector in the past decade? Here are fifteen of them, culled from my writing. By no way is this list exhaustive. More than interviews, these are more like conversations that offer a glimpse into the enormous changes that the nation's banking and financial sector has been witnessing in the past decade and also the evolution of these leaders.

The notable absentees are Uday Kotak, vice chairman and managing director of Kotak Mahindra Bank Ltd; Chandra Shekhar Ghosh, founder, MD and CEO of Bandhan Bank Ltd; Vijay Shekhar Sharma, founder of the mobile payments company One97 Communications, which is behind the well-known consumer brand Paytm; and A.P. Hota, former managing director and CEO of National Payments Corporation of India. Sharma and Hota are the poster boys in the Indian payments space; they have brought in phenomenal changes as an entrepreneur (Sharma) and as a professional (Hota).

I stayed away from interviewing Ghosh because of perceived conflict of interest (I am attached to Bandhan Bank as an adviser) and did not interview other three in the current format. None of the interviews were done for this book; they were done while I was covering the banking sector as a journalist.

The list includes regulators, commercial bankers, professionals-turned-entrepreneurs, investment bankers and a fund manager. One is an expat who offers an outsider's perspective on doing business in India.

Barring two, all were written after the collapse of Lehman Brothers. The two I profiled in 2001 and 2006 are still relevant as big-time influencers in the Indian financial sector—K.V. Kamath and Deepak Parekh.

Former managing director and CEO of ICICI Bank, Kamath now heads the New Development Bank, a multilateral institution set up by the BRICS grouping of Brazil, Russia, India, China and South Africa. Even in the worst of times, when the economy faltered in the wake of the global liquidity crisis, Kamath refused to accept official figures, and instead spoke about growth's different components—that which was counted and that which was uncounted.

In 2001, Kamath, the guru of Indian retail banking, predicted the changes that would grip the financial sector, the overarching role of technology in banking, the speed at which the sector would change and the importance of scale. All these are playing out today. Certainly, he has his detractors. Many believe his love for speed and scale (Chinese banks are his model) comes with inherent problems.

Parekh was once on every key government panel—the Malhotra committee on insurance reforms, the Narasimham committee on banking reforms, the panel that did the groundwork for a housing finance regulator. He helped chalk out the rescue plan for the former Unit Trust of India during its first crisis in the late 1990s. More than a decade back, he eloquently spoke about the importance of critical reforms, many of which are being rolled out now.

The commercial bankers profiled here have been key players in the changes that have been taking place in the Indian financial sector and the challenges that accompany such changes.

In 2009, in the thick of the crisis just ahead of formally taking over the mantle from Kamath as ICICI Bank boss, Chanda Kochhar admitted that the lender had grown at a scorching pace when interest rates were low and the economic climate was different. She would need to do things differently. Kochhar actually shrank the balance sheet of ICICI Bank. It is another story that she misread the economic trend later and accumulated bad assets.

The 2014 interview of Arundhati Bhattacharya, the first woman 'chairman' in State Bank of India's two-century-old history, was candid in saying that India's largest lender was paying for its own rapid growth. It gave money to companies when the economy was growing at a healthy pace, but when the climate turned adverse, they were not in a position to repay loans. She also spoke about helping such companies hive off and monetize non-core assets by identifying strategic investors and even looking for a new management—something which the banking regulator is forcing banks to do now.

Another State Bank chairman is featured here—O.P. Bhatt, one of the few chiefs of the bank to have got a five-year stint. We met in 2008, months before the Lehman collapse. Bhatt spoke about merging the SBI's associate banks to build scale. He initiated this exercise with a proposal to merge the State Bank of Saurashtra, the smallest of the associate banks. Bhattacharya later took this forward and recently the SBI absorbed five associate banks, along with the Bharatiya Mahila Bank, reinforcing its position as India's biggest lender and one among the world's top fifty.

It was around the same time, 2008, that the chat with Aditya Puri took place. As boss of India's most valued lender, HDFC Bank, Puri is India's longest-serving bank CEO. At that time, HDFC Bank was taking over the Centurion Bank of Punjab. Almost like a soothsayer, Puri had said, 'We have no desire to run a treasury-operated hedge fund overseas. I am not into making an unworthy borrower into a top-rated customer through financial engineering. In principle, I am against any exposure to very sophisticated instruments. Anything that does not make common sense may land you in trouble.'

The meeting with Pramit Jhaveri, then an investment banker and not the CEO of Citibank India, took place in 2007. The first question I asked him was about the price that Tata Steel was paying for the European steelmaker Corus. His answer was: 'This is an incredibly bold and aggressive move by the Tatas. Whether they are paying more or less, time will tell.' The answer to that is now evident.

Shikha Sharma admitted in 2014 that running Axis Bank had been her toughest assignment. Five years into heading it, she said, 'It's always difficult when you take over a healthy, well-run franchise as you can end up spoiling it.' This is when the bank was growing at a healthy pace and the stock market was rewarding it handsomely. It's a different story now.

Inflation slayer, former Reserve Bank of India governor Raghuram Rajan, launched a sustained campaign to address the rising bad loans of Indian banks. Deputy governor of RBI, Viral Acharya, is now carrying on that task.

A year after he took over as the RBI governor, in our interview, Rajan had said, 'I see my job as a kind of a mission. I have to keep doing what I do. And take the decision without looking to who's happy and who's not.' He also admitted: 'There's immense pressure on the RBI from different quarters—I can certainly attest to that—to relax on every front of our regulations and supervision.'

Former Securities and Exchange Board of India chairman U.K. Sinha had a six-year term with two extensions. In SEBI's twenty-five-year history, only one chairman had a longer tenure—D.R. Mehta for seven years. Sinha also holds the unenviable record of being the only regulator against whose appointment five public interest litigations, or PILs, were filed. During his tenure, Sinha took on several high-profile businessmen, including Sahara's Subrata Roy, the big boss of India's largest shadow bank. On corporate India, Sinha's take was: 'There is too much abuse of related-party businesses.'

Leo Puri heads UTI Asset Management Co. Ltd (UTI AMC), a teen with the soul of a fifty-one-year-old institution. UTI has been losing its market share for many reasons. The solution, according to Puri, is going public and making UTI AMC a widely regarded institution. He had submitted a proposal to the government after he took over, but there's been no decision yet.

The two professionals who have turned entrepreneurs are Jaspal Bindra and V. Vaidyanathan. Bindra, Standard Chartered Bank's chief executive officer for Asia and group executive director till early 2015, picked up a 20 per cent stake in Centrum Capital Ltd, a non-banking finance company, and become an entrepreneur. Centrum's business has been surging. For Bindra, money is not a problem. There are plenty of funds available both as debt and equity. His challenge is to grow and build a solid track record and be in the reckoning to set up a bank. 'If available, we can buy a bank too,' he said, echoing the aspiration of many.

Vaidyanathan, who prefers to be called Vaidya, was among the earliest bets Kamath made while building the retail banking team in ICICI Bank in 2000. By the time he was thirty-eight, Vaidyanathan was an executive director on the bank's board and later headed its life insurance arm, ICICI Prudential Life Insurance. Leaving a flourishing career, he acquired a 10 per cent stake in a real-estate-focused NBFC in 2010. He built a retail team and developed products based on non-conventional models of credit underwriting and collections. The loan book jumped from Rs 940 million in 2010 to Rs 27 billion in two years.

He then pitched to PE players for a management buyout and secured an equity backing of Rs 8.10 billion from Warburg Pincus in 2012. Pulling this off despite the challenges of a slowing economy during 2010–13, rising interest rates and weak markets was no mean achievement. The company has grown since to a worth of Rs 200 billion and has lent to over four million customers, and its market cap rose tenfold to over $1.2 billion. In March 2017, Vaidyanathan sold 1.5 per cent of his stake to retire the debt that he had taken to acquire his holding five years ago.

The only non-Indian in the list is Brooks Entwistle, who came to Mumbai in February 2006 to set up shop for Goldman Sachs in India. He was the only employee for the first few months. Operating out of a hotel suite in south Mumbai, every time he answered a call, he would say, 'Goldman Sachs' and if the caller was looking for him, 'Let me see if Brooks is around.' A few seconds later, to make it seem like there was a large staff on the ground, he would pick up the phone in another room, stir his coffee and say, 'Brooks speaking.'

What is his advice to expats who come to India to build a business? 'There is no manual on how to do it. You must go local from day one. Make India your home. Don't think about your next posting,' he said. One morning in 2007, while dropping his daughters to school, they saw a few cows, a goat, a horse, and finally, on Linking Road, an elephant. His eldest daughter Bryanna screamed with joy: 'Daddy, it's just like living in a movie.'

Yes, the India story has been a bit like a movie with a lot of drama and plot twists. The profiles of these fifteen men and women provide context for a complex story, providing a setting for the melting pot of Indian finance and banking—along with the enormous changes and challenges that are a part of this evolution.

1

Deepak Parekh

BANKING ON A 'SLOWDOWN'

11 January 2005

On 26 December 2004, Deepak Shantilal Parekh attended five weddings. That's par for the course; there are days when the sixty-year-old Housing Development Finance Corporation (HDFC) chief attends half a dozen parties.

Hectic networking? I tease. No, there's no need for that, he replies with equanimity. 'It's just that I can't say no to anybody.'

I can vouch for the fact that he's pretty good at demurring, though. He never quite refused my invitation for a leisurely lunch, but it took me the best part of the year to actually pin him down.

So here we were, finally, at Wet Wicket, the bar at the Cricket Club of India (CCI).

The choice of a bar instead of a more conventional restaurant was not driven by the need for a midday drink. Parekh rarely drinks at the myriad parties he attends, restricting himself to the odd glass of thirty-year-old Ballantine, with a friend at home. He chose Wet Wicket because it was not crowded, so conversation would be easier. The added attraction was a cricket match between CCI and Lords & Commons (a team of select British MPs from the

House of Lords and the House of Commons) on the lush green CCI grounds. Parekh is a self-confessed cricket fanatic. Just that morning, he'd switched on to catch the Pakistan–Australia Test match at Melbourne. Of course, it's not cricket that's kept him from accepting my invitation. Running one of India's largest financial services companies, 'with activities ranging from housing finance, banking, insurance, credit rating, mutual funds, and even BPO operations' is work enough.

But Parekh also seems to have had a monopoly on memberships to key government committees—the Malhotra committee on insurance reforms, the Narasimham committee on banking reforms and the panel that did the groundwork for a housing finance regulator.

He helped chalk out the rescue plan for the former Unit Trust of India during its first crisis in the late 1990s. Now, he is on the Manmohan Singh government's newly set up committee on foreign direct investment.

We decide to order before small talk settles into more serious conversation. Parekh opts for a beer to give me company with my minestrone soup. For the main course, we opt for Parsi fare; he insists I eat prawn, but I opt for mutton *dhansak* while he chooses *akuri*, the spicy Parsi scrambled egg and toast.

I ask him about his role as the government's unofficial crisis consultant; it turns out that he's also a stringent critic. His current irritation is at the dilly-dallying over airport privatization.

'Five and a half years ago our panel recommended that airports should be privatized. Jaswant Singh and George Fernandes were on that panel. Nothing has happened till now. Is the government concerned about the state of the airports and customer service?'

As he points out, the government has received expressions of interest for Delhi and Mumbai. Why does it have to wait for six months for the technical bids? 'Why can't it put a gun on the heads of the bidders and tell them to put in the technical bids right now?' Parekh asks.

He answers his own question. 'Once a State Bank chairman told me that he was there because he did not take any decision. The biggest decision is not to take any decision so that you can never go wrong. That's our system . . . The government does not want to take decisions.'

Parekh detects the same penchant for non-action when it came to Dabhol Power Company (DPC). 'It's over two years and we have not been able to sort out the DPC problem. Its assets are rotting. Every stakeholder must take a hit and get the project going. The power situation is grave in Maharashtra. But nobody bothers about this,' he says.

He points to the progress in the telecom sector as an example. 'If we can do this for telecom, why can't we move forward in power, airports and ports?' he asks.

For roads, Parekh's suggestion is to go for the annuity-based system where the builder of the road is given the responsibility for its maintenance for the next ten years or so, at a cost that is factored into the construction.

Housing and tourism, according to him, are the two most crucial sectors for India, which can generate employment both directly and indirectly. For the housing sector, Parekh has some valuable suggestions. 'Flats must be sold based on the carpet area and not the super built-up area. Why should customers pay the price for space they don't get? Similarly, when a consumer buys a car or a TV there is warranty for the goods. Why can't there be warranty for flats, which are the most expensive fast-moving consumer good?' he asks.

As Parekh finishes his akuri and helps himself to a bit of the dhansak gravy and a spoon of rice, I ask him what went wrong with the Infrastructure Development Finance Company (IDFC). Why did the government want to merge it with the State Bank of India?

Parekh, who is also chairman of IDFC, says a few bureaucrats and some of the financial institutions were against it when Chidambaram, during his earlier stint as a finance minister, gave Rs 10 billion to start IDFC.

'It was never meant to be a term-lending institution. Its job was to lead the private sector into infrastructure and help the government decide on policy matters. It has not failed. If the government delays in taking decisions for infrastructure projects, what can IDFC do?' he says.

Now I come to the big question: How long will HDFC continue to stand alone? Why is Parekh resisting its merger with HDFC Bank? Parekh's explanation is that the merger will require Rs 90 billion worth of investment in securities to meet the statutory liquidity reserve ratio.

'In a rising interest rate scenario, when you mark the investment portfolio to market, it will kill both HDFC and HDFC Bank.'

Does that mean they will continue to remain separate entities? 'There are many options. What's the harm in remaining separate entities? The parent does not come in the way of the bank's growth. We have allowed it to go for a second ADS [American Depositary Share] even though it will bring down HDFC's stake in the bank.'

And he's proud of HDFC's performance, so much so that he can reel off statistics on it at will. HDFC on a year-on-year basis has been growing its balance sheet by 30 per cent, and profit by 20 to 25 per cent.

'Our cost to income ratio is 13 per cent against HDFC Bank's 48 per cent. We will keep the spread intact at 2.2 per cent in the next seven to seventeen years. What's the problem?' asks a confident Parekh.

I get a plum cake as dessert as part of the fixed menu while Parekh asks for chocolate ice cream. I remind him of his dream of making HDFC India's GE Caps. He admits that this dream cannot be fulfilled unless the regulator allows the group to set up a holding company.

'Globally, the holding company concept is accepted. HSBC has seventy-six subsidiaries under its umbrella. Ideally, HDFC should be listed and all other outfits should be its wholly-owned subsidiaries. But that's not possible unless you have one regulator.'

As he points out, HDFC is regulated by the National Housing Bank, the HDFC bank by the Reserve Bank of India, the mutual fund by SEBI and the insurance companies by IRDA.

'How do I go for the holding company structure in this scenario? It is high time the government set up another Narasimham committee to explore the UK's Financial Services Authority model for the Indian financial sector,' he says.

I finish my cake, but there is no sign of Parekh's ice cream. I ask him about his plans. 'I have lived a full life. I would like to slow down now. Next year when my term expires as chairman of HDFC, I will request the board to excuse me from the executive post. I will continue as the non-executive chairman. I would like to indulge in golf . . . I need to give three hours to golf every day, which is not possible now,' he says.

Instead, he indulges in bridge for four hours every Saturday at Congress MP Murli Deora's house. His other passion is chocolate cookies, which he buys by the bagful during every trip abroad. 'I mainly like plain chocolate, but I think Britannia has some excellent chocolate cookies,' he says.

His chocolate ice cream arrives after much delay (the waiter thought he had asked for iced tea and not ice cream).

When the bill comes, Parekh insists on settling it. It's a small price to pay, he explains, for the inordinate delay in accepting my invitation. As he jokes, being a banker he cannot deny me the interest.

2

K.V. Kamath

GREEN CHILLIES AND UNIVERSAL BANKING

21 June 2001

The first time I met Kundapur Vaman Kamath on the day he took over as managing director of ICICI in 1996, I remember the photographer remarking that he was a tall man. Since then, Kamath has grown in his stature in the Indian financial sector in the way he has steered ICICI. Despite that he remains easily accessible.

When I called his office to invite him for lunch, he agreed readily, but with a rider—can we leave out the South Mumbai five-star hotels from our orbit because he doesn't want to spend three hours over a meal? His suggestion: 'Let's eat at the executive lunchroom at ICICI and if you wish you can foot the bill.' I agreed with a caveat—it has to be an exclusive affair between two of us with no other ICICI executives around. (Normally, when Kamath meets journalists, he always has somebody around to tell him what he should not tell the press.)

When I walk into Kamath's cabin on the tenth floor of the ICICI headquarters in Mumbai's Bandra Kurla Complex, it is with relief I overhear his secretary instructing somebody to lay a table for two of us. Kamath and I take the spiral staircase to the executive lunchroom where a bowl of green salad and another small plate with slices of onion and fresh chillies had already been laid.

We are quickly served with a vegetable soup into which Kamath sprinkles some pepper for additional spice. He had returned from Hong Kong just that morning, tying up some loose ends for an insurance venture ICICI was doing with Prudential, but shows no signs of tiredness.

When I remark on this, he says, 'I take vitamin capsules today—A, E, C and one multivitamin capsule daily—and they give me tremendous energy. The pace at which I work today is scorching, one and a half times more than what I did in the eighties.' Helping himself to the salad, he says, 'I never get tired.'

The waiter comes with *rawa* fish fry and a dry Mangaluru-style preparation of chicken, while Kamath continues to detail his dietary regimen. 'I'm on Dr Atkin's diet,' he says, 'no carbohydrates, no sugar—but I am allowed to take any amount of protein and fat.' Helping himself to the chicken, he says, 'I can have 100 grams of rice or a paratha. I prefer paratha to rice.' For the moment, he seems satisfied tackling the boneless chicken. 'I like this,' he says. 'Normally, I eat one meat preparation and some fish,' edging the fish bones aside with his fork.

It may be a coincidence that the preparation is of Mangaluru style, for Kamath hails from Kundapur which is sixty kilometres away from Mangaluru.

He graduated from Karnataka Regional Engineering College in Surathkal and did his postgraduate diploma in business administration from IIM, Ahmedabad, before joining ICICI as a project officer in 1971 at a monthly salary of Rs 975.

Since then, he has done stints elsewhere, but is thrilled to be back to steer ICICI through one of its most interesting phases. The blueprint for the new ICICI was drafted in Jakarta in late 1995.

'It was a remote-control exercise. I was using email as the medium and constructing the new structure of the organization with the people I knew between 1971 and 1988 when I left ICICI to join Asian Development Bank,' he explains. The waiter has brought parathas for both of us, but Kamath is still enjoying his fish and chicken. He, in fact, asks the waiter for a second helping of chicken.

By the time he joined ADB, Kamath had been through virtually every department of ICICI—strategy, planning, treasury, leasing, and even being the executive assistant to S.S. Nadkarni, his mentor.

'When the ADB offer came, Vaghul [Narayan Vaghul, the then ICICI chief] asked me to keep a lien on the ICICI job. I did so, but finally, in 1991, I parted with ICICI,' recollects Kamath with a tinge of nostalgia.

Life at ADB was considerably cushier with a handsome salary, eight hours of working a day, and a couple of vacations a year. 'In early 1995, I told my wife I wanted to retire and come back to India and study liberal arts,' he remembers. 'She did not like the idea."

The waiter is back. This time with *methibhaji* which Kamath takes, and tomato *bharta* to which he says no. 'I like leafy vegetables, palak,' he explains, 'and some green stuff at dinner too.' So far, his paratha has remained untouched.

Quitting ADB, he was wooed by the Barkie Group in Indonesia with an offer of a blank cheque and the task of consolidating the conglomerate. He agreed, but on the condition that it would only be for a year, a period that was stretched by a few months when Vaghul met him in Singapore and asked him to take over ICICI. It was an offer Kamath could not resist.

'I did not even ask what my compensation package would be,' he says. 'I just returned with an open mind in April 1996.'

We have already spent an hour at lunch, but are far from over. Kamath takes his first bite of the paratha and methibhaji, helping himself to one of the green chillies on the plate. 'I love green chilli and onion,' he says, 'it adds spice to my food.' The waiter returns with rice and dal, but neither of us wants any more.

'All of us here work on a twelve-hour module,' Kamath says, reviewing the situation at ICICI. 'The business is different now, and changes are no more incremental but so significant that there is a big chasm which we have to jump to overcome.' He adds, 'There are so many opportunities. We have to move with the pace; we cannot buck the pace.'

Is it because of this pressure-cooker atmosphere that so many people are leaving ICICI? 'There is always huge paranoia about changes,' he says, 'but we don't have a very high turnover. And in a way, when some people leave, others get a chance to grow.'

Biting into another green chilli, he says, 'As in any growing organization, when someone leaves, it creates opportunities for others.'

Away from work, Kamath is a speed maniac, watching motor sports with an avid fascination. 'I watch motor sports to relax. Outside work, that's the only passion I have. It's interesting to watch how to manage speed.'

It obviously has some lessons for him at work too because at ICICI, strategy changes every three months.

'Changes are so radical that you cannot have a fixed strategy,' Kamath insists. 'Today you think you are competing with ISPs [Internet Service Providers], but tomorrow the face of competition could change to portals, telecom outfits, B2B and B2C. You have to be on your toes always, checking out the competition.' He bites into yet another green chilli.

The waiter brings us bowls of fresh fruits—mango, *chikoo*, papaya. Both of us start with mango. Is he happy the way ICICI is moving? 'I have achieved more than I thought I would be able to. I strove to put ICICI on the forefront of technology, but never guessed that it would be a leader.'

Pausing over his mango, Kamath says, 'The work is fun. In Indonesia, with Bakrie Group, I was getting three times [what] I am making here. At ADB, I was paid a lot to do nothing, but I am enjoying every moment here.'

The waiter offered us *kesharpeda*s which are returned untasted. I ask for a cappuccino. Even though we spent a good deal of time together, Kamath shows no hurry. I ask him how he would like to see himself described—as a man of action or a visionary?

'Where is the question of vision?' Kamath shoots back. 'We are reacting to changes. If you ask me to give marks to ICICI for its ability to change as an organization, I will give it 7–7.5 on a scale of ten. Ideally, it should score fifteen on a scale of ten. Till you cross ten, you are only reacting to changes. You must be proactive. The question of vision comes after that.'

I picked up two paans, shooting a last question: now that he has achieved so much in ICICI, does he have any immediate retirement plans?

'No, no, there's a lot of work,' he says. 'We are getting ready for universal banking.'

He gets up—somebody has been waiting for him in his office. Looking back at our lunch table, I find that all the green chillies have disappeared from his plate.

Postscript

In 2009, Kamath handed over the mantle to Chanda Kochhar and moved himself into the role of a non-executive chairman. Beyond banking, he got involved in other areas (he became the non-executive chairman of India's second-largest software exporter, Infosys Ltd) before taking over as the first boss of the New Development Bank of BRICS countries.

3

Chanda Kochhar

STEPPING INTO HER OWN NEW SHOES

17 April 2009

In 1999, Chanda Kochhar, then a general manager and head of the major clients group at Industrial Credit and Investment Corporation of India Ltd, or ICICI—the old avatar of ICICI Bank Ltd—made a presentation to her managing director and CEO, K.V. Kamath. The topics were about changing the reporting structure, cutting down time for product development, ending duplication of efforts, and other ideas for optimization. At the end of the hour-long presentation, Kamath gently asked her who had given Kochhar the go-ahead for the study. Kochhar fumbled, groped for words, and finally confessed—she had not taken anybody's clearance. Kamath loved her answer.

Ten years later, Kochhar, forty-seven, is all set to move into the corner suite, replacing Kamath and becoming the youngest CEO in the bank's fifty-four-year history. She is currently the bank's joint managing director.

The pair first met twenty-five years ago. It was in March 1984 that Kamath, then group head of both the leasing and strategy divisions of ICICI, interviewed the fresh MBA for the post of management trainee. 'He did not ask any academic questions. He was probing and the focus was more on common sense and practical issues,' reminisces Kochhar, as she nibbles on a raw papaya salad at Mumbai's Taj President Hotel's Thai Pavilion restaurant. Kochhar is dressed in one of her signature saris—this one is a pink *bandhani*—and matching gold sandals.

There have been much better times for anyone to take over as chief executive of a large bank. Bad loans are growing against the backdrop of an unprecedented global credit crunch, and ICICI Bank is now shrinking its balance sheet. Moreover, the bank's shares have underperformed for over a year now. Till early last year, the bank was India's most valued one in terms of market capitalization, comfortably ahead of the much larger State Bank of India despite a smaller asset base. But in the past twelve months, ICICI Bank's shares have lost around two-thirds of their value.

Kochhar, however, isn't one to be ruffled by sudden changes in plan. In 2000, Kamath asked her if she'd move from the corporate operations to the retail side of the business. It was a steep move—corporate loans at that time accounted for around half of the balance sheet and an even larger portion of the profits. Retail was less than 1 per cent of the business. Kochhar took a day to think before accepting.

Over the next six years, she ramped up the retail business to about 67 per cent of the bank's balance sheet. 'Domain knowledge helps, but only to a certain extent, and the available data are never complete. We need to depend on logic, gut feel and our ability to react. There is risk and one must take risks,' Kochhar says, explaining her methods.

After we order the main course—red Thai curry, steamed rice and some noodles—I ask her what ails the bank. Why are depositors perennially worried about their money and why do investors dump the stock often on sheer rumour? Why does she have to appear on TV so often to reassure the world?

'We have always done things ahead of time. We started [the] retail business when others couldn't even dream of it. We went international ahead of others. There is always scepticism [about the ICICI Bank],' she says. Do her TV appearances help? 'They do, because we have a very broad consumer base—from very large corporations in metros to small farmers in Tamil Nadu. We are a very complex organization and communication is a challenge.'

Looking back, and in the light of recent hardships for banks, does she regret being involved with any of the businesses? Kochhar gathers her thoughts before replying: 'Perhaps we could have got out of the small-ticket personal loan business earlier. We did it last year, but it could have been done one year before. Collection is difficult. The consumers of these loans are not used to the payment rigour.'

What about credit-linked notes, credit default swaps and other structured products where ICICI Bank lost money? 'We were never there in a big way. We were just testing [the] waters, learning. The market turned bad suddenly, but we moved out pretty fast. One must know when to cut positions.'

Now that she is taking over as CEO, what is top on her agenda? Will she spend time correcting mistakes? 'There was no big mistake. We grew at a scorching pace when the interest rates were low and the economic climate was different. Now, we need to do things differently,' Kochhar says, dismissing the idea that her actions will be corrective in nature to start with.

As part of the new strategy, she wants to increase low-cost current and savings accounts, or CASA. This is around 26 per cent of the bank's deposit portfolio now. If CASA grows, the cost of deposits comes down and a bank's net interest margin—or the difference between what it spends on deposits and earns on loans—goes up. Also, the bank will roll out 600 branches this year, taking its total branch network to 2000, thereby reducing its dependence on direct sales agents.

Kochhar also sees 'muted' growth in overseas assets, which currently account for around 25 per cent of the bank's overall assets— around Rs 3.92 trillion. 'Overseas, we have been depending on public deposits, bonds and interbank borrowings to build assets. The cost of bonds is high. We will use deposits to replace bonds,' she says, virtually laying the blueprint of a new ICICI Bank on the table.

There is no time for dessert as she has to rush to a meeting. With time running out, I jump to a critical question: Won't she find it difficult to run the show as quite a few seasoned ICICI hands, heads of group companies, are planning to quit after she becomes the boss?

'Even if such things happen, there won't be any destabilization in the group. We have a huge talent pool. My advantage is that I have worked with most people in the organization as I had been through almost all divisions.'

And indeed, Kochhar has been associated with most divisions in the bank. As a management trainee earning Rs 2300 a month, she was part of a projects group that oversaw industries such as textiles, paper, sugar and petroleum, and was named a junior officer three months before her training period ended. She built the bank's retail business from scratch and she was also the ICICI Bank's first employee. In 1993, after the financial institution got the central bank's nod to float the bank, she worked on the concept, recruited from forty-odd different organizations, selected the core software platform, and even designed the bank's first chequebook.

Finally, I ask about her fetish for saris, jewellery and pearls. Be it meetings with institutional investors or regulators, Kochhar is always seen in a sari. Kochhar says it's because the sari is the 'most graceful attire for women'. As for jewellery, 'I have no particular fetish for pearls. I love all kinds of jewellery. I love to coordinate my clothes, jewellery, pair of sandals. I spend time on that. At heart, I am still a middle-income family girl who loves good clothes.'

As we get up, I ask the obvious last question: how difficult will it be to fill Kamath's large shoes? 'I will do the job to the best of my ability. I won't need to fill anybody else's shoes. All of us must create our own shoes and make sure that we don't trip.'

4

Arundhati Bhattacharya

CRACKING A MALE BASTION

1 March 2014

Arundhati Bhattacharya, fifty-seven, the first woman boss in State Bank of India's 208-year history, calls herself chairman of the bank—not chairperson. Immediately after moving into the corner room at the bank's headquarters on Madam Cama Road in Mumbai's business district of Nariman Point, Bhattacharya printed her business cards as chairperson, but the bank's legal department advised her against it as the SBI Act does not have any provision for chairperson.

Even before we settle down at the Belvedere Club at the Oberoi in Mumbai, she expresses her unhappiness with the media. 'You always try to sensationalize things . . . I remember reading hundreds of stories saying how rotten our midday meal scheme is, but there was not a single article on how successfully some of the midday meal schemes have been run,' she tells me with equal gusto while ordering 'toddy'—a mocktail of lemon, honey, ginger, pepper, cardamom and clove, boiled in hot water—tonic for her cold. I opt for watermelon juice. For starters, we order shami kebab that melts in the mouth and dahi kebab, made with hung curd.

Born in north Kolkata, Bhattacharya, the youngest of three children of an electrical engineer, spent her childhood in the steel cities of Bhilai in Chhattisgarh and Bokaro in Jharkhand, where her father clocked long hours at the plants while her mother studied homoeopathy. She graduated in English literature from Lady Brabourne College in Kolkata and before completing her postgraduation from Jadavpur University, she tried her luck at becoming a probationary officer in the SBI, along with half a dozen classmates. The immediate provocation for looking for a job was her father's retirement. In 1977, when she got the appointment letter and a first-class train ticket to travel to Hyderabad, where the orientation course would be held at the bank's staff college, the entire hostel celebrated.

Did she have any inkling when she joined the bank that one day she would become its chief? 'Theoretically, every probationary officer has a chance to become chairman. In that sense, all in our batch might have dreamt of bagging the top job,' she responds.

Why did it take so many years for a woman to become the head of the bank? 'It took time as initially not too many women were coming for an officer's job at SBI and many among those who were coming, gave up their careers midway for their family,' Bhattacharya says. In 1977, less than 20 per cent of the new officers were women. Now, the figure has doubled. Still, the percentage of women employees in the SBI is not very high. Among officers, it's about 17 per cent and among all employees, about 23 per cent. 'Your ability will get you the job, but you also need to have age on your side. So if you started your career at twenty-one, you have an advantage over others in your batch who started at, say, twenty-four,' she says.

Bhattacharya, who took over from Pratip Chaudhuri as the SBI chairman in October, has been able to balance home and office as she does not consider herself indispensable in either place. 'That comes from a sense of insecurity. But more important than that, once you step out, the team should take over. I always focus on team building—both in office and at home.' When she goes for a long tour, her husband, a software professional based in Kolkata, comes to Mumbai to give company to their daughter.

Bhattacharya got a whiff of the top job when she was made deputy managing director and corporate development officer in 2010. In her journey to the corner room, she superseded three senior colleagues—Hemant Contractor, A. Krishna Kumar and S. Vishvanathan—with whom she will have to work at least for a year. Isn't that difficult? 'This is not new . . . A senior colleague not getting the top job is accepted in State Bank. What's important is respecting their abilities and giving them enough space. They are high performers. At State Bank all decisions are collective decisions. I have created the comfort zone,' says Bhattacharya.

As a professional, Bhattacharya always wants to be out of her comfort zone. Which is why, looking back, she doesn't see her thirty-seven-year career in the SBI as one job; it's a combination of eleven jobs that began with her first assignment at the foreign exchange wing in the Kolkata main branch, and has run the gamut of retail banking, corporate banking, a stint in the US, treasury, rural banking, new businesses, metro business, HR, investment banking and finally, her posting as the bank's chief financial officer, ahead of the chairmanship.

The most challenging assignment has been her involvement in new businesses, where she contributed to the setting up of general insurance, a private equity fund, a mobile application platform and pension funds. Between December 2007 and May 2009, as chief general manager of new businesses, she cobbled together three joint-venture arrangements—with the investment banking and financial services group Macquarie for the private equity fund, Insurance Australia Group (IAG) for general insurance, and the financial services company Societe Generale for custodial service.

She finds customer service at the bank 'patchy' and wants it to be 'uniformly good'. All the verticals of the bank now work as silos and Bhattacharya wants them to collaborate with each other. 'You will find branches of State Bank and its associates in the same location. On an average, a customer is sold 1.7 products, but it can be scaled up to five . . . we are not playing to our strength.'

The SBI's profits have been on the decline for the past four quarters and bad assets have been on the rise. In the December quarter, the gross bad loans rose to 5.73 per cent of the total loans and net bad loans to 3.24 per cent. If one adds restructured loans to gross bad loans, the pile is 9.06 per cent. Bhattacharya says any solution will depend on how the economy does. 'The bank is paying for the growth. It gave money to companies when the economy was growing at a healthy pace, but now with the sudden decline in growth, companies are not in a position to pay back bank loans.'

Bhattacharya sees massive stress in the mid-corporate group and small and medium enterprises that do not have a diversified business model. They are suppliers to large companies who have stopped payments because of stress. Banks are helping such companies hive off and monetize non-core assets by identifying strategic investors and even looking for new management. 'New players need to step in. We are seeing some silver linings . . . The highly leveraged companies are not asking for unrealistic valuations, and companies sitting on cash in their balance sheets are looking for value buying. If the trend catches up, things will look up,' says Bhattacharya.

Apart from managing bad assets, Bhattacharya is focusing on raising productivity and leveraging IT to do many more things smartly. 'My guys work hard . . . That's fine, but they also need to work smartly,' Bhattacharya says. She is communicating with them through a blog on the bank's internal social networking site and is also planning a Rs 10-billion employees' stock purchase scheme.

After a light Indian dinner of chicken curry, *achari bhindi* and dal with rice and *phulka*, I ask for *rasmalai* while she opts for Darjeeling tea. As a parting shot, I ask her for one thing that she wants to change about the bank immediately. 'The service quality. I hate to hear complaints when I meet people at functions.' I grab the opportunity to share with her my wife's experience as an SBI customer—she doesn't get mobile alerts for banking transactions even though she has registered for the service. By the next morning, the problem is sorted out.

Postscript

On 1 October 2016, five days ahead of the end of her three-year term, Bhattacharya's tenure was extended by one more year—the first instance of an SBI chief getting an extension after the age of sixty. More time was given to her as she was in the process of merging five associate banks with the SBI as well as the Bharatiya Mahila Bank.

5

Aditya Puri

BANKER IN THE SPOTLIGHT

15 March 2008

Aditya Puri, managing director of HDFC Bank Ltd, one of the most expensive banks in the world in terms of price to book value, didn't start out as a banker. As an executive assistant to the finance director of automobile firm Mahindra and Mahindra Ltd, Puri was jealous of his cousin, a Citibank trainee who used to live in an air-conditioned, carpeted apartment with his batchmates on the posh Carmichael Road in Mumbai. There was even a cook and a butler on call. On top of that, the young men were to be trained in Beirut.

'What the hell am I doing living as a paying guest in Colaba, surviving on a toast and half a cup of tea in the morning, and catching a train to Kandivli every day?' Puri wondered. So, he asked his cousin to get him an interview with Citibank, believing banking could not be very different from accounting. Puri got the job, the above-mentioned comforts and a 'hefty pay hike'.

My guest arrives at the ITC Grand Central in Mumbai a few minutes before me, but that is not surprising because he doesn't stay in office beyond 5.30 p.m. 'I am the first person to reach office at 8.30 a.m., and the first to leave. I believe in a work–life balance, and I don't want to be the martyr for my office. I take a month's holiday every year,' says Puri as we walk into Hornby's Pavilion.

Puri has been in the news for the merger of Centurion Bank of Punjab (Centurion BoP) with HDFC Bank. As he orders a Glenmorangie, I ask for the inside story. 'There is no story. It all happened within a week. They first approached Deepak [Parekh, chairman of Housing Development Finance Corporation, HDFC Bank's promoter], and we took it forward. Rana [Talwar, chairman of Centurion BoP] and I are old friends. He was my senior in Citibank,' he says matter-of-factly. Both Puri and Talwar are from Chandigarh, and their fathers are good friends.

Isn't he paying too much for Centurion BoP? I ask. 'Not at all. We are paying a 10 per cent discount to the market price of Centurion BoP. The price to book value is not relevant here. We are paying for the value of the franchise, which is highly underutilized.'

Puri believes that the true value of Centurion BoP lies in its network of more than 400 branches, three million customers, and a portfolio of personal loans and two-wheeler loans. 'It's a steal,' he says. The bank also comes with 6000 employees, but there will be no retrenchments, according to Puri.

'We need more people. Very few senior people may have some issues, but one needs to figure out whether one wants to remain a big fish in a small pond or become a small fish in a big pond,' he says.

What about Centurion CEO Shailendra Bhandari? 'What about him? He is an old HDFC Bank hand. He will be one of the executive directors managing portfolios such as treasury, private banking, agriculture, commodities, international banking—major growth areas for the bank,' he says.

Puri is not worried about integrating Centurion BoP, which is less than a quarter of the size of HDFC Bank. Times Bank, which his company took over in 2000, was bigger, he points out.

I ask him why HDFC Bank is shy of international banking. Global business now accounts for about 25 per cent of the balance sheet of its peer, ICICI Bank Ltd, but HDFC Bank has no presence outside India. 'Aren't you glad that we are not making losses because of our foreign operations? We have no desire to run a treasury-operated hedge fund overseas. I am not into making an unworthy borrower into a top-rated customer through financial engineering. In principle, I am against any exposure to very sophisticated instruments. Anything that does not make common sense may land you in trouble,' he says.

HDFC Bank will open a branch in Bahrain and a representative office in Dubai, but will not borrow short to lend long. 'We will have matching funding and look for a reasonable margin,' Puri lays the outline of his overseas business on the table.

He has always been a straight talker. At Citibank, when Victor Menezes, the former India head, asked him to go to New York, he opted for Saudi Arabia instead, where he could save more money. In 1994, when Parekh landed up in Malaysia to woo him back to India to create a world-class bank, he had one condition—that he be given a 'completely free hand' in running the bank. Parekh agreed and Puri did not think twice before forfeiting the special options given by Citi Chairman John Read and taking a 'huge salary cut' to shift to Mumbai. He was HDFC Bank's third employee, after its chairman and financial controller.

'The bank consisted of me and a table. When we looked for more space and rented a floor at Kamala Mills compound, rats ate the computer wires after the office was set up,' says Puri, recounting his early days at the bank.

We shift to Shanghai Club, the Chinese eatery, for dinner and the rest of his story. Here, he orders a Johnnie Walker Gold Label. 'We hired the best available talent from Bank of America, Citi and UBS to head different divisions, and told them to hire people of their choice to run their businesses,' Puri narrates the untold story of the making of India's most expensive bank.

HDFC Bank began with five clients—the Tatas, Birlas, Reliance Industries Ltd, Hero Honda Motors Ltd and Siemens Ltd. Today, there is hardly any firm in India which doesn't bank here. 'We do not want to be in any business where we are not a market leader or among the top three,' Puri says. The next big business opportunity, according to him, is commodities. 'We are developing products for middlemen and farmers and traders. This will be larger than the stock market business,' he predicts.

Puri is a great believer in technology. He is often seen discussing banking technology at various forums, sharing the dais with tech gurus such as John Chambers and Steve Ballmer. But he doesn't use a mobile phone and never checks his own emails. His senior colleagues get handwritten notes when he wants to discuss business with them. 'Why should I open my emails and respond to them? My secretary types faster than me. I don't need a mobile phone as you'll never find a file on my table. Before leaving office, I clear every file. For emergencies, there is my wife's mobile,' Puri says.

He loves to spend time with his wife and children every evening and on weekends. 'As a banker, I do network and build relationships with corporations, but not necessarily by attending parties. I visit them at their offices,' Puri says. Every alternate weekend, he heads to his farmhouse at Lonavala to unwind. He grows strawberries, mulberries, guavas and Italian lemons there, and plays with his dog, Bushka, a mix of Great Dane and Dobermann. He has used his favourite Makrana marble extensively in this house, and Persian carpets cover the floor.

So, who runs HDFC Bank—Puri or Parekh? Puri answers, unfazed: 'HDFC Bank is run by Aditya Puri and its board of independent directors. Deepak and me have an excellent personal and professional relationship.'

We have egg fried rice with Hunan chicken, steamed fish and stir-fried Chinese vegetable, and Puri wants to skip dessert. I suggest that his acquisition of Times Bank in 2000 could be likened to a breakfast and the Centurion BoP takeover to a meal. Does he still have an appetite for dessert when it comes to banking? I ask him while we wait for our cars at the hotel portico. 'Why not? We are open to acquisition even today, if it's the right fit,' he says with a smile.

6

Pramit Jhaveri

'I WISH I WAS A JEWELLER'

11 February 2007

It is not easy to take an investment banker out for a drink, especially if the person is Pramit Jhaveri, who believes firmly in the philosophy of keeping his mouth shut as 'loose lips sink ships'. We first met in 2000 when he took over as head of investment banking at Citibank. Soon after, I watched him playing tennis with George Bush Sr at Bombay Gymkhana at a bank event.

Jhaveri commits to an evening out only after I assure him we will not discuss any deals-in-progress. 'I am not one who brags about his deals over a drink. Investment banking is all about client confidentiality and trust. Only after a deal is done do you have bragging rights,' Jhaveri says.

Before we can settle down in a quiet corner of Opium Den at Hilton Towers in Mumbai, the waiter pours cold water on our plans, literally. It's a dry day, thanks to the Brihanmumbai Municipal Corporation elections. Jhaveri, known for his networking and relationship management skills, tries every trick to get us a glass of wine—white or red—or a single malt, but the waiter is firm. No one drinks on a dry day, not even a foreigner, we're told. So, we settle for *nimbupani*, sweet and sour.

The first thing I want to pick his brains about is the price the Tatas are paying for the European steelmaker Corus. Munching masala peanuts, Jhaveri states the obvious, 'The Tatas have delivered a message to the world that Indian corporations need to be taken very seriously.'

Isn't that a diplomatic answer, I ask. 'I am not being diplomatic,' Jhaveri counters. 'This is an incredibly bold and aggressive move by the Tatas. Whether they are paying more or less, time will tell.'

Jhaveri comes from a family of jewellers. His father, a second-generation businessman, was a jewellery manufacturer and diamond trader. But before Pramit could complete his education, the joint family had split and the business closed down.

'In a sense, finance was in my blood. I was a campus recruitment and did not think twice before accepting the Citibank offer as it had glamour,' Jhaveri says, sipping his fresh lime water. His first salary back in 1987 was Rs 3100. It's the perfect chance to ask how much he earns now. 'Well, it's something you don't talk about openly. It's not a state secret and the industry has a reasonable sense of who gets how much,' he says, choosing every word. He also dislikes the term, dealmaker. 'There is no individual dealmaker any more. Very few deals can be done by one individual. They are all done by institutions. Globally, individual dealmakers have no space. The domestic investment banks will possibly adopt the same model,' he says.

Taking the cue, I ask him whether so many investment banks can survive in India. Over the last one year, at least four global investment banks have set up shop—UBS, Goldman Sachs, Lehman Brothers and CSFB. Is there so much business?

Jhaveri's take on this is simple. Indeed, the business is growing. In 2000, India accounted for about 2 per cent of total Asian business. Now, this has gone up to about 15 per cent. The market is growing by 50 per cent every year.

But costs have also been growing. Five years back, the cost of Indian operations was at a significant discount in comparison to Hong Kong and Singapore, which is no longer the case; however, now the cost advantage does not exist any more as the prices of people and real estate have been growing phenomenally. On the other hand, investment bankers' fees are being squeezed.

So, do we see a shake-out in the industry? 'Wait for three years,' says Jhaveri laconically. To generate revenue, investment bankers must look for other routes such as leverage financing and structured financing, he feels. Citibank has been doing this very aggressively. The first such deal was KKR's $900-million buyout of Flextronics in the software space and General Atlantic Partners' buyout of GE Caps' business processing unit, Genpact.

Citi investment banking has been particularly aggressive in foreign currency convertibles and equity raising. It topped the equity and debt league tables in 2006 and was placed third for the M&A deals. In 2003, it handled only two equity issues. In the next three years between 2004 and 2006, the number of such issues rose to fifty-five. 'Things are happening very fast. It's just like a fast train, stopping at stations very briefly. If we don't jump on, we'll miss the train,' Jhaveri says, highlighting the scorching pace of investment banking activities in India.

I want to know his recipe for success. 'I am a relationship man. Once we do a deal for a company, I try to make sure that we are involved in all future deals. Five years ago, we did a small $40-million private placement for UTI Bank; since then, we have done all its issues—GDR [Global Depositary Receipt], overseas bond, foreign currency borrowing. Ditto with Tata Motors and Bajaj Hindustan. I enter into a relationship and carry it forward.'

Jhaveri makes it a point to squeeze in short family holidays through the year, to places like Thailand, Switzerland and South Africa. He is also an avid art collector. 'We have restrictions on investing in shares. I put my money in mutual funds and real estate, but my passion is collecting Husain and Souza. Art is a better performing asset class than equity,' he says.

He also has an eye for jewellery. If he was not an investment banker, he would have been a jeweller, he says. 'I love intricate jewellery designs. On my wife's fortieth birthday, I gifted her a lovely necklace,' he says. His wife too was an investment banker with DSP Merrill Lynch. She quit her job as two investment bankers from rival institutions cannot live under one roof. 'I make phone calls at midnight and early mornings to the US. These calls are extremely sensitive. You can't have another investment banker in your bedroom,' he says.

Does she regret quitting an exciting career, I ask Jhaveri as we get up to leave. 'Not at all. She is the actual art collector. The yield on her investment is much more than what I earn.'

7

Shikha Sharma

THE LIBERAL BANKER

14 June 2014

There are two reasons why Shikha Sharma, managing director and chief executive officer of Axis Bank Ltd, India's third-largest private lender, considers this the toughest stint in her thirty-four-year-old career. First, though she spent twenty-nine years with the ICICI Group in diverse roles—from setting up its investment banking arm to running consumer lending and personal services units as well as its insurance company for close to a decade—she was not a seasoned commercial banker before she joined Axis Bank. She has just completed five years in the current role.

Second, there was nobody to handhold her there in the initial days. Her predecessor P.J. Nayak had left in a huff when she was chosen to lead the bank (Nayak may have preferred an internal candidate to succeed him). 'It was like taking over a flying aircraft. You are suddenly asked to sit on the pilot's seat mid-air,' Sharma says.

She orders Chilean sea bass and stir-fried vegetables at San-Qi, the Asian restaurant at Four Seasons, Worli, Mumbai, while I settle for a set thali of green Thai curry.

Sharma, fifty-six, is on a diet. 'These days I am into swimming, but more than a hobby, it's a real struggle,' she says with a smile. She is a Hindi film buff, and watches movies on weekends. At one point in time, inspired by her mother-in-law, who was a Hindustani classical singer, she even learnt classical music, intending to introduce her own son and daughter to it. But now her primary personal goal is to lose weight under the supervision of nutritionist and fitness consultant Suman Agarwal.

Her bank, however, has been growing bigger. The balance sheet is spreading even at a healthy pace and the stock price is at its lifetime high.

After taking over in June 2009, she formulated the Vision 2015 document and has reached most of the milestones she set for the bank. The suite of products has broadened; the retail business has grown to create a balance with the corporate business; and systems and processes have been institutionalized. 'It's always difficult when you take over a healthy, well-run franchise as you can end up spoiling it. While you are setting up a new venture you can do things the way you want, but here you have to build on the existing strength, which is what I have been doing,' she says, explaining her role as the CEO.

A predominantly corporate bank since inception in 1994, Axis Bank now has about 36 per cent retail assets and Sharma wants to push it up to about 45 per cent. The growth of its low-cost current and savings account, or CASA, has been the strongest among the top ten banks in India, and it has been topping the list in debt syndication for years.

Now, the bank is formulating its Vision 2020 document. The three main constituents of the vision are growing CASA, maintaining the growth in return on equity (18.2 per cent now) and profitably reaching out to 5 per cent of India's bankable population (currently, its reach is restricted to 1.5 per cent). 'We have a customer-oriented culture and we will continue to emphasize on that by filling in customer-facing technology gaps,' Sharma says. She doesn't want to expand overseas; the bank's overseas presence is required only to meet domestic clients' offshore needs, not to do local business there.

So how is Axis Bank different from ICICI Bank Ltd? 'Unlike ICICI Bank which had migrated from a project finance institution to banking, Axis was born as a bank and so it has more banking depth,' she says. According to Sharma, ICICI Bank has a flatter structure and a very competitive environment, while Axis Bank is hierarchical and friendly. 'And, of course, Axis Bank has fewer women executives,' she adds. After she took over, Sharma has tried to change the company's work culture by rewarding employees on performance and not seniority, and encouraging different points of view. 'The boss is not always right, you can have a different point of view,' she says.

This liberal approach is perhaps a result of her upbringing. The eldest child of a brigadier in the ordnance corps, who was an ammunition expert and fought in two India–Pakistan wars, Sharma studied at seven schools in different parts of the country. At all their homes, empty shells were used as flower vases. At Loreto Convent School in New Delhi, she was passionate about physics, but her *tauji* (father's elder brother) convinced her to study economics, considered to have better professional prospects, at the Lady Shri Ram College for Women. She says she ended up at the Indian Institute of Management Ahmedabad (IIMA) under peer pressure.

In the 1978 batch of 180 students at IIMA, there were five women. At the interview, she met Sanjay—a tall, dark and handsome man, straight out of a Mills & Boon romance (incidentally, Sharma was addicted to Mills & Boon romances till her mid-forties). It was love at first sight. 'I found in him someone who was well read and had novel ideas.'

In the summer of 1980, she was picked up by ICICI Ltd, as it was known then. She worked there for twenty-nine years. K.V. Kamath, the current chairman, and Mark Tucker, the former group CEO of Prudential Plc and now CEO of AIA Group Ltd, mentored her in the ICICI Group. 'Both of them were tough, hard taskmasters and always gave feedback.' In 2009, Egon Zehnder headhunted her for Axis Bank's top post.

The rivalry between Sharma and Chanda Kochhar, the current MD and CEO of ICICI Bank, was once the talk of the business world, and many believe Sharma left ICICI because Kochhar got the top job, which she too had coveted. I can't resist the temptation of asking her about the rivalry. She brushes it aside, saying: 'We were not friends, but had healthy respect for each other. Now, after leaving ICICI, we spend more time together as both of us are on the Visa Global Advisory Council and the board of IBA (Indian Banks Association).'

Sharma's journey at Axis Bank has had its share of hurdles. The bank's net non-performing assets are only 0.40 per cent, but many analysts apprehend it has more bad loans hidden in its cupboard. Sharma refutes the allegation of 'hiding', saying the Institute of Chartered Accountants of India (ICAI) has awarded the bank for excellence in financial reporting for three years. She admits, however, that the analysts have a 'legitimate worry' because of Axis Bank's relatively high exposure to infrastructure projects—about 12 per cent of the total loans.

She believes the worst is over—growth has bottomed out, interest rates have peaked—and hopes that with the government's push, stalled projects will start moving.

The bank's acquisition of Enam Securities Pvt. Ltd, an investment banking firm, is not among the high points of her stint. The day the deal was announced in November 2010, the bank's stock lost 5 per cent on the bourses as the analyst community felt it had paid too much. Two years later, the deal was closed, after paring the valuation of the transaction by almost one-third, to Rs 13.96 billion.

Sharma defends her decision to acquire Enam, saying it filled a strategic gap for the bank, but admits that it hasn't been able to extract the full value of the deal till now. She says, however, that she has no regrets, for this will happen over the next ten years. Did she pay more than she should have? She sidesteps the question, saying, 'Maybe we should have negotiated hard.'

There's a romanticism in the way Sharma looks at life and her career. She describes with almost childlike enthusiasm her recent visit to a leopard park near Udaipur in Rajasthan that opened in October—she saw four leopards.

Sharma is a Hindi film buff. Typically, the Sharma couple wait for the reviews and rush to the theatre over the weekend to watch any film that gets three stars and above. Usually, they watch 'happy' films. She doesn't have a favourite actor, but likes Ranbir Kapoor and Deepika Padukone. In recent times, Sharma has enjoyed watching *Queen* and *Chennai Express*. Her all-time favourite film is *Casablanca*, the 1942 American romance by Michael Curtiz. She has watched the Shah Rukh Khan and Kajol starrer *Kuch Kuch Hota Hai* ten times.

'I believe in making the most of the day; I don't think of the past or the future,' she says, adding that she is not a prisoner to data. 'I always balance data with intuition while taking decisions. I could be impulsive while buying a home, but not when I am doing business.'

Beneath the romantic is a shrewd banker who senses every business opportunity passing her way. During our lunch, I casually mentioned I was in need of an auto loan. The next day I got a call from a gentleman from the bank's retail division to ask how much money I needed, and whether he could drop by to see me.

8

Om Prakash Bhatt

THE CHAIRMAN IN A HURRY

3 May 2008

Even after spending an exhausting day at Mundra Port in Gujarat, Om Prakash Bhatt is as sprightly as ever. Arriving in a black T-shirt, the fifty-seven-year-old boss of India's largest commercial bank, the State Bank of India, looks smart and immediately apologizes for being a few minutes late.

'Don't ask me the brand of my T-shirt; I don't know. My wife buys my clothes,' Bhatt says as we enter Jewel of India at Nehru Centre, Worli. This is hardly surprising. Bhatt is a busy, hands-on man. A firm believer in the adage 'seeing is believing', he often visits ports, factories and even a business process outsourcing unit. 'You must know whom you are lending money to, and the competition. This is the best way to know your borrowers and their industry,' he says.

Bhatt likes red wine, but orders a Laphroaig to give me company. 'I hope you'll like its smoky taste,' he says, and calls for the bottle to check the age of the single malt whisky.

Bhatt is one of the few chairmen of the SBI to have got a five-year stint. Ironically, banking was not his first choice for a career. He joined the bank as a probationary officer only after he proved to be 'underage' to appear for the Indian Administrative Service.

Did he know that he would eventually head the bank one day? A postgraduate in English literature, Bhatt first says 'it's luck' and then, almost as an afterthought, adds: 'I have all along been hard-working, innovative and a team person. I can relate to people well.'

And for a reluctant recruit, Bhatt has performed remarkably well. Within a year of taking over as chief general manager of the bottom-ranked north-eastern circle of the SBI, Bhatt lifted the circle to the number one position.

In his next assignment as the managing director of the State Bank of Travancore, Bhatt changed the profile of a traditional traders' bank into a retail bank, and aggressively sold mutual fund and insurance products. The State Bank of Travancore is one of the seven associate banks of the SBI and many SBI bosses, including Bhatt's predecessor A.K. Purwar, were groomed for the top position at these banks.

His route to the top of the SBI, though, was anything but a cakewalk. Bhatt became a managing director of the SBI after a keenly fought run-off with four of his colleagues—all belonging to the same batch of probationary officers. All five were interviewed in September 2005, three months before the managing director's post fell vacant, but Bhatt got the government nod in April 2006. 'Although I was an SBI representative in the US, people who wanted to block my way dubbed me as a liaison officer,' says Bhatt.

Bhatt was later elevated to chairman in July 2006. The first thing he did was to stop the rollout of core banking solutions in the SBI branches. 'We were mechanically rolling out technology without checking if it was beneficial to customers. I asked TCS [Tata Consultancy Services Ltd], which was implementing the project to read the riot act. Everybody was shocked at my audacity. But we needed some 700 modifications before the project restarted, and TCS rose to the occasion splendidly,' says Bhatt.

With the same 'audacity', Bhatt is now on a branch-opening spree. In the past five months, he has opened 955 branches— more than six branches a day on an average.

Why does the SBI need so many branches when there are alternative channels such as mobile phones and the Internet that everyone is keen to hop on to? 'One of the reasons behind SBI's market share going down is its absence in strategic locations. Over the last ten years, we have been saying SBI has 9000-plus branches. Yet, there are 2000 semi-urban centres where the SBI group does not have a single branch. So, now we plan to open 2000 branches every year and take the network to 20,000 and almost triple the number of ATMs, from 8500 to 25,000. Why should the ATMs be only cash dispensers? We want to use these machines for many other business transactions such as issuing chequebooks, bill payments, and so on,' Bhatt says. To support this business plan, the bank has been recruiting people aggressively. Last year, it recruited 9000 people, and the plan is to get 15,000 people this year.

The results, Bhatt claims, are showing. 'Our home loan portfolio has grown 27 per cent this year, higher than the competition. Similarly, the auto loan portfolio's growth has been 30 per cent. You can't call SBI a sleeping elephant any more,' says Bhatt with a wide grin.

Bhatt also wants to merge the associate banks with the SBI to build scale. He initiated this exercise last year with a proposal to merge the State Bank of Saurashtra, the smallest of the associate banks. The proposal is awaiting government approval. 'It is taking a little time, but the merger is inevitable. Currently, there is a positive environment created for consolidation within the SBI family. We will not push for it but [will] pursue individual cases. It will be easier to merge the unlisted banks first,' he says.

In the mid-1990s, the consultancy firm McKinsey and Co. had suggested the merger of seven associate banks with the SBI or among themselves. But none of Bhatt's predecessors made any move in the face of stiff resistance from trade unions. Bhatt also has an 'open mind' about acquisitions abroad and the Rs 167-billion kitty raised through a rights issue may come in handy. 'We will use the money to grow our assets, and overseas acquisitions are possible,' he says.

It's time to fill his glass, but this time he sticks to his favourite red wine to wash down a spartan meal of tandoori roti, *sabzikadai* and dal.

The SBI is buzzing with activity nowadays. The bank is looking to cover 100,000 villages under the financial inclusion programme, enter the private equity and pension businesses, launch custodial services—and is not very far away from identifying a partner for the general insurance business.

In the private equity space, it has already acquired 19.75 per cent in Sage Capital Fund Management, an Indian private equity firm that plans to raise a $200-million fund. The bank is floating an infrastructure fund with the Macquarie Group and talking to Unitech Ltd for a realty fund. A deputy managing director (DMD) of the bank now looks exclusively at business innovation.

Does the bank pay its employees performance-linked incentives? Bhatt does not believe in incentives that are not in conformity with the SBI culture. 'I am for those kinds of incentives that help them inculcate value and not encourage greed,' he says. Early this week, around twenty branch managers with their spouses were invited for dinner at his bungalow in south Mumbai. These branch managers were chosen as members of the chairman's club, based on their performance. The ritual is not new, but Bhatt gave it a personal touch by hosting it at his home. 'This is one incentive they will cherish for long,' Bhatt says.

He seems to excel at getting the best out of his colleagues. So, before we get up, I ask him a very uncomfortable question: why is he taking away powers from his managing directors? Earlier, the bank's two MDs were looking after national banking and corporate banking. Now, these portfolios have been split and distributed among DMDs and the bank's current MD has been looking after risk management. Isn't Bhatt making himself more powerful?

Changing business realities, Bhatt explains, are behind his reshuffling exercise. Indeed, big corporations were the bank's major borrowers, but now the SBI's exposure to these companies is Rs 350 billion while its mortgage portfolio is Rs 420 billion. 'Things are not static and the relative importance of business groups is changing. With the economy becoming more and more complex, risk management is the most important job in any bank. Shouldn't I have the authority to decide who will do what in the bank? I am doing this to increase the efficiency of the bank and not to make myself more powerful. And besides, it is well within the rules set down by the SBI Act.'

As we wait for our cars, Bhatt whispers into my ears: 'Write anything you want about me. But the bank is more important than any individual. Don't harm the bank.'

9

Raghuram Rajan

IN STEP

30 August 2014

When Raghuram Govind Rajan came to India as the government's chief economic adviser two years ago, everyone warned him about the bureaucracy. 'People told me the bureaucracy here will be very difficult to deal with—very smart people, but with very different agendas.'

Rajan, fifty-one, hasn't found much truth in that. 'If you have paid attention elsewhere and if you are not completely naive, there isn't a whole lot that is surprising or different. It is slightly different here inasmuch as there isn't often a sense of urgency. Things that need to be done yesterday are still not done, in some cases. But that's not surprising.'

When he took over as the Reserve Bank of India governor on 4 September, he was handed a report by a committee he had headed in 2008 which recommended differentiated bank licences (where different kinds of banks do different things as opposed to the current crop of universal banks). Predecessor Duvvuri Subbarao had liberalized branch licensing right up till tier-2 cities but had then hit a roadblock. 'So my initial effort was to pull all those things that were in the planning stage and say let's finish. There's no reason for things to season.'

Rajan even has a term for this style of policymaking. 'One way to do things is to say let us think in theory, develop the best plan possible and then implement in one go. I call this the Brahminical way. But this may not work as at the implementation stage you will realize that some aspects were not considered. The alternative is, roll up the sleeves, don't minimize the thinking phase, but do it quickly. I am trying to do that. There's this Chinese phrase, 'cross the river by feeling the stones'. It's basically step by step, but take that step, don't theorize about how you're going to cross the entire river, not knowing where the steps are . . . Take the first step and feel your way through the next step, be more practical about it.'

Extended Honeymoon

We're having lunch in the RBI visitors' room, adjacent to Rajan's eighteenth-floor corner office in Mumbai's Fort area. The menu features everything you could possibly think of, from green pea soup and stuffed pomfret to prawn *balchao* and *badami murg*—all from the RBI kitchen run by chef Brian Pais.

Rajan walks in a few minutes past 1 p.m. A warm handshake later, I ask him bluntly whether he offered to resign when the Bharatiya Janata Party–led National Democratic Alliance government took over in May. After all, he was appointed by the Congress-led United Progressive Alliance government. Rajan doesn't seem annoyed, but prefers not to answer this question, even off the record. 'Of course, if I lost the confidence of the government at any point, I would go the next day,' he says curtly.

Was the governorship part of the arrangement when he took over as chief economic adviser? I ask him even before we sit down to lunch.

'There was no arrangement,' says Rajan.

We plough through all the food, with the portraits of sixteen of the RBI's twenty-two past governors (Subbarao is still not there though it has been a year since he stepped down) looking down at us.

Rajan had two conditions when I invited him for lunch: One, let's meet at the RBI and two, no personal questions. He is a vegetarian, although he doesn't mind eating eggs. So, the onus of eating all that meat and seafood is on me, but I find him keeping a close eye on my plate. 'Are there too many bones? Would you care for a fresh plate?' he asks me while eating a chapatti with *paneer birbali*.

In August last year, the UPA government announced the name of the next RBI governor a month before the position fell vacant, and Rajan, then chief economic adviser, was sent to the RBI as an officer on special duty—something that had never happened in the RBI's seventy-nine-year history.

It was a tough gig. Inflation had been high for years, but what added to the problem was a record high current account deficit, a falling local currency against the greenback and the real threat of a ratings downgrade.

One year on, the rupee has stabilized, the current account deficit is manageable. Rajan is not shy of raising policy rates to fight inflation and, most importantly, the government is backing him to the hilt in his fight against inflation. He is under no pressure to cut interest rates to boost growth in Asia's third-largest economy.

Unbelievably, Rajan's honeymoon with the industry and people in general continues. What's the secret? 'Look at the Indian cricket team. They are gods, they can't do any wrong, and then they come down to earth after they lose a few matches. I am waiting for something to happen to bring me down there, even though I can't say I am looking forward to that. I see my job as a kind of a mission. I have to keep doing what I do. And take the decision without looking to who's happy and who's not,' he says.

Born in Bhopal in 1963, the third child of a police officer, Rajan's rise in the world of economics has been meteoric. A gold medallist at both the Indian Institute of Technology Delhi and the Indian Institute of Management Ahmedabad, he did a short stint at Tata Administrative Services as a management trainee before getting a doctorate in management from the Massachusetts Institute of Technology's Sloan School of Management in the US.

In 1991, he joined the University of Chicago Booth School of Business as an assistant professor of finance and worked there till August 2003, when he was appointed chief economist at the International Monetary Fund (IMF).

In 2005, at Jackson Hole, Wyoming, at the annual central bankers' conference, Rajan tore apart US Federal Reserve board chairman Alan Greenspan's work and reputation. A 2009 *Wall Street Journal* report on his presentation says Rajan even argued that the banking system itself would be at risk and banks would lose confidence in one another. 'The inter-bank market could freeze up, and one could well have a full-blown financial crisis.' Two years later, that's exactly what happened.

Rajan still believes that financial reforms take 'a hundred small steps', the title of a 2008 paper by a committee that he headed, where he spoke about inflation targeting and a floating exchange rate, among other things. 'Whatever you put in place, the success of that you will see in years down the line, especially in the financial sector, where things have to catch on . . . There is a sense in India that we are uniquely different from the rest of the world. In some ways we are, but in many ways some of the issues we find here are similar to the issues you find anywhere else.'

Rajan plays squash or runs daily. In January, he participated in the Mumbai Half Marathon. When it comes to work though, he's been more of a sprinter than a marathon man from the beginning. 'We have stabilized the currency. We need to bring inflation under control and bring NPAs down—those two things are still ongoing. They will take time to fully get tackled. But at least we made a quick beginning. Going forward, it was also to show that we could put down the agenda for revitalizing the financial sector—banking, markets, inclusion. We are taking steps and we have to see how they play out. For example, the interest rate futures market in India is picking up in liquidity, but still at about Rs 15 billion a day, it's relatively small. This has to grow. We need to have more players coming in. Let's move and let's keep fiddling [with] the structure to get it right,' he says.

Of course, it's not easy to work fast in an organization like the RBI. The central bank has been known to sit on things, but rarely says no. 'This is an organization with tremendous capabilities, but it is also a bureaucracy, in the non-pejorative sense of the word. Sometimes the bureaucracy delays things in order to essentially say no without saying so. Especially in a country where sometimes saying no is seen as a slap in the face, it's better that the issue slowly dissipates over time rather than having to take a decision. Some policies that seem inordinately delayed should be seen in that light—perhaps there's a fundamental disagreement over the policy, and therefore the best way to kill it without prompting a confrontation . . .' he says.

Rajan agrees that people are always trying to see how far they can push the central bank to see their point of view. 'Of course, there's immense pressure on the RBI from different quarters—I can certainly attest to that—to relax on every front of our regulations and supervision. People asking you to relax on those fronts sometimes are trying to see how far they can push you. Of course, if the system gets into trouble, the RBI will bear the blame because it's the stability regulator, but before that everybody will push you to be "flexible". There will be pressure, but the appropriate response RBI may have found is dignified silence.'

Restructuring the RBI

Meanwhile, work is on to modernize the behemoth. After all, it was set up in the 1930s, at a time when the world was reeling under the Great Depression, and since then its objectives have remained unchanged. 'We are undertaking some internal reorganization of RBI's structure and how it functions. There will be concerns, like any other reorganization, and we have to take the staff along with us. But the whole idea is to make it an organization which is fully capable of meeting the challenges of the twenty-first century. We need to figure out how to move towards specialization. Training and support is a second issue. We need good performance evaluation and once we evaluate weaknesses, we need to offer support in terms of skill building,' says Rajan.

The RBI board has already approved Rajan's ambitious plan. He refutes the idea that he plans to import talent from outside. 'In an organization that has grown as it has, it's better to grow the internal talent than bring too many people from outside as they will be seen as competing for the existing jobs. You can bring people in if you are expanding, but you have to be very careful in doing it and do it in small doses only.'

Rajan declines the fresh fruits and ice cream, and opts for coffee instead. It seems like the right time to ask him about commentators who have described him as India's newest sex symbol (in Shobhaa De's words, 'the guy's put "sex" back into the limp Sensex'). Many of my female colleagues at *Mint* swoon over him and even those who don't know the way to the RBI headquarters on Mint Road are keen to attend his press conferences.

Rajan, 6ft 1 inch, blushes, but soon recovers to say: 'My wife, Radhika, teases me a lot about this. I worry that there is a real danger that you distract from the very important and sober task of policymaking. But that said, the value of having glamour introduced into some professions is that it attracts young people into that profession. If a boring economist can become glamorous, maybe economics is something worth pursuing.

'When I was young, I read about [John Maynard] Keynes. And I said what a glamorous guy, doing great policies, writing great books; wouldn't that be a good thing to do? And what did he do? Economics. We look at people who catch our eye, and then we learn more about what they do and that helps attract us to the field. I think we need more economists, so in that sense I am not upset.'

It's well past 2.15 p.m. and I see him looking furtively at his watch. I ask him what he does when he is not writing monetary policy and not thinking about financial stability. 'Squash in the evening or in the morning, depending on the day and depending on if I haven't torn any muscles. Now my son is home [he is studying in the US], we play video games together. I talk to my daughter [who is also studying in the US]; occasionally go out with my wife to visit friends. I love reading, and sometimes I write. I do write all my speeches. I like to run, if I can find the weather cooperating. I like to visit places, if we can go out to a new place for a board meeting, I try to look around. Eating out is a little difficult these days simply because people recognize . . . They don't interrupt you, but still I feel a little embarrassed, my son feels even more embarrassed.'

The liveried RBI waiter appears with a tray of paan, formally signalling the end of our meeting. I pick up two and without losing a moment, shoot my last question to Rajan: he has achieved so much in such a short time. Even if he remains RBI governor for five years, he will be only fifty-five. What will he do after that?

'I like writing and thinking. What next is back to the future, go back to writing and thinking, with the idea that I have learnt a lot about India and will write more about it—what I think is going right and wrong. Not a "tell-all" book, but a thought-piece like my other books. But I have no fears about a life of quiet contemplation. Actually, that's my other side. I think my wife is perfectly happy staying quiet and going underground. And we have no desire to be in the limelight.'

He may not like this, but I am sure the limelight will always chase him.

Postscript

Unlike his predecessor D. Subbarao, Rajan did not get a second term. He has gone back to the academic world in the US 'as he lost the confidence of the government', but is 'willing to return to India if the nation wants' him.

10

U.K. Sinha

SMART AS A WHIP

20 September 2014

Upendra Kumar Sinha holds the unenviable record of being the only regulator against whose appointment four public interest litigations, or PILs, have been filed. Hundreds of RTI (Right to Information) applications were moved and his eligibility challenged—not only for the Securities and Exchange Board of India) chairman's post, which he currently holds, but even for his previous appointment, as head of UTI Asset Management Co. Ltd.

Who's behind this? I ask him. 'It's a mystery to me. I guess those who don't want me at SEBI are behind this,' says Sinha with nonchalance. We are at Jiggs Kalra's Masala Library at Bandra Kurla Complex in Mumbai on a Monday afternoon.

Sinha opts for a fresh lime soda while I choose the burnt curry-leaf martini. In addition to handling the PILs he has been in the news for fighting Subrata Roy of Sahara India Pariwar. 'I have been branded as an activist who wants to curb Sahara. I am just doing my job,' says Sinha.

(Sahara India Pariwar filed a Rs 2-billion defamation suit against this author in December even before his book *Sahara: The Untold Story* was published. An out-of-court settlement was reached in April and the book was published in June.)

By nature, Sinha, sixty-two, loves a challenge and his fight against the collective investment scheme (CIS) is testimony to this. Nowhere in the world does a market regulator oversee the complex, murky arena of CIS; it's the job of the state. A CIS is a scheme formed by any company under which the contributions or payments made by investors are pooled and utilized to make profits. There has been rampant misuse of this vehicle, using regulatory loopholes, and SEBI initiated fifty cases, many of which it is battling in the courts. 'When people lose money, I must intervene,' Sinha says.

The chicken tikka starter comes in a jar; the amuse-bouche is molecular *khandvi* with a miniature *bun maska*. For mains, we order tandoori roti, dal and *meen moilee* (river sole served with a coconut-based sauce). Ahead of that, a mishti doi lollipop with a dash of strawberry sauce arrives to cleanse the palate.

On Sahara, says Sinha, SEBI was meticulous. For instance, when Sahara sent records of millions of investors in its contentious money-raising scheme in some 31,000 cartons in 127 trucks in September 2012, SEBI was prepared with the space to store these records.

Readers will remember the battle that was waged publicly too, through full-page advertisements in national newspapers. I ask Sinha about Sahara's allegation that SEBI has never seriously checked whether the investors exist or not. In 2008, when the Reserve Bank of India closed down Sahara's para-banking operation, there was no case of missing depositors. Sinha's explanation is that unlike in the previous instance, this time the Supreme Court told Sahara to deposit the money with SEBI. 'We were not allowed to advertise in newspapers and on TV channels, asking depositors to reach out to us. We did that only on our website. Now, with the court clearance, we will do so,' he says. Roy has been in New Delhi's Tihar jail since March for alleged non-payment of money to the bond holders.

Sinha has got even more on his plate after the recent amendment to the SEBI Act which empowers it to clamp down on CIS worth at least Rs 1 billion. Will we see SEBI cracking down on all Ponzi schemes? Sinha says there needs to be more coordination among SEBI, the RBI, the Union Ministry of Corporate Affairs and various state governments, as such schemes need to be stalled early. The new law also gives SEBI special power for recovery and faster resolution of cases through special courts. 'We have got more powers and along with that more responsibility and accountability,' Sinha says.

He has already embarked on an exercise to restructure SEBI to prepare it for the new regime. The consulting firm Oliver Wyman has studied several weaknesses of SEBI; it wants the regulator to be more proactive. SEBI typically gets into enforcement action after an event has happened, but does not do much to prevent things from happening. Penalty for offences is also pretty low in India. This needs to be raised, particularly for insider trading and market manipulation. Sinha wants the market regulator to be accountable for what it does and remove discretion from the decision-making process. He has already made some critical changes. For instance, serious offences like insider trading or front-running are no longer part of any consent process. SEBI has also formulated a new takeover code and norms to govern market infrastructure institutions.

Music and Urdu Poetry

A love for music and Urdu poetry helps Sinha fight stress. During his morning walk, he listens to music on his iPod. After reaching home from office in the evening, he listens to music for at least an hour. Another way of unwinding is playing bridge. Sinha can recite Sahir Ludhianvi's famous poem 'Taj Mahal' and Mirza Ghalib's poems flawlessly.

Sinha is a seasoned bureaucrat. Early in his career, he was district magistrate of three districts in Bihar. As a district magistrate in Patna, he worked under four chief ministers. Later, in the finance ministry, he worked under four finance ministers.

The son of a freedom fighter who was jailed for three years for participating in the Quit India movement, Sinha started his career as a probationary officer in the State Bank of India after completing a postgraduate course in physics from Patna Science College (he has a bachelor's degree in law from Patna University). At the SBI, at the age of twenty-three, Sinha learnt his first lesson of finance looking after a Rs 0.6-billion portfolio of commercial and institutional finances. IndusInd Bank Ltd's managing director and chief executive officer, Romesh Sobti, was his colleague at the bank.

In 1976, Sinha quit the bank and joined the Indian Administrative Services, despite the better salary at the SBI. However, during his joint secretary days in the Union home ministry, he got a somnolent portfolio—joint secretary (freedom fighter and rehabilitation)—to oversee refugees from Pakistan and rehabilitate them. There was virtually no work, but even there Sinha excelled and within six months was given a key assignment of handling the election in Jammu and Kashmir in 1996. 'I believe that whatever assignment is given to me, I must do it sincerely. If I do this, the system will recognize me,' he says.

He sees his entire career as an exercise in connecting the dots. The circle that started with his assignment in early IAS days as managing director of Bihar State Credit and Investment Corporation Ltd was completed when he took over as SEBI chief in 2011. As joint secretary in the banking division of the Ministry of Finance, he played a key role in the merger of ICICI Ltd with ICICI Bank Ltd to create India's first universal bank; and as joint secretary in charge of capital markets, he supervised the restructuring of Unit Trust of India, the country's first mutual fund.

'The UTI recast has been the finest financial engineering in the Indian financial market—the financial involvement of the government was limited, the fiscal outgo was staggered over a period of time and the government ended up making money,' he reminisces.

I ask for his views on corporate India. 'There is too much abuse of related-party businesses,' he says. 'Compensation of key management people should be scrutinized thoroughly—this has been a global practice.' He also emphasizes independent remuneration and audit committees of the board. 'We need to focus on these if we want foreign investors to have confidence in the Indian market.'

It is well past 3 p.m. now and I see him looking at his watch. Without wasting time, I shoot the last question: why is SEBI taking so much time to decide on the Reliance Industries Ltd's (RIL's) alleged insider trading case? Sinha pauses for a moment, gathers his thoughts, and tells me with a straight face, 'You would need to find out who is to be blamed.'

In 2013, SEBI rejected the RIL's consent proposal. Since then, the case has come up for hearing sixteen times at the Securities Appellate Tribunal. Who is to be blamed? I look at him confused, but he refuses to say more. I am well aware that sometimes one needs to focus more on what a regulator doesn't say than what he reveals.

11

Viral V. Acharya

THE CHANGE AGENT

24 June 2017

Within a month of taking over as a deputy governor at the Reserve Bank of India on 20 January, Viral V. Acharya, addressing a banking technology conference of the Indian Banks' Association, chose to speak 'with a certain sense of urgency' on the need and ways to 'decisively resolve Indian banks' stressed assets'.

This speech of Acharya, forty-three, the RBI's youngest deputy governor post-liberalization, reminds us of another one—also by a deputy governor—two decades ago. At an annual gathering of foreign exchange dealers in Goa in August 1997, Y.V. Reddy had said, 'As per the real effective exchange rate, it would certainly appear that the rupee is overvalued.' The next day, the local currency tumbled.

There are many differences between the two speeches. In 1997, the central bank wanted to push the rupee down against the dollar; now the problem centres around the rising bad assets of the banks. Reddy's message was subtle; Acharya's, direct. On both occasions, however, the RBI wanted to send out a message and test the market reaction. Reddy and Acharya were chosen to be the messengers, and presumably both speeches were cleared by the governors—Bimal Jalan in 1997 and Urjit Patel now.

When I invited Acharya for a meeting in May, he was hesitant. I was intrigued by his way of doing things differently. He does not go to office wearing a suit and tie unless there is a formal meeting; he doesn't stay at the house reserved for a deputy governor in south Mumbai's tony Napean Sea Road, living instead with his parents and brother's family in the western suburb of Vile Parle (*'Mere paas Maa hai!'* he says); he often takes a shower in office. He plays tennis every day on the lawns of Ashoka Towers at Parel or the Bombay Gymkhana, and football with the neighbourhood children when his nine-year-old US-based son is in town.

After much persuasion, he agreed to meet me at the RBI guest house in Kolkata, where he had arrived to give a speech at an industry chamber seminar. Since it's not a public place, I made another request—I wanted to hear him sing his favourite Kishore Kumar song. Acharya is reluctant. Although he started an Indian film music band while studying at the New York University Stern School of Business (NYU Stern) in 1998—calling it Surbahaar, after the music event at the Indian Institute of Technology Bombay—he insists he is just a 'bathroom singer'. He says his wife, Manjiree, who prefers jazz, once got him to train under Hindustani classical singers Pandits Rajan and Sajan Mishra in London, but the apprenticeship lasted only a week.

Over a vegetarian meal at the guest house in Alipore, we begin with the obvious appetizer—his relationship with former RBI governor Raghuram Rajan. Is Acharya a Rajan protégé? Not exactly.

While doing his bachelor's in computer science and engineering at IIT Bombay, Acharya got tired of algorithms and thought he probably wasn't cut out for computer science. So he picked international finance as an elective subject in his final year in 1995.

In the same year, he wrote to Rajan seeking admission at the University of Chicago Graduate (now Booth) School of Business. He also applied to NYU Stern and Cornell University. Acharya chose NYU Stern—he wasn't sure at the time if he wanted a life at Wall Street or in academics. Acharya says the research friendship with Rajan really blossomed in 2006, the last year of Rajan's term as chief economist and director of research at the International Monetary Fund, when he invited Acharya for a project and they began writing research papers together. 'Raghu has been sort of a role model,' he says.

Poor Man's Rajan

Acharya, I remind him, is often referred to as the 'poor man's Rajan'. He laughs. 'In 2004, on a flight to the Western Finance Association meetings, a New York Federal Reserve member was sitting next to me. I was scribbling something on a piece of paper. He asked me, "Are you Raghu?" My answer was, "No." He looked at my scribbling and asked the next question: "Banking crisis model?" And then again, "Indian . . . banking . . . Are you sure you aren't Raghu?" In retrospect, I should have told him, "I am a poor man's Raghu!"' Acharya says cheerfully. Of course, there are similarities, howsoever superficial, between the two—both studied at IITs before shifting to finance and economics; and both love cricket.

Did he want to be a central banker all along or did he arrive at the RBI by accident? Acharya confides that he had sent his CV to Rajan for an opening at the RBI and also asked Patel whether he should apply. The current governor, of course, had answered in the affirmative.

Since his entry into the RBI, Acharya, who had been a big supporter of the bad bank idea as an academician, has changed his stance notably even as the bad loans of the Indian banking system have inched towards Rs 8 trillion. 'We need to deal with the situation in a very swift manner and decisively. I am not pushing for a bad bank at this time as it is a quasi-government structure, it takes long to get it going, and there is upfront impact on the fiscal situation. Also, as we lose time, the underlying companies get more and more adversely affected,' he says.

'We need to focus on the banks and the companies, both. Of course, we will need government support for the bad assets in the infrastructure space.' With behind-the-scenes work on resolving bad assets in full swing, Acharya understandably chooses his words carefully. I ask how he proposes to fill the holes that will be created after the banks take deep haircuts to clean up their balance sheets. 'We need to be creative. We need government intervention, but continuous recapitalization is not a good idea. We need to look at effectively selling the banks' loan assets, deposits, customer base, non-core assets . . . everything to solve the problem.'

Acharya has a theory about the mess we are in. According to him, public-sector banks mobilized more deposits than the private banks after the 2008 credit crisis, but capital allocation was poor. Besides, the government came out with a stimulus package. 'We talk about boom and bust. But this was somewhat different. The boom did not last long and the bust hasn't yet ended,' he says.

In the second half of 2015, the RBI under Rajan launched the asset quality review for banks, but that has proved ineffective in cleaning up bad loans. Now, it wants to be involved directly in the process. I ask him bluntly if this is the job of the banking regulator; Acharya remains unperturbed. He doesn't agree that AQR is a failure, believing that 'after the AQR, we are pushing the banks harder to come clean. Probably we should not have done this chronologically, one after the other; it could have been a simultaneous process.'

The regulator, he believes, has to intervene, for the big problem is coordination among banks. 'Why were the banks not forthcoming? There was no incentive to push. This has happened in other countries too, in Japan in the 1990s and in Europe recently. Now, we are launching a two-pronged attack: The banks must realize that capital is not cheap and at the same time, the promoters will feel the threat of RBI moving the bankruptcy court directly or if the restructuring fails to resolve in a time-bound manner. So, both the lenders and the borrowers will have the urgency to resolve bad assets.'

Acharya has always been known as a workaholic, and since he joined the RBI, the number of hours he sleeps has come down. Every month he takes his parents out for dinner one weekend, rushes to Pune to spend time with his mother-in-law on another, catches up on some sleep on the third and, on the fourth, takes a United Airlines non-stop flight to Newark to spend time with his wife and their son, Siddhant, in New York. There has been at least one occasion in the past few months when he's been to the US just for a few hours—to attend Siddhant's musical at school.

Music is very close to Acharya's heart. Over a dessert of succulent Himsagar mango, he tells me of his love for Hindustani classical music and how he believes that lyrics give further meaning to music. He listens to a lot of Kishore Kumar—his all-time favourite songs are '*Kuchh Toh Log Kahenge*' and '*Phoolon Ke Rang Se*'—Lata Mangeshkar, Mehdi Hasan and Pandit Bhimsen Joshi. On my insistence, Acharya hums his favourite songs, but refuses to sing them out. Songs picturized on Amitabh Bachchan are also a favourite—'*Khaike Paan Banaraswala*' and '*My Name Is Anthony Gonsalves*'.

The C.V. Starr professor of economics at NYU Stern has taken a three-year leave from the university to fulfil his role at the RBI. Given a choice, will he stay on? 'At the moment, I look at this as a three-year assignment. That's the understanding I have with my wife, who will remain in New York with my son. I am not thinking beyond this,' he says.

We get around to the fact that in the last fiscal year, bank credit growth was around 5.5 per cent, a historic low. 'We are not overtly worried on this per se . . . As we resolve stressed assets and banks get recapitalized, investment and credit growth will return. Also, the non-banking finance companies and corporate bonds are complementing the bank credit; what is happening is we are seeing different sources of credit,' he says, while agreeing that corporations are over-indebted, excessive capacity is leading to loss in pricing power, and supply is far in excess of demand.

Optimistic, Acharya believes the Indian economy is resilient, with good signs on most fronts—macroeconomic stability, consumption and growing financialization, illustrated by the swelling portfolios of mutual funds and insurance firms. 'We need some structural reforms to give the big push to the economy and enable greater job creation . . . I am a firm believer in economic inclusion before financial inclusion.'

I ask him about the functioning of the monetary policy committee, of which he is a member, and media reports on government pressure on the committee to cut interest rates and push growth. He declines to comment. I ask him another uncomfortable question: as a deputy governor, his mandate is monetary policymaking, but his core focus seems to be on the banking crisis. Acharya admits that he is an 'outsider' in this area, but has the 'freedom to be part of the process', and adds that the RBI is a 'well-oiled machine that gets things done in the end'.

Acharya's determination to clean up the banking system may not be music to the ears of our bankers, but he is certainly a change agent at the RBI, someone who's not afraid to take the bull by the horns. We should be ready for some action.

12

Jaspal Bindra

RETURN OF THE PRODIGAL SON

28 January 2017

On 15 January, at least 42,000 runners lined up at the starting point of the Standard Chartered Mumbai Marathon, the largest road-run event in Asia. Jaspal Bindra, who came up with the idea in 2004, was nowhere to be seen. In 2016 too, he was not around.

Bindra, the bank's chief executive officer for Asia and group executive director till early 2015, had not missed a single Mumbai Marathon till 2016. He had been living in Hong Kong from 2008, but would fly down for the event—always held on the third Sunday in January—and cheer the runners.

A few days ahead of the Mumbai Marathon, Bindra, fifty-six, is a few minutes late for our luncheon meeting at the NRI (Not Really Indian) restaurant at the Bandra-Kurla Complex in Mumbai. To avoid the hassle of choosing individual dishes, we opt for *jugalbandi*, a meal for two, accompanied by a glass of Chandon Brut each. The starters are South African periperi wings, BBQ prawns and a Burmese green tea salad; this year-old restaurant serves Indian-inflected cuisine from around the world.

As always, Bindra is dressed immaculately, in a white shirt and sky-blue turban. Some fifteen years ago, over dinner at a different restaurant in south Mumbai—he was then regional general manager, India, and CEO of Standard Chartered Bank—Bindra, digging into his chicken satay and prawn tempura, had commented, 'As long as I have an active sex life, I don't need to play golf.' Those were not Twitter days, so it did not get wide publicity, but the banking community took note. He was perceived to be aggressive, someone who calls a spade a spade.

During his two-year tenure as head of corporate and institutional banking at StanChart (1998–2000) and later as the head of both StanChart and ANZ Grindlays (he oversaw the merger of the two), Bindra showed 3200 employees the door—nearly 50 per cent of the employee strength then.

By a twist of fate, he himself had to quit the bank where he was one of the top five executives. Did he feel insecure after the StanChart board, under pressure from shareholders, asked CEO Peter Sands to leave? Bindra's answer is quite logical. He was one of the top four executives of the bank reporting to Sands. The others were Mike Rees (overseeing the wholesale and retail assets), Andy Halford (group chief financial officer) and V. Shankar (another banker of Indian origin, in charge of Europe, the Middle East, Africa and Americas). 'Had the new CEO come from within the bank, I would have got a different responsibility. But since Sands's successor came from outside, all four of us would have continued to do the same job. At mid-fifties, I was looking for a different responsibility,' he says.

Was he eyeing the top job? 'Well, maybe not at that point of time, but yes, if I had stuck around, I would have liked the challenge,' Bindra says, nibbling on the spicy wings.

He was the first to leave after Sands. By end-February 2015, he had put in his papers. Shankar and Rees followed him. Did he get a ton of money as a severance package? The standard practice in the bank is one year's remuneration when a board-level executive quits. And he was not allowed to take up any job in the financial sector for a year after resigning.

I cannot resist the temptation of asking how StanChart got into a situation in India where its bad assets ballooned and profits plunged. India, which accounts for anything from 15–20 per cent of the bank's global profits, and is probably the second most important market along with Singapore, after Hong Kong, has gone through a real bad patch in the past few years. Was the local management (which was reporting to Bindra) reckless? Was it greed for balance-sheet growth that got the bank into trouble?

Bindra says the bank actually weathered the collapse of Lehman Brothers well and continued to show growth in profit until 2012. Thereafter, it suffered on account of a severe structural shrinkage in the commodity prices. What he means is that the companies to which the bank had exposure were in the commodity space and once they suffered, their ability to service bank loans was dented.

Why did StanChart take such large exposures to so many companies in India which have in any case been overleveraged, laden with loans they couldn't repay? Bindra says this assumption is not entirely correct. 'Our internal norms do not allow the bank to take more than 50 per cent exposure in any loan. This means that even if it gives, say, a $1-billion loan to a particular company, it sells down 50–75 per cent of it to other lenders within ninety days of disbursing the loan. So, we were as affected as others. It is not fair to say only StanChart accumulated bad assets.'

As the main course arrives—Sri Lankan *potli murg* and *dal makhani* with tandoori roti and rice—I decide to shift my focus to the present. Like quite a few other global Indian bankers, he is back in the country to do something on his own. Is it the proverbial return of the prodigal son? Also, what made him pick up a stake in Centrum Capital Ltd, a non-banking finance company, and become an entrepreneur?

'I was fifty-five when I was leaving StanChart. I had three choices before me—I could have got a similar job overseas and probably run a smaller bank as CEO; partially retire and join a few boards of companies and offer advisory services; or become an entrepreneur. And if I were to be an entrepreneur, it had to be in India,' he says.

'The Best Time to Be in India'

'Where else can you grow business in the banking and finance space? The public-sector banks are losing their market share, foreign banks are shrinking business by design . . . This is the best time to be in India. I could not afford to miss this window,' Bindra says.

Last April, he reportedly picked up close to a 20 per cent stake in Centrum, started in 1995 by Bindra's long-time friend Chandir Gidwani and Khushrooh Byramjee at the Bombay Mutual Building in Fort. It is a financial services firm with a presence in corporate finance, foreign exchange, wealth management, institutional broking and investment banking. It manages around Rs 100-billion assets in its wealth management portfolio, but does not have a balance sheet as such, for it does not give loans. Bindra is adding that piece to Centrum. He has started giving loans ranging from Rs 50–200 million to small- and medium-size entrepreneurs. Not too many banks dabble in this segment where financing is based primarily on cash flows, not balance sheets.

He has already built a portfolio of Rs 4 billion in this business. Another new business is small and affordable housing finance in the range of Rs 1 million–2.5 million. Again, there is a huge opportunity with the government's big push for affordable housing and drop in the cost of money. The third new fund-based business is private equity. 'We need to compete with some of the private banks and a few other NBFCs, not the entire banking system,' Bindra says.

When he picked up the stake in Centrum, the market value of the NBFC was Rs 4.5 billion. Now it has crossed Rs 15 billion. I assume that at Rs 4.5-billion market value, for a 20 per cent stake, he would have put in Rs 900 million. But Bindra says that may not be the correct figure as he has picked up a stake in the holding company, not the listed entity. Now all three partners—Gidwani, Byramjee and Bindra—hold equal stakes of around 20 per cent each in the listed entity.

After graduating from XLRI, a management school in Jamshedpur, Bindra joined the Bank of America, where he spent ten years. He spent another five at the Union Bank of Switzerland as head of business development in India before shifting to StanChart in August 1998, where he remained for seventeen years.

Brought up in Kolkata and many district towns in West Bengal (his father was a police officer), Bindra's Bengal connection is still alive. His wife is from Asansol, and he visits his in-laws often. He can speak fluent Bengali, but has not developed a sweet tooth. So, while I choose butterscotch ice cream for dessert, he orders coffee.

The last round of conversation predictably revolves around demonetization. He joins the discussion a bit diplomatically. He agrees that digital banking in the unorganized sector is not easy, but says that once we go cashless, the cost of operations will definitely come down and size will become less relevant for the NBFCs. Currently, Centrum employs 2000 people; for the foreign exchange business, its biggest earner, it has a presence at nineteen airports and 100 outlets spread over forty-five cities.

'Money is not a problem. There are plenty of funds available both as debt and equity. My challenge is to grow and build a solid track record and be in the reckoning to set up a bank. If available, we can buy a bank too,' he says. All these, if at all, will happen after 2020. Till then, he wants to build a solid NBFC which can compete with private banks effectively.

Like the Mumbai Marathon, StanChart's Indian Depository Receipts, or IDR, was also Bindra's baby. He agrees with me that it was a flop. 'There have been issues such as tax and the class of investors who could buy IDRs. The insurance firms were never allowed to buy . . . It was an experiment that failed,' he says. StanChart remains the first and only foreign company to launch an IDR.

But all that is behind him.

I remind him of his life-size bronze statue on the eighth floor of Standard Chartered Bank Plc's old headquarters at London's 1, Aldermanbury Square—a unique initiative of the bank to showcase the diversity of its employee base. In June 2013, the headquarters were shifted to 1, Basinghall Avenue in London. Does the new office still have his statue? He shrugs his shoulders. Bindra doesn't really care much for such things now.

That day, the Centrum stock hit its lifetime high of Rs 34.50. In 2016, when Bindra took over as the executive chairman and a promoter, it was trading at around Rs 10.

13

V. Vaidyanathan

'I BOUGHT MY FIRST CAR WHEN I HAD RS 10,000 IN MY POCKET'

10 March 2007

The ICICI Bank Ltd's executive director, V. Vaidyanathan, is learning the guitar these days. This Boyzone song is one of the few that he has been practising whenever he finds time between playing golf, attending board meetings, growing the bank's booming retail business and running the Mumbai marathon.

As we settle down at Dublin, the bar at ITC Grand Central Sheraton, I ask him what his latest favourite is. Vaidyanathan hums a few lines of R. Kelly's 'I Believe I Can Fly':

I believe I can touch the sky
I think about it every night and day
Spread my wings and fly away
I believe I can soar
I see me running through that open door
I believe I can fly. . .

'I really believe that I can fly,' Vaidyanathan says. He does not look tired after a long day in office, preparing for the next day's board meeting at Jodhpur. At thirty-nine, he is the youngest board member of the ICICI Bank.

'You know what I mean when I say I can fly . . . I want to make the most of life. There are so many things to do. I sleep very little and pack my day as much as possible,' he says, nibbling a chilli pepper crispy. By this time, I know why the ICICI Bank's retail business has been growing at a phenomenal pace.

In 2000, when Vaidyanathan joined the ICICI Bank leaving his first job at Citibank, the bank's retail business had 100 employees and a book of Rs 4 billion. Today, 28,000 people are involved in India's largest private-sector bank's retail business, which is as big as Rs 1.2 trillion and accounts for more than 65 per cent of its total business.

How has he managed to grow this business, I ask. Vaidyanathan gives credit to his deputies, the heads of mortgages, auto loans and credit-card business, and then lays his trump card on the table, 'I make them believe they are the owners of the organization. When you are the owner, you give your best.' I ask him for an incident about how he went about it. He says he sometimes managed a double role of being in the head office and branches at the same time. He travelled by the evening flight to a city, hired his team in the night, and returned to BKC office by the morning flight, was at work all day, and flew out to another city the next night and could do this for a week.

With the rise in interest rates, does he see retail loans growing at the same speed? Over the last one year, the ICICI Bank has raised its home-loan rate at least six times. Vaidyanathan makes a mild protest, saying the bank has not raised the loan as many times, but admits that the average home-loan rate has gone up by about three percentage points over the last one year—from 8 per cent to 11 per cent. 'This will slow down growth. We have been growing at 35 per cent. The growth rate will come down to 20–25 per cent, but there will not be any drastic cut in demand. There is a shortage of thirty-five million homes,' he says.

After finishing from the Birla Institute of Technology, Vaidyanathan joined Citibank and worked at various departments, ranging from sales to credit, collections and even phone banking. He was a campus recruitment at Citi. Why did he quit Citi, I ask him rather bluntly. His answer is even more blunt: 'I took six months to make up my mind. Finally, what attracted me to ICICI Bank was stock options. And it was a big job.'

His candid answer encourages me to ask him what he does with so much money. Once again, he is quite forthcoming. 'I spend today what I will earn tomorrow. In 1993, I bought my first car when I had Rs 10,000 in my pocket. And for the EMIs. I don't wait for years to see the returns on stocks growing multifold. I sell stocks and take holidays because I believe in India, our future will be brighter than our past. And contribute to Give Foundation regularly.'

Since he likes Indian food, we order spicy tandoori aloo. We discuss the issues he is likely to manage in the retail business in the coming years. An important challenge, according to him, is tackling consumer education. 'The concept of availing loans to spend and consume is rather new to Indians. So we need to educate and carry the market along with us. I always give the benefit of the doubt to my customers. If somebody says he did not clear his credit-card outstandings because he did not receive the bill, I say fine, let's waive the penalty. As a matter of principle, I don't fight for the last penny on any deal. I leave something on the table and make sure that it's a win-win deal for both the bank and the customer,' he says.

Vaidyanathan also believes that it's high time banks moved to the next model of retail banking.

'We should not fall in love with what we create. We must go for the next wave, that is selling retail loans real time,' he says, eating the spicy tandoori aloo. 'So far, we have depended on data and looking at the past, and then we try to predict the future behaviour of a customer. For instance, if a customer bought a small car three years back and his bank account shows a healthy balance, we know that he will go for a big car. Now we need to react instantly. We need to react to every bank transaction and every purchase at electrifying speed. That is possible. We are working on it,' Vaidyanathan says.

He should know about speed. Every other Sunday morning, he runs 24 km from Worli Seaface to the National Centre for Performing Arts and back to Worli Seaface, in two hours and forty-five minutes. He ran the Mumbai Marathon, 42 km, in January, but missed his target. 'I was hoping to finish it in about five hours, but took twenty-eight minutes more,' he says.

Now I ask him the obvious question. Will he succeed K.V. Kamath at the ICICI Bank? Kamath has no retirement age, but he will complete fifteen years at the bank in 2010 and may not continue beyond that. For the first time, I see Vaidyanathan groping for words and trying to come up with a diplomatic answer. 'ICICI Bank is full of talented people and it's up to the board to decide on Kamath's successor. For the time being, my aim is to learn new things and understand different businesses,' he says. As we get up to leave, I hear him humming 'I Believe I Can Fly'.

14

Leo Puri

THE ACCIDENTAL MANAGER

17 January 2015

In the summer of 2012, Leo Puri went trekking to the Mount Everest Base Camp with his wife and teenage children. But climbing up to 5,364m in Nepal is perhaps not as tough as his current job: managing director of UTI Asset Management Co. Ltd (UTI AMC), a twelve-year-old company with the soul of a fifty-one-year old institution.

Regulated by the Securities and Exchange Board of India , UTI AMC now operates under the Companies Act. The government holds the majority stake of 74 per cent through four sponsors, all public-sector institutions, but it is not a government enterprise. It is a schizophrenic entity—on the one hand, it has an institutional legacy and memory; on the other, it is a relatively new entrant which is still finding its identity in the professional asset management space. Born out of a repeal of the UTI Act in 2001, this is UTI's second life.

We are at Oh! Calcutta at Mumbai's Tardeo. Puri hasn't chosen the restaurant, known for its Bengali cuisine, because I am a Bengali. Born in Kolkata, he loves Bengali food. His father used to work for Metal Box India Ltd, a blue-chip British multinational packaging company, which eventually succumbed to the politics of labour in the Left Front–ruled Bengal. Puri studied till class five at St Xavier's Collegiate School in Kolkata before moving to Mayo College, a boys-only independent boarding school in Ajmer, Rajasthan. He vividly remembers his Kolkata days, playing hockey with Armenian, Chinese and Anglo-Indian school friends.

His parents had come from Lahore to Kolkata after Independence. His paternal grandfather was a professor of zoology at the Government College University in Lahore, and his butterfly collection, says Puri, is still preserved there.

Puri's career is as eventful as the history of UTI. A dual master's degree holder from Oxford University and Cambridge University (a master's in politics, philosophy and economics from Oxford and one in law from Cambridge), Puri had two stints with McKinsey & Co. Inc.—first as a director and then as an adviser—and was managing director of Warburg Pincus LLC before moving to UTI AMC in August 2013. The post had been lying vacant for more than two years; U.K. Sinha had left in February 2011 to become chairman of SEBI, India's capital market regulator. The executive search firm Egon Zehnder approached Puri, but the appointment process took longer than usual.

First, the Union finance minister at the time was strongly in favour of an IAS officer for that post. Once the minister changed, the officer was pushed out of the race, but Puri's academic background didn't exactly match with what the UTI management was looking for.

'There is always an element of accident in my career—I don't plan it,' Puri, fifty-three, says, nibbling on *kakrachingri bhapa* (steamed crab meat and shrimps with mustard and chillies) as a starter. To wash it down, we order a fresh ginger-mango-orange drink. For the main course, Puri's preferences are *chorchori* (a mix of leafy vegetables) and Kolkata *bhetki* with mustard and steamed rice.

His first love was the civil services. After graduating from Oxford, Puri sought the permission of the then prime minister Indira Gandhi to take the IAS exam at the Indian high commission in London, but he did not get it. Then he wanted to become a lawyer. With a postgraduate degree from Cambridge, Puri's enrolment as a member of the Bar Council of India was automatic, but his stint at the law firm J.B. Dadachanji and Co. in New Delhi did not last beyond a few months. He was convinced he couldn't make a decent living through the legal profession. 'The legal profession was a cottage industry then and you needed to be the son or nephew of an eminent lawyer to get it going for you. The firm even forgot to pay me for a few months,' Puri recollects.

Leo Puri doesn't read business or management books; he reads history and political biographies. Currently, he is reading *Lives of Others* by Neel Mukherjee. He enjoys Western classical music and theatre. Recently, he saw *The Curious Incident of the Dog in the Night-Time* and *Behind the Beautiful Forevers*—both National Theatre, UK, productions. An avid sportsman in school, he used to play hockey till the university level; now he plays golf. He loves holidaying with family, trekking, visiting historical sites and going on safaris.

For him, the UTI assignment is more than just a job. 'It's not an asset manager only; it's an integral part of India's financial-sector architecture which contributed a lot to the development of financial markets. It was born out of a sense of purpose and now I need to anchor its transformation in terms of business and corporate governance.'

I remind him that UTI AMC has lost substantial market share and been pushed to the fifth position in the Rs 10.96-trillion Indian asset management industry, with just about an 8 per cent market share. Puri says the slide, which began in 2011, has been arrested: 'We are the third most profitable asset manager with 9.56 million investor accounts—one-fourth of the total investor base.'

UTI is also the most overstaffed asset manager, with 1300 employees and two trade unions—an employees' union as well as an unrecognized officers' union. Puri admits that human resources is a challenge, but believes it's not insurmountable. 'We are professionalizing a bureaucracy. Yes, we have more people on the payroll than we need, but I have no plan to get rid of them; once the business grows, their presence will be justified,' he says, somewhat diplomatically. He has made two key appointments—head of HR and of sales and marketing—and has created his top team. The salary structure is being reworked and made market-driven to attract talent.

The strength of UTI, according to him, lies in that it's the largest independent asset manager not promoted by a financial institution or a corporate entity, and this allows him to take decisions on asset allocation without fear or favour. But it is an orphan. The Life Insurance Corporation of India, the State Bank of India, the Bank of Baroda and the Punjab National Bank are reluctant sponsors. After the repeal of the UTI Act, when the organization was restructured, they walked in on behalf of the government, but they have never been interested in running the show—they have their own asset management companies. There is also a clear conflict of interest, for SEBI norms do not allow one entity to be involved in running more than one asset management company.

The US-based global investment management firm T. Rowe Price holds a 26 per cent stake in UTI AMC and has board representation, but clearly it cannot do much without the support of the sponsors. The fact that it took more than two years to get a CEO after Sinha left is a testimony to this.

Puri agrees. 'We don't have the culture of governance, say, like Singapore. In some sense, we work with one hand tied behind our back. We need to have a debate on the limits of reforms under public ownership,' he says. The solution, according to him, is going public and making UTI AMC a widely held institution. He says he has submitted a proposal to the government, but doesn't seem optimistic about it happening soon.

To counter the pungent aftertaste of the Kolkata bhetki, we decide to share a *nolengurer* ice cream (home-made date palm jaggery). After spending two hours talking, we leave discussing UTI Mutual Fund's new TV advertisement (a young son takes his father, a former Ranji Trophy player, to watch a match at Lord's, UK) with the tag line, *Haq Ek Behtar Zindagi Ka* (The Right to a Better Life).

In the universe of asset managers, will UTI AMC regain its fortunes, and reclaim its right to a better life? Puri's five-year term will be a test.

Postscript

Puri has completed four years in office. He is still persuading the government for UTI AMC's initial public offering.

15

Brooks Entwistle

THE INSIDER WITH OUTSIDE CONNECTIONS

24 September 2010

In February 2006, when Brooks Entwistle came to Mumbai to set up shop for Goldman Sachs in India, he was the only employee for the first few months. Operating out of a hotel suite in south Mumbai, every time he answered a call he would say, 'Goldman Sachs'— and if the caller was looking for him, 'Let me see if Brooks is around.' A few seconds later, in an effort to portray an image of a larger force on the ground, he would pick up the phone in another room, stir his coffee and say, 'Brooks speaking.'

Today, Goldman Sachs has a team of 100 employees in India, including those at the firm's service centre in Bengaluru.

When I approached the normally reticent managing director and country head of Goldman Sachs for this meeting, he insisted that it would have to be at Koh by Ian Kittichai, the new Thai restaurant at InterContinental Marine Drive. He stayed at the hotel when he came to Mumbai to head Goldman Sachs. More importantly, he loves spicy Thai food. Entwistle attributes his love for spices and the mountains to a childhood spent in Colorado, US, where he grew up eating spicy Mexican cuisine.

As we settle down, I discover Entwistle's Thai connection goes beyond food. He lived at Preah Vihear, in remote northern Cambodia, bordering Thailand, for two years in the early 1990s as part of a UN team to prepare Cambodia for free and fair elections. In the war zone, where shelling was a daily occurrence as the Cambodian People's Armed Forces and the Khmer Rouge fought each other, Entwistle learnt to 'manage cross-cultures and to build businesses under difficult circumstances'. He served as a district electoral supervisor, effectively the governor of the district; his partner in the mission was a woman from Sweden; the civil police in Choam Khsan, where he was based, was from Ghana; the military observers from Russia, Uruguay and Poland; and a young Australian soldier ran the radio station. Then there was the Pakistani peacekeeping force.

Entwistle, forty-three, started his career in Goldman in 1989 as an analyst in investment banking in New York. While working in Hong Kong in 1991, he came across a UN advertisement in the *Far Eastern Economic Review* seeking volunteers to conduct elections in Cambodia and decided to jump at the opportunity.

Indeed, there was a deeper reason. He was looking for Long Se Bina, a Cambodian boy whom Entwistle's parents had adopted under a sponsorship programme of World Vision, an international relief and development organization. In April 1975, when Khmer Rouge forces began their final assault on Phnom Penh, fifty-odd small children from the same orphanage where the boy lived had been airlifted out. But Bina and others, who did not meet the cut-off age, were left on the streets to fend for themselves. At the request of Entwistle's family, the Red Cross launched a hunt for the boy, but the file was closed in 1978, a year before Vietnam took over Cambodia.

Now, Entwistle's eldest daughter Bryanna, nine, is of the same age at which Entwistle lost his 'brother'. He plans to take his three daughters to Cambodia this Diwali to complete the circle.

Back at Goldman Sachs in New York in1995 after completing his MBA at Harvard Business School, he periodically used his vacation time to serve as an election monitor with the Carter Center in places such as Liberia and Mozambique because he loves to work in 'countries emerging from conflicts'.

The Cambodia elections were free, fair and technically perfect. But the Khmer Rouge took over his district after six months, undoing at first blush almost two years of hard work by the team. Entwistle knows well that elections are but one piece of the puzzle of getting a country back on its feet. 'Nation building is an incredibly complex, long-term process. Elections alone cannot do it. There are many issues such as leadership, governance and rule of law . . . This takes place over a generation,' he says.

Had he not been an investment banker, Entwistle would probably have been a diplomat with a deep interest in international affairs and foreign policy. He has tracked India closely since the late 1990s, when he returned to Hong Kong for a second stint to help start the Asian technology group of Goldman Sachs. In 2000, both he and wife Laura came to the Indian Institute of Management Ahmedabad for campus recruitments, competing with each other: Entwistle for Goldman, and his wife for her firm, the Boston Consulting Group.

In 2003, when he went back to New York, the family thought it was for good, but when the bank chose to end its decade-old relationship with Kotak Mahindra Bank Ltd and go it alone (as it wanted to offer the whole suite of products, while the joint venture was only for securities and investment banking), the mantle fell on Entwistle to head it.

In October 2005, he came here on a secret trip with Laura, one that convinced them India was the place to be. Within a few months, only a duffle bag in tow, he was here, on his fiftieth trip to India, to 'dig into a once-in-a-lifetime opportunity'. Laura joined him a few months later with their daughters.

Since then, Goldman Sachs has invested at least $2 billion (around Rs 92 billion) in forty-five firms. It now offers investment banking, broking, offshore asset management, fixed-income securities, private equity and non-banking finance business. It has applied to the banking regulator for a licence to get into commercial banking and the business of buying and selling government bonds. It is also keen to start its domestic asset management business.

Its employees include sixteen managing directors, some of them hand-picked from rival banks such as Bank of America, Merrill Lynch, Deutsche Bank, Morgan Stanley and UBS. Initially, at least 25 per cent of the employees of the Mumbai office were from the global office, to help build the culture, but now Entwistle is the only non-Indian here.

Won't he move out soon after mentoring Sonjoy Chatterjee, his newly hired co-head in India, for the top job? Entwistle says there is no immediate plan as they have a 'full life' here, deeply embedded in the community. His wife is the president of the American School in Mumbai and heads the Mumbai chapter of Room to Read, an international non-profit organization. They have church meetings in their home every week. 'I wake up every morning and see there's so much to do,' he says, digging into jasmine rice mixed with green chicken curry.

Entwistle collects old travel posters, antique maps, first-edition books and old movie posters. His office has a poster of Nargis Dutt's superhit film *Mother India*. Her son, Sanjay Dutt, and thespian Dilip Kumar are his neighbours in Bandra's Pali Hill. 'I have a reading problem,' he tells me sheepishly, adding he could be Amazon's biggest customer in India. Coincidentally, he spent his last birthday with actor Aamir Khan, discussing movies and education over dinner at a friend's place.

Entwistle doesn't consider himself an outsider in India. He is an 'insider in India with strong outside global connections'. What is his advice to expats who come to India to build a business? 'There is no manual on how to do it. You must go local from day one. Make India your home. Don't think about your next posting,' he says.

One morning in 2007, while dropping his daughters to school, they saw a few cows, a goat, a horse, and finally, on Linking Road, an elephant. His eldest daughter, Bryanna, screamed with joy, saying, 'Daddy, it's just like living in a movie.'

For Entwistle, unlike his daughters, life in Mumbai is not surreal. It's real and hectic, and he is still trying to figure out how to find zones of silence. But he is not complaining. He sleeps five hours a night, gets up for an early run through the quiet lanes of Bandra and packs in as much as possible to live life fully, completely submerged in the local culture.

Epilogue

INDIAN BANKING 2025

Through the essays in the book, I have tried to chronicle the developments in Indian banking and finance over a tumultuous decade. And, through this epilogue, let me attempt to play the role of a soothsayer, peer into the crystal ball and foretell Indian banking 2025.

What we have been witnessing in the past few years is, to use a cliché, a conundrum. Banks in India, particularly most state-owned banks, have been piling up bad assets and the health of some of them is in such a state that both the government and the Reserve Bank of India have been pushing for consolidation in the industry. At the same time, the RBI is also opening up the sector for new entities.

Consider the fact that since Independence till July 2015, in sixty-eight years, India got twelve new banks (all of them have not survived).On the other hand, since August 2015, we have got two new universal banks, ten small-finance banks (at the time of writing this, eight of them are operational) and eleven payments banks (not all are operational as yet even as a few have surrendered their licences). What more, the RBI has put the licence for universal banking on tap. This means, there is no special window for seeking a new bank licence. Any entity can knock at the regulator's door any time and walk away with a licence to set up a bank if it is 'fit and proper'.

The RBI is also planning to open the turf for new kinds of banks such as wholesale banks and depository banks. Besides, the foreign banks operating in India are being encouraged for local incorporation (one of them has already got the nod for its Indian subsidiary) and it won't be a surprise if the large cooperative banks are asked to migrate into full-fledged commercial banking over the next few years.

There is an apparent contradiction in the trend but consolidation (in the public-sector banking industry) and expansion (in overall banking services) are probably both sides of the same coin. The banking regulator wants to intensify competition by opening up the sector and forcing some of the public-sector banks to merge and consolidate. While the blueprint for this is being drafted, it is for sure that the public-sector banks which currently account for around 70 per cent of the industry will lose their market share probably to 60 per cent by 2025.

Similarly, the credit offtake in past few years has been tardy. For fear of creating more bad assets, many banks are afraid of giving new loans. That has led to the resurgence of the non-banking finance companies. Both their balance sheet growth and the rise in the value of their shares in the stock market in the past few years have been phenomenal. Does this mean the next decade will belong to the NBFCs? Will India cease to host a bank-led financial system by 2025? This is something we need to watch out for. Till the NBFCs complete one full cycle—say, of eight to ten years—it will be difficult to declare all of them winners. They are subject to light-touch regulations and it's not easy to predict which entity will end up showing big holes in their balance sheets in the future. Only when the tide goes out, we will discover who have been swimming naked.

Talking about NBFCs, the flavour of the next few years will be financing affordable housing. The government is betting big on this. Its mission is 'Housing for All by 2022' and it is backing this up with fiscal incentives. A burgeoning housing sector fuels economic growth as it has a multiplier effect in terms of sale of cement, steel and other housing material, and can create jobs, and lead to increased investment in education.

There are about twenty new entrants in the affordable housing space even as the fourteen existing lenders are significantly expanding their portfolios of low-cost home loans by broadening their distribution channels through direct sales and community-based loans. They are all using technology to reach out to the lower end of the customer segment. There has also been a rate war to woo the customers. A burgeoning middle class, rising disposable incomes and fiscal incentives on home loans have increased the affordability of homes, and the average age of a new home buyer in India is now thirty-two years, down from early forties a decade ago.

Even though the little over Rs 12-trillion Indian mortgage market has been growing at around 18–19 per cent every year, its size is too small in relation to the economy—around 9 per cent of the GDP, less than half of what it is in China. Singapore's mortgage market is 32 per cent of its GDP, lower than Hong Kong's 41 per cent, and in the US and the UK, it is 81 per cent and 88 per cent of the GDP, respectively. In Denmark, the southernmost and smallest of the Nordic countries, the mortgage market is 104 per cent of the GDP.

Most bankers are seeing enormous opportunities in the market with a shortage of close to 19 million units in urban India and around 40 million in the rural pockets. One hopes that no one is losing sight of the affordability of the customers in this segment, compromising on loan appraisal and risk management, and that bubbles are not seen after a few years.

One set of NBFCs will definitely find it difficult to maintain the growth—the microfinance institutions. A few years down the line, I will not be surprised if I hear the experts shouting, 'Microfinance is dead; long live microfinance!' The market of microloans will continue to grow, but the process of intermediation will change.

The proposed merger of Bharat Financial Inclusion Ltd with IndusInd Bank Ltd signals two new trends: one, the high-margin business of the MFIs is under threat by the new set of small-finance banks as well as some of the existing commercial banks which are seriously planning to penetrate semi-urban India; and two, at the right prices, the banks will be willing to buy the good MFI franchises to expand in the hinterland.

For the MFIs, the pitch has been queered for multiple reasons. For instance, for a large MFI, the spread or the difference between the cost of funds and the price of its loan is capped at 10 percentage points. This means that if such an MFI is raising loans from other banks at, say, 10 per cent, it cannot charge more than 20 per cent for its loans. The banks which have access to lower-cost funds in the form of deposits do not have any such cap; - they can charge their borrowers as much as they want. For the small borrowers, access to bank loan is more critical than the cost of the loan.

Also, a small borrower cannot take money from more than two MFIs, but the banks are not subjected to any such restriction.

Most importantly, cash has been the medium of transaction in the segment where the MFIs operate. The increasing focus on digitization is hurting their business. To survive and flourish, the MFIs will have to forge alliances with different kinds of banks—small-finance, payments and universal banks—as well as digital wallet service providers, and disburse and collect money through the banking channel. Theoretically, this new architecture will make money expensive for the small borrowers as the money cannot be disbursed at their doorsteps any more. They would need to travel to the nearest bank branch or the banking correspondent, and in the process, they may lose halfaday's wage and/or incur costs in transport.

On the other hand, the operational cost for the MFIs will come down as they would not need so many people for the disbursements of loans and collection of repayments. This will help them bring down the price of loans and compensate for the additional cost that the borrowers will incur. However, this is a theory. In reality, the MFIs will find the going tough. The universe of small loans is big but the banks and other NBFCs will gradually replace the MFIs on this turf. A few successful small banks will become universal banks by 2015 while others forge alliances with banks; a few more strong MFIs will migrate to the path of small-finance banks and many MFIs will be taken over by the banks.

All these will give a big leg up to the financial inclusion drive. Till mid-September, at least 302.5 million accounts have been opened in the Pradhan Mantri Jan-Dhan Yojana scheme, the most ambitious financial inclusion drive globally, launched in August 2014. The money kept in these accounts is only Rs 666 billion, and many such accounts do not have any money kept or they are zero-balance accounts, but the fact remains that they have served a critical purpose—access to banking for the people at the bottom of the pyramid, the first step towards financial inclusion.

We all know that it will take a while to achieve financial inclusion in the truest sense of the term—access to credit at a reasonable price without much hassles. We also know that social and economic inclusion must precede financial inclusion. But let's admit that the PMJDY, to start with, is giving a big push for inclusive finance by opening millions of bank accounts and routing subsidies through these accounts. By 2025, most adult Indians should have access to bank deposits, credit and remittance facilities as well as insurance and mutual fund products.

Finally, technology will play a big role in this transformation. Ideally, this book should have a chapter on technology in banking, but I didn't dare to attempt that as it has been difficult to keep pace with the changes in this space. I thought anything I write on banking technology would be irrelevant by the time the book gets published.

In 2015, in the run-up to its launch, IDFC Bank Ltd, India's newest universal bank, was desperately looking for a unique selling proposition, or USP. How could it become different from other banks of its ilk in Mumbai where it is headquartered? It decided to showcase the ease of transactions as its USP or the differentiating factor from other banks. However, even before IDFC Bank was formally launched in October 2015, other banks such as HDFC Bank Ltd, ICICI Bank Ltd, Kotak Bank Ltd, Axis Bank Ltd and the State Bank of India took giant strides on the technology front, creating mobile wallets, offering their customers ease of transaction and cutting down the time for sanctioning loans.

Use of Big Data, artificial intelligence, and even robots are the in-thing in Indian banks now; many private banks are showing the door to thousands of employees who are not needed in the new landscape. By 2025, or even before that, the point of sales, or PoS, machines and even ATMs and credit cards can become obsolete as the smartphone will be the main mode of all banking transactions.

And, to meet the young, impatient customers' increasing demand for prompt and smart services, the banks will have to operate like air-traffic controllers, working 24X7. By 2025, at least a few banks will consider themselves as technology companies and feel tempted to say, 'We also do banking.'

Will that be the slogan of 2025? Many believe that we don't have to wait for that long; it can even happen by 2020. I have a different take on this. In India, it can happen, but in `Bharat', the banks will have to continue to treat technology as an enabler; technology by itself cannot be a product, at least in the foreseeable future. For various reasons—ranging from connectivity to lifestyle and the pattern of cash flow of individuals and small businesses—'Bharat' will continue to depend on relationship banking for small borrowers, and technology will cement that.

The challenge before us is to merge India and 'Bharat' on the banking turf. Yes, only technology can achieve that, but it is too ambitious to expect that to happen by 2025.

List of Abbreviations

ABI: Authorized Bank Investor
ACC: Appointments Committee of the Cabinet
ADB: Asian Development Bank
ADS: American Depositary Share
AGT: Amtek Global Technologies
AIG: American International Group
AQR: Asset Quality Review
BBM: BlackBerry Messenger
BC: Banking Correspondent
BPLR: Benchmark Prime Lending Rate
BSFL: Bhartiya Samruddhi Finance Limited
CAG: Comptroller and Auditor General
CAR: Capital Adequacy Ratio
CBI: Central Bureau of Investigation
CCI: Cricket Club of India
CD: Certificate of Deposit
CDR: Corporate Debt Restructuring
CIS: Collective Investment Scheme
CMD: Chairman and Managing Director
CP: Commercial Paper
CRR: Cash Reserve Ratio
CVC: Central Vigilance Commission
DISCOM: Distribution Company
DMD: Deputy Managing Director
DoP: Department of Posts
DPC: Dabhol Power Company
DSA: Direct Sales Agent
EBIT: Earnings Before Interest and Taxes
ED: Enforcement Directorate
EPC: Engineering, Procurement and Construction

FCCB:	Foreign Currency Convertible Bond
FDI:	Foreign Direct Investment
FIPB:	Foreign Investment Promotion Board
FSA:	Financial Services Authority
FSDC:	Financial Stability and Development Council
GDP:	Gross Domestic Product
GDR:	Global Depositary Receipt
GST:	Goods and Services Tax
HDFC:	Housing Development Finance Corporation
HLCCFM:	High-level Coordination Committee on Financial Markets
HUL:	Hindustan Unilever Limited
IAG:	Insurance Australia Group
IBA:	Indian Banks Association
ICAI:	Institute of Chartered Accountants of India
ICICI:	Industrial Credit and Investment Corporation of India
IDFC:	Infrastructure Development Finance Company Limited
IIMA:	Indian Institute of Management Ahmedabad
IMF:	International Monetary Fund
IOB:	Indian Overseas Bank
IPPB:	India Post Payments Bank
IRDA:	Insurance Regulatory and Development Authority
IRR:	Internal Rate of Return
ISP:	Internet Service Provider
JLF:	Joint Lenders' Forum
KYC:	Know Your Customer
LIBOR:	London Interbank Offered Rate
LIC:	Life Insurance Corporation of India
MCLR:	Marginal Cost of Funds-based Lending Rate.
MFI:	Microfinance Institution
MFIN:	Microfinance Institutions Network

MIBOR: Mumbai Interbank Offered Rate
MPC: Monetary Policy Committee
MTM: Mark to Market
NABARD: National Bank for Agriculture and Rural Development
NBER: National Bureau of Economic Research
NBFC: Non-banking Finance Company
NCD: Non-convertible Debenture
NHB: National Housing Bank
NPA: Non-performing Asset
PAC: Public Accounts Committee
PLR: Prime Lending Rate
PKSF: Palli Karma-Sahayak Foundation
PPA: Power Purchase Agreement
PSB: Public-sector Bank
PSU: Public-sector Undertaking
RBI: Reserve Bank of India
R-Com: Reliance Communications
RFP: Request for Proposal
RIL: Reliance Industries Limited
RTI: Right to Information
S4A: Scheme for Sustainable Structuring of Stressed Assets
SARFAESI: Securitization and Reconstruction of Financial Assets and Enforcement of Security Interest
SBI: State Bank of India
SDR: Strategic Debt Restructuring
SEBI: Securities and Exchange Board of India
SFIO: Serious Fraud Investigation Office
SHG: Self-help Group
SIDBI: Small Industries Development Bank of India
SME: Small and Medium Enterprise
SRO: Self-regulatory Organizations
TCS: Tata Consultancy Services Limited

UBI: United Bank of India
UDAY: Ujwal Discom Assurance Yojana
ULIP: Unit-linked Insurance Plan
UPA: United Progressive Alliance
USL: United Spirits Limited
WWG: Worlds Window Group